Maj.-Gen., Count Cherep-Spiridovich

THE SECRET WORLD GOVERNMENT

OR

"THE HIDDEN HAND"

The Unrevealed in History

100 Historical "Mysteries" Explained

MAJOR-GENERAL, COUNT CHEREP-SPIRIDOVICH

This picture was taken in Washington at the personal request of the late President Theodore Roosevelt by his photographer.

INTRODUCTION

This book is mostly about Jews; it is not against the Jews.

These painstaking researches have been made in order to re-write history "with conscience;" as Lamartine urged, as Washington Irving admonished. The results are presented to the thinking public to enlarge its intelligence, not its prejudice. The book should appeal to Jew and Gentile alike, that they may join hands in purging society of its enemies, be they Jewish plotters or Gentile participants; each group more contemptible than the other according to the point of contemplation.

The Jews should bring to bay the "satanists," who corrupt the countries in which they have found asylum; the Gentiles should make harmless every Judas, who accepts the bribes of the Jews.

Together they should eliminate from authority the man who "sells his birthright;" equally with him, who, taking advantage of his weaker brother, "buys it for a mess of pottage;"

"But he that is greatest among you shall be your servant." (St. Matthew).

Count Cherep-Spiridovich springs from Norse gentility. His remotest ancestor on record was prince Rurik, who, being one of the "Worthies" of his time, was in 862 called by the Slavic people to Novgorod, where he founded a dynasty and gave Russia its name.

Nordic tradition, coupled with exceptional education and training, have given to general Spiridovich the spiritual ardor, the constructive impulse, and the extraordinary perseverance required to make his vast knowledge serve the exigencies of the present by his peculiar power to forecast the future, but it devolves upon the individual reader to make practical application of it, by refusing to participate in the practices, which engage "Enemies of Humanity." A Chicago Rabbi recently said:

"We have been told, long enough: 'You cannot change Human Nature; but, I say to you: Human Nature can be changed; and, what is more: Human Nature must be changed."

And, how may it be changed? A Danish philosopher has given the formula. He speaks of traditions of caste as undeniable obstacles to the realization of Freedom and Equality; but suggests how these obstacles may be converted into opportunities saying:

"In the nature of Inequality is a secret. Equality becomes inhuman under forced abolition of Inequality; Inequality becomes inhuman when we neglect to promote Equality: it is upon inequality as a basis, that equality must be reared. The agony of society arises from this simple thesis being misunderstood on opposite sides."

These are the jewels of thought of a century; they blind the evil eye of bolshevism; may each reader set them, firmly, in the diadem of his deeds. Count Tolstoy prophesied:

"A man shall come from the North to save civilization."

Is that man Cherep-Spiridovich? Who knows?—Read his book and the world will never again seem the same to you.

Chicago, July 4, 1926. Herjulf Vikingson.

PREFACE

"Will our civilization survive?,"

Mr. J. D. Rockefeller Jr. and others anxiously ask.
It will, if this book is read and its message spread.
It surely will not, if this book is trampled upon!
Count Okuma, the farsighted and clever statesman of Japan, affirmed this war will lead to the death of Aryan civilization. Though he knows how it will be destroyed, he, as a Mongol, did not reveal it. Therefore, I shall do it.

Why did a score of the best British (among them the famous President of the British Empire's Press, Mr Robert Donald) French, Slav and other editors call me "Prophetic Genius" or "Prophet" with "astounding," "marvelous," "preter-natural," "miraculous" foresight and intuition?*

Because they found in my 7 pre-war books 80-odd political predictions all of which were later realized, as if prophecies,

Why have I been so successful in all my predictions?

Only because I most humbly agreed with the warnings of OUR SAVIOUR (St. John VIII, 44, St. Matthew XXIII, 15 etc.).

Never did I think that I "know better," or that I ought to be "less prejudiced" or not so "full of racial hatred," as He.

That is why everything concerning World affairs and the future of America and of the Aryan Race is clear to me, while all the statesmen, writers, preachers and politicians are puzzled.

Here are some samples of this. Mussolini in perplexity said:

"Yet, the why of war, which has followed human society since its origin, never has been explained, and apparently must be put into the domain of unexplained matters." (New York American, April 3, 1925).

If Mussolini were a Christian, he would not thus blunder...

Because CHRIST said clearly that there is a "Satan's lust of murder and that the Jews — his sons — will do it." And History, as we shall see, daily confirms this OUR SAVIOUR'S warning which means: "Gentiles, keep far away from the Jews!"

The Talmud is today preached in every synagogue! It teaches:

"Thou (Jew) shalt smite the other nations, which the Lord delivers in your (Jewish) hands"..."kill the best goym" (gentiles.)

*In the New York Times of April 17, 1907, was published my prediction about the two Balkan and this wars.

1

A WAR IS BUT A "LEGALIZED MASS-MURDER."

A war is only a "legalized mass murder." Thus CHRIST pointed out those, who arrange all wars and revolutions, and that their chief cause is Satan's and his sons' "lust of murder."

But "Christians" never seem to agree with CHRIST.

The same with ex-Premier of France Joseph Caillaux. When asked how to save France, he wrongly answered:

"The public seems to believe that there exists some half secret remedies as yet unemployed to cure the impecuniosity of States. Work and economy. That is the regimen. Such are the only remedies."

If France follows Caillaux's advice and works and economizes without following CHRIST'S indication, then in five or ten years she will become rich again. Then Rothschild V-th or VI-th will order his Lloyd Georges, Clemenceaus, Woodrow Wilsons, *Bethmann - Hollweg - Rothschilds, Aerenthals, Sazonovs, Sonninos Kemal-Pashas, Venizelos, Masaryks, et al, to start a new world war.

And all that the French nation would have earned according to Caillaux's advice, would be spent in silly mutual self-extermination of the Aryan race, or in payment of indemnity to Germany.

Edouard Rothschild V-th in Paris and the 300 Judeo-Mongols, who are composing the World Government (the Hidden Hand), made 100 billions out of this First World War. Of course, not counting their "lust of murder," they are willing to stage a Second World War. They are preparing it against rich America.

Controlling the World press, they can easily stage any war.

"If Wall Street should say the word tomorrow, all the editors and preachers would be for the war" (Eugene V. Debs, The Sun, May 4, 1925).

One needs not to be a prophet to foresee such imminent an issue if the French follow the Caillaux way of salvation.

Thus the Dictator of Italy and the presumed Dictator of France show the same serious lack of judgement.

But the necessity of growing statesmen is most vital.

What is a difference between a statesman and a politician? Demosthenes and Edmund Burke explained it:

"A statesman must know how to foresee the future. A politician grasps only the present" (which is already the past).

"To govern — means to foresee," says a wise old proverb. Otherwise — "without foreseeing one cannot govern."

As soon as one agrees with CHRIST, one becomes more bright.

*As ex-Senator R. F. Pettigrew says in his "Triumphant Plutocracy," Mr. Woodrow Wilson pushed the Americans into war against their will.

2

WHY IS CHRISTIAN CIVILIZATION IN DEADLY DANGER?

Because "Christianity" has become positively Christless!

Not only do we not execute the commands of our SAVIOUR, but nearly all our Aryan so-called ruling class, and even clergy, seem to believe that HE was "wrong" and that they "are wiser."

They think that they must not be as full of "racial hatred" and "religious prejudice" as they imagine HE was (St. John, VIII, 44) when HE condemned the scribes, whose criminal books called the Talmud are being followed by an entire race, which is killing us!

Out of each 100 gentiles 99 will surely shout:

"CHRIST ordered us to love even our worst foes."

Precisely; that is why we are obliged to prevent the Jews from "doing their lust of murder."* The more we love somebody, the more must we endeavor to cure his criminality.

"I must be cruel only to be kind," Hamlet said.

Love and connivance with crimes are different matters.

Would you tell your beloved child: "Go and murder?"
Love the foes of CHRIST, but check their "lust of murder."

My book is not religious but purely scientific. It is not my intention to claim any merit of discovery, for the facts themselves prove day by day how amazingly right CHRIST is.

To follow HIS commands is hard and irksome.** The least that we could do would be to recognize HIS Wisdom and HIS desire to guide us safely even here—on earth. But, as I said, our ruling classes refuse, perhaps unconsciously, to believe HIS warnings.

"When a nation forgets God, God sends an earthquake," said the French genius, Victor Hugo. We are witnessing a political earthquake in Russia, in fact on one-sixth of the surface of our globe. By the news from that country we get daily information that "numerous people convicted of counter-revolutionary activity were shot to death today." The reason why so many persons are being killed is not because of their counter-revolutionary activity, but is nothing more or less than **the deliberate murder of the intelligent Aryan classes in order to substitute the Asiatics.**

*The murder may be moral, mental and physical.

**The Jews deceived many of us, that CHRIST has never said, that the authors of the Talmud (now followed by a whole race) are the "sons of the devil." CHRIST could not fail to warn thus, because, otherwise, the above truth is so obviously proved by the true history, that we would have the right to reproach OUR SAVIOUR for not having thus warned us.

The Jews lied that the Gospel of St. John was written later ,on, and even might be apocryphal. Be it so (though it is not), but does not CHRIST'S other statement (St. Matthew's XXIII. 15) corroborate the St. John's?

3

THE WORLD GOVERNMENT AGAINST PEACE

"The problems of unrest must be solved, if the Republic is to be preserved" (Mr. Arthur Hobson Quinn, the Dean of the University of Pennsylvania).

Yes! But to solve the "problems of unrest," and thus to save the White Race, we must know that the World Unrest is caused by the "lust of murder" of the Judeo-Mongols and their firm desire to smash the Aryans and to overthrow everything Christian.

This is well understood by Mr. Madison Grant, who wrote in the introduction to Mr. Lothrop Stoddard's "Rising Tide of Color":

"Now Asia, in the guise of Bolshevism with Semitic leadership and Chinese executioners, is organizing an assault upon western Europe."

The assault of Asia is not to be upon Europe only, but upon the Aryan Race as a whole, especially upon wealthy America.

The wild Bolshevist meetings in New York prove that the same "earthquake" that is destroying Russia, the former Eastern guardian of Christian civilization, is beginning in America. Few Americans paid attention to the fact that all the speakers were Asiatics*.

Why are the Aryans so stupidly blind?

"Whom the gods wish to destroy, they first make mad."

And do we not see the mass-madness of the Aryans in the question of the "League of Nations," "World Court," "War on War," and so forth? Indeed, millions of well-meaning persons in every Aryan country are working hopelessly, as if pouring water into bottomless barrels, or like squirrels turning their endless wheels. They imagine that the quantity of their work would recompense for the miserably poor quality. They all ignore CHRIST'S warnings. **Only by checking the Jews' lusts could peace be kept.**

When at a political convention in Chicago I begged several professors to explain the wisest statement of the late Vice-President Hon. T. R. Marshall: **"The World Government will not permit the establishment of peace,"** asking them, **"What is the World Government"** and **"why will it not permit the establishment of peace,"** they became confused and could find no answer!

How astoundingly right was Professor Charles E. Merriam of the University of Chicago, when he exclaimed in a lecture:

"What advantages will we reap if science conquers all the world, except the World Government."—(The Chicago Tribune, Jan. 24, 1924).

*History proves, and the Jewish Encyclopaedia confirms it, that the so-called "German, Russian, Polish and Eastern Jews" are Mongols, who accepted the Jewish Talmud, which is not the creed given to Moses. The Talmud seems more like the by-laws of a gang of murderers than a religion, yet it is strictly followed by the so-called "Jews."

Among others things the Talmud teaches: "The best Gentiles must be destroyed," and similar commands. However, many politicians have the effrontery to declare that this "religion" ought also to be "respected," while it ought to be exposed in the Courts, as inciting to murder.

4

I said that the Christian Civilization could still survive, if this book be read and its message widely spread. Why! Because it illustrates my "Science of Political Foresight," which has proved its value in such numerous cases and verifying all of my eighty and more predictions in my seven pre-war books.*

Here is one of the proofs of the usefulness of my science: After a long discussion with General McDonough, the Chief of the War Intelligence Department in London, and with the British Foreign Office, I submitted on September 17, 1918, a report advising the signing of peace with Bulgaria, which, as I foretold in the above report, would provoke an uprising of the Slavs in Austria and a panic in Germany and the immediate surrender of her armies. My advice was accepted and two weeks later peace with Bulgaria was signed; two weeks still later the Slavs in Austria rose, and Austria was prostrated: and two weeks after the Austrian defection, Germany was thrown into a panic and surrender forced upon her.

The First World War was thus ended, thanks to my advice!

The self-extermination of the Aryans was stopped. Otherwise, fighting would have continued for many months more and at least some five million more Aryans would have lost their lives in vain, of whom not less than two millions would have been Americans.

Asiatic Bolshevism would have jumped from Russia into Germany, then all over Europe, and eventually to America. Further the thousand million Mongols of China, Japan and other Asiatics and Africans would have found the moment propitious to have repeated the historic invasions of Attila (defeated near Paris in 471), and of Baty, who lost his army in 1240 at Fiume.

These two possibilities were not taken into consideration by those who thought that the Allies should have fought longer,—that Germany should have been crushed and peace signed in Berlin.

I did not advise the Allies not to go to Berlin!

The above has remained an **"unrevealed"** fact in history!

The only publication in Great Britain confirming it was the Christian Commonwealth which published it in February, 1919. The only newspaper in America was the New York Staats Zeitung, which, although furiously attacking me (April 29, 1921), proved that it was my advice to England to sign peace with Bulgaria that brought about the prompt surrender of Germany.

*See my "Vers La Debacle (Towards the Debacle). Dangers et Remedes," published in October, 1913, in which I warned Russia about what since has happened and offered "the Remedies," which could have saved her.

ALL HISTORIES AND THE PRESS ARE "BUNK"

The Staats Zeitung blamed me for Germany's disaster, forgetting that if Germany had not surrendered, Europe by now would have been drowned in an ocean of blood, spilt by the Bolsheviks, or perhaps even by the Mongol invaders.

Why was this fact of my saving some five million Aryans so carefully silenced by the press? Because, if by one report I were able to save five million Aryans one would reasonably expect that I could save many more. But that is precisely what the World Government does not want. Its aim is bloodshed.

Why? As the 300 Judeo-Mongols, who compose it, are converted Mongols, they are "twofold more the children of hell" than the regular ancient Jews (St. Matthew XXIII, 15).

The "mystery" of this silencing by the press of such vital facts is explained by the Hon. W. Jennings Bryan, who said:

"Newspapers do not give facts, they fool the people regularly."—(New York Times, May 16, 1921).

"Americans know nothing about what is going on overseas" (Shaw Desmond, The Chicago Tribune, March 1, 1924).

"The United States is not getting the truth of conditions in Europe" (Mr. Ch. Edw. Russell, Socialist leader, May, 1925).

"The newspapers are the dirtiest and filthiest things that ever happened" (Mrs. Bjurstedt Mallory, Chicago Tribune, July 21, 1922).

"Europe is descending towards dissolution. We are willing to check the descent. But we are unable to determine, how we can help! We are not well informed as to the facts! The danger of complete collapse is nearer than ever" ("Chicago Tribune," Febr. 7, 1923).

The newspapers have hundreds of informers, but they remain silent.

Why? Because the press is controlled by the "sons of the devil"!

Men of genius, such as Voltaire, Napoleon, Lamartine, Henry Ford, have warned us that history is "untrue," still it seems that, with the exception perhaps of Washington Irving and the President Emeritus of Leland University, Dr. Starr Jordan, nobody has demanded that "History be rewritten and revised," thus to expose "the organizers of all wars." On the contrary, when Mr. Henry Ford placed incontrovertible facts, bearing on the causes of the world's unrest, before the public, newspapers generally trampled upon his words and endeavored to discredit him.

For fifty years history has been my beloved "hobby."

When, thanks to my advice, the Armistice was signed, I went to the Library of the British Museum and practically lived there for thirty months, reading, studying and copying much of the substance of this "Unrevealed in History." It took me forty months more to create the ONLY "History With Conscience."

6

AMERICA FACING THREE UNITED MONGOL FOES

The crushing of our civilization, predicted by Count Okuma, may be undertaken even to-day, probably beginning with a Judeo-Mongol attack upon the United States or a Judeo-Mongol attack upon Europe, as it is being now done in Bulgaria, in China, etc.

Even the best informed Americans ignore the fact that they are today facing **simultaneously** three **Mongolian** foes:

(1)—**The Judeo-Mongolian World Government**—"the Hidden Hand," which controls in 1925: (a) three hundred billion dollars of available capital; (b) the world's press, and (c) many governments.

(2) **Mongolian Japan,** whose assault is inevitable, as Mr. H. G. Wells and others predicted. Japan is conspiring today with the Judeo-Mongolian Soviets of Moscow, and they are both now using every means to take entire control of China and force her to join them in crushing the Aryan Race.

(3) **The Judeo-Mongolian Bolshevism,** which, according to the late Samuel Gompers, is being financed with millions by the so-called International Bankers ("Germano-Anglo-American"), who are all Judeo-**Mongols.** Bolshevism is inflaming at least five million Judeo-Mongols and some three or four million "secret Judeo-Mongols" in America; also the heads of twelve million Negroes here, and seven million more of all kinds of "reds," "pinks," "radicals," "utopians, "pacifists" and other discontented persons in the United States, who are willing to "improve" it, as Russia was ...

"Most of the people of Wisconsin are on the Trotzky side" (Sen. Brookhart, Febr. 7, 1923).

Thus there are nearly twenty-five million revolutionists within the United States, which are menaced from without by a coalition of the Mongolian Japan, China and other Asiatics with the Soviets; by the half-Mongolian Mexico (which is practically ruled by a Judeo-Mongol Dictator, Roberto Huberman) and by some Aryan powers controlled by the World Government (the Hidden Hand).

In this critical moment some American Senators seem to be deliberately trying to provoke the indignation, and to arouse the animosity of England, France, Italy and Germany by much timeless and useless talk about their war-debts to America. Such optimism is futile and contrary to her best interests.

The speech of the Ambassador, Mr. Alanston Houghton, demanding that Europe change her policies was considered a threat. And we read in Japanese newspapers, that she finds "the American naval manoeuvre plan **too boldly provocative and a great menace to the safety of Japan**" (N. Y. Times, May 3, 1925).

7

Americans are lulled into a sense of false security by memory of nearly complete safety during the past one hundred and fifty years, but this security was due to two main reasons which now are inoperative:

(1) A Czar of Russia would not permit any overt attack on the United States, just as he prevented it in 1863-64.

(2) Until a few years ago the two oceans protected the American shores, but these natural defenses have been abolished by the nature of perfected aggressive warfare.

Therefore, the optimism which has always prevailed in America, due principally to the protection above mentioned, is no longer based upon solid ground. America must, therefore, recognize and face the danger and prepare for any eventuality.

Americans are somewhat intoxicated by the laurels of the First World War, when fate gave America **fifteen months** of interval and absolute security at home, between her declaration of war and her real entrance upon the battlefields, where the American troops met the Germans, worn out by four years fighting.

In the Second World War which is being staged by the World Government **against America,** she will not be given even **fifteen minutes** for her preparations; this war will not be declared. . . .

All of the above mentioned three Mongolian groups of foes of the United States were "pro-American" in 1918. They were then busy in attempting to destroy or undermine the Christian rulers of Russia, Germany, Austria, England and Italy, and bending these countries nearly to the state of bankruptcy.

The World Government **"kept America out of war,"** as long as the Czar, "the traditional friend of America" (according to President Roosevelt) needed her help. **It forced America into the war** as soon as the Czar of Russia was overthrown. Even the Chicago Tribune of July 27, 1922, repeated the rumor, that a Judeo-**Mongol,** Justice Lubitz Brandeis, **"ruled the White House by secret telephone,"** and a Jew, Bernard M. Baruch, literally "spat" in the face of the Senate that he was the **"most powerful man"** in America.

In his interesting "The Triumphant Plutocracy" ex Senator R. F. Pettigrew wrote that when the American nation elected Mr. Woodrow Wilson "because he kept America out of war," he was already preparing to declare it.

The World Government threw America into it even against the will of the nation, by ordering the "American" press to make it!

THE UNITED STATES WAS NEVER IN GREATER DANGER.

Now all the world is against America!

Yes! The eleventh hour of America is here! And I appeal to America in the same terms as I did to the Czar in his own newspaper "Zemschina" in Petrograd on August 24, (11), 1916:

"The catastrophe is approaching like a hurricane; each second is to be counted. Reconciliate the Christian Churches and proclaim the Slav Union and you will be saved."

He was dissuaded from following my "way of salvation" and an unparalleled disaster swept him, his family and the Nordic Aryan classes of Russia into oblivion.

Now a worse catastrophe is menacing America, the backbone of the White Race, and again I show the "way of salvation." In order to make it easy for Americans to adopt this remedy, I shall try to persuade them to realize that two main dangers exist:

(1) That the World Government really does function.

(2) That the Second World War is being staged.

To those who, like Mrs. Wood Parks, are sure that "America is too rich and strong to be conquered," I shall point to Russia, which is not conquered, but where is a real hell on earth.

What is the reason for the distress of Russia?

She had scorned CHRIST'S warning and now lets the Jews rule.

Do we not see the same blunder in America today?

In Washington was created a "Big Four Entente." A "scrap of paper," the late Senator Cabot Lodge implied. It is provoking a tacit Chino-German-Russo-Italian "Counter Alliance," and nothing will prevent England, Japan, Mexico and other powers from joining it in due time, because they are all under such an omnipotent influence of the Satanic Forces,* which are now ruling the World (see my "Science of Political Foresight"), that at any moment their press could stage a "casus belli" against the United States. The rebukes to Europe and the refusals to join her Conferences give to Euro-Asia the pretext to unite in hostility.

"America is quite isolated," Rev. L. H. Hough of Detroit says. And no Conference did touch the worst foe of our Christian civilization, the Judeo-Mongol World Government, referred to by Hon. T. R. Marshall and by Prof. C. E. Merriam and known as the Hidden Hand which is enslaving and misguiding the foreign and domestic politics of all great countries. Its chief aim now is to repeat its attempt of 1861-65, and by destroying the United States, "knock out" Christian civilization.

Only by spreading this book could be such fratricide averted.

*"Japan is invaded by Mohammedanism."—(N. Y. World, on May 1, 1921). "Mohammedanism is ruled by Judaism" (Science of Polit. Foresight) "Japan is worshipping Satan" (Morning Post, Aug. 28, 1920).

"We (the Jews) are nothing but the world's seducers, its destroyers, its incediaries, its executioners" (Dr. Oscar Levy of London).

EVERY EXPERT FORESEES WAR OR DISASTER.

The final crushing of our civilization, I repeat, foretold by Okuma and others, may be attempted even today, and may begin with the Judeo-Mongol attack upon the United States first, or by a Judeo-Mongol assault upon Central Europe. Russia is at the disposal of the Judeo-Mongol Hidden Hand, and having ceased to be the **Eastern vanguard of Christian civilization,** has become the **Western vanguard of the Mongols. The Soviets arouse China!**

In July, 1921, I submitted a detailed report to President Harding about the World situation and the Hidden Hand's plan. The report was read in my presence by the President's Secretary, Mr. George B. Christian. Later on I published it in English and in Russian, entitling it "Let Us Prevent the Second World War, Already Prepared," and spread it in Europe in tens of thousands of copies.

The neighbors of Russia, and especially the Balkan States, became cautious, knowing my foresight, and took every possible means to prevent an eventual assault of the Judeo-Mongol Bolsheviks. Their various efforts in the Balkans were carefully watched, and therefore, have all failed up to the present day.

Since then the Hidden Hand has shown a feverish activity in the Far East, which means that the first assault will be against America.

If my book is heeded this assault may fail also!

The Generals J. J. Pershing, G. Bell, G. V. H. Mosely and Marshal Fayoile foretold a new war; as Clemenceau, ex-Ambassador H. Morgenthau and many others have done.

Even France has chosen to take offense, and Clemenceau declared: "We in France have to act as if we were alone in the World." This means complete isolation of the United States and practically it sounds like a threat.

An imminent catastrophe for Europe (and thus for the whole White race) was foretold by Mr. Frank Vanderlip, the ex-American Ambassador G. Harvey, Senator M. McCormick and by many other leaders; unless Europe should find financial aid from other than American sources, but it can only be found here.

"Europe will make every effort to get her gold back."—(Isaac Marcosson in his book "The War After the War").

"I am putting before England precisely the policy of Disraeli," confessed the late Prime Minister of Great Britain, Hon. Bonar Law, i. e., the most aggressive and faithless policy which ever existed. And Hon. Bonar Law's party is again in power... Thus we may expect that Disraeli's policy will be followed again.

But Disraeli was a mere tool of the Rothschilds.

And according to Bismarck (La Vieille France, N-216) it was Disraeli and his patrons, the Rothschilds, who invented the plan of destroying the United States by fomenting a Civil War here, and by a foreign attack in 1863-64 by five powers.

10

THE SATANIC FORCES NOW VS. THE UNITED STATES.

The Civil War was started in 1861 and the British, French, Spanish, Belgian and Austrian* troops were already in Mexico City, ready to profit by the Civil War, staged by the Hidden Hand!

But then the Czar Alexander II. warned Napoleon III. that he would invade France if this coalition helped the Southerners to smash the North. **The Czar even sent his squadrons at the disposal of President Lincoln to defend New York and San Francisco.** President A. Lincoln had the right to order this fleet to fight any of the above five Powers.

Only thus the United States was saved!

Nothing prevents the above plan from being renewed again in 1925-26. There is no longer a Czar in Russia, and the Judeo-Mongol Soviets are the worst foes of the United States.

China, Japan and Mexico are kept wrongly indignant.

Even the Judeo-Mongol New York World states:

"Japan has ordered 140,000 machine guns from the Vickers Company. The Scrutton Company is executing large Japanese orders. Japan is making amazingly rapid strides in air armaments" (Augnst 5 and 6, 1924).

Behind Vickers is the "mysterious" Judeo-Mongol Sir Basil Zaharov, who, according to the Chicago Tribune (April 8, 1924) "has opened immense credits with London banks to finance the purchase of war materials for Russia"... and bombs for Sophia.**

Yei Ling, a Chinese Senator, issued a letter challenging us:

'If you (the White Race) should regard them (his demands) as excessive and unreasonable, China with her 400,000,000 people will unite with the weak and small races of Asia and the suppressed peoples of Europe and Africa and meet you on the field of battle to fight out the issue."—(New York Times, August 25, 1924).

And the Moslems are on the eve of an uprising, as in Morocco!

"The whole vast world of Islam (250,000,000 souls) is today in profound unrest."—(Mr. Lothrop Stoddard in Scribner's).

"The Islamic world will not rest our labors, nor sheath our swords until every Moslem nation enjoys complete independence."—(Mustapha-Kemal, the Judeo-Mongol Dictator of Turkey).

"Mohammedanism invaded Japan" (New York World, May 1, 1921).

"Bolshevism the creed of which contains the very highest precepts of Islam, has just triumphed over an enemy, who was threatening our existence" (Mustapha Kemal, a Jew, Dictator of Turkey, on August 14, 1920).

"The ideals of Bolshevism at many points are consonant with the finest ideals of Judaism" (The Editor of the Jewish Chronicle, London).

"We Jews, are still here, our last word is not yet spoken, our last deed is not yet done, our last revolution is not yet made." (Dr. Oscar Levy.)

"The Colored races will exterminate the   ites."—(Dr. Inge of St. Paul's Cathedral in London).

I could quote any number of such warnings.

*"The Nineteenth Century and After," p. p. 867, 872, 926, by Edwin Emerson, Jr. and Marion Mills Miller.

**As CHRIST foretold it (St. John VIII, 44).

But almost nobody knows, that all the so-called Satanic Forces: Pan-Asiatism, Pan-Britanism, Pan-Germanism, Pan-Islamism, are all autocratically led by Pan-Judaism, headed now by Edouard Rothschild V-th in Paris, a Judeo-Mongol!

I repeat that he and 300 other Judeo-Mongols compose the above World Government, or the Hidden Hand.

Only blind people do not see the hand writing on the wall: The Russo-Chino-Japanese treaty has been signed. The three signatory countries represent a combination of some 600,000,000 persons.

The talented Mr. Arthur Brisbane wrote:

"It interests us, because the three nations are united chiefly in their dislike of the United States. Skilful propaganda has made China think that America represents contempt for Asia's people."—(New York American, Feb. 22, 1925).

But why not expose the why and who is financing this skillful propaganda? The Judeo-Mongolian Soviets of Russia? Yes! But who provides the money? Mr. Gompers explained it (May 1, 1922):

"The Anglo-German-American Bankers," i.e., the same 300 members of the Hidden Hand. Brisbane adds:

"Russia dislikes us because we persist in maintaining what they call a capitalistic Government. The success of it annoys Russia, while the fact that we won't admit Asiatic masses to full partnership, annoys Japan."

Here Mr. Brisbane is "regularly fooling" his readers.

Real Russia likes Americans and admires their "capitalistic Government." It is the Judeo-Mongols who are ruling Russia who hate America, not because she is "capitalistic," but because she is Christian and is the "backbone" of the White Race.

Meanwhile the Judeo-Mongols are a "yellow" race and they are aiming to "do the devil's lust of murder," as CHRIST foretold it. How can we continually forget HIS warnings when we discuss World problems?

Brisbane assures: "We won't admit Asiatic masses." But that is not true, because real masses of the worst Asiatic Judeo-Mongols are pouring daily and nightly into the United States.

Many Jewish offices are forging false passports for the Jews.

"Scarcely any but Jewish immigrants are coming over (to New York). They pose as Poles, Russians, even Irish."—(Plain English, August 13, 1921).

Such outrageous injustice towards Japan exasperates her, and Brisbane is right in foretelling that America "may have trouble in that direction." Yes! She will have disaster, unless Americans at least understand that all dangers facing them are being purposely staged by the Judeo-Mongol Hidden Hand.

The ex-Ambassador Mr. Cyrus E. Wood wisely stated:

"The Japanese exclusion act was an international disaster of the first magnitude."—(Jan. 24, 1925).

ALL TALK ABOUT PEACE IS PREPOSTEROUS.

Numberless hypocrites or ignoramuses are preaching "Good Will," "Friendliness," "Peace." But sheep in the stockyards are full of "Good Will" and are most peace loving. However, millions of them are slaughtered by few butchers. Just the 300 "butchers" (the Hidden Hand) sent (in 1914) 20,000,000 men to their death.

Instead of babbling about peace and "Good Will" we must reveal these 300 butchers and check their **"Bad (Satanic) Will"**!

Otherwise, all these "peace" efforts are absolutely useless, even harmful, because they lull America to a state of security and thus encourage her foes to attack.

"No man would have war," said Senator Hiram W. Johnson. No! Except these butchers who are preparing in the United States a revolution and Civil War (Protestants vs. Catholics; Labor vs. Capital; Negroes vs. Whites); and a combined foreign attack and disaster, as I said, perhaps even in 1926, unless this book should awaken this splendid nation and the rest of Christendom.

"Only by a vital and permanent joining of the nations in a union can mankind be saved from another conflagration which **will leave the world in ashes**," wrote S. Colcord in his "Great Deception."

Yes! But the Hidden Hand **will not allow** any such union and no kind of peace, as Hon. T. R. Marshall wisely warned us. Thus the dreams of ignorant "peace-lovers" who scorn CHRIST are vain. The Hidden Hand rendered fruitless 30 Peace Conferences.

The only reason for Russia's unheard of tortures is: she ignored the Hidden Hand ,as does the United States now. And Russia, like America, scorned the above mentioned warnings of CHRIST.

The chief danger to America is its **blind optimism**. Thus the Pres. of the League of Women Voters, Mrs. M. Wood Park said:

"Our country is too rich, too large to be conquered." At this the editor of the Chicago Tribune (November 7, 1922) wisely answered: "NONSENSE!"

It is precisely the rich countries that have been attacked and destroyed. But let us suppose, that the United States in the end could not be conquered, must its sons be plundered and drowned in an ocean of blood? But many millions of Americans are thinking just as Mrs. Wood Park and other optimists foolishly believe, that not enough money can be found for a combined attack.

The Hidden Hand now controls 300 billion dollars and would willingly advance the needed amount for such an assault, because the Hidden Hand would gain some 100 billions, as it did from the First World War, as I proved it in my "Gentiles Review."

WAR MIGHT OCCUR AT ANY MOMENT.

R. F. Pettigrew proved, the Hidden Hand's agents here are "self elected Dictators, who wreck and rule, and can at any moment wreck financial institutions and inaugurate panics. They are endowed with the power of Government!"*

The above **Judeo-Mongol Dictators within America** can take even here any number of billions in order to finance the assault against the United States, just as they helped Germany during this war. The Hidden Hand is behind all the Socialist, Communist, Bolshevist, Anarchist, "Pacifist" and all kinds of "red" organizations everywhere. Why? Because its main aim is bloodshed at any price.

"The future wars will come with increasing suddenness," wisely stated Gen. Tasker Bliss. When the general strike paralyzes everything and these clashes are started, then, **without declaring war,** as Gen. Brancker, the ex-Chief of the British Air Forces, foretold, the enemy forces will simultaneously assail all the American ships in night attacks by torpedo boats (as in Port Arthur in 1904) submarines and airships. The voyage of the American Atlantic fleet gave the Japanese a pretext to inflame their nation and to suddenly attack every American ship at night, **without declaring war!**

What General William Mitchell is stating in 1925, I had submitted to Pres. Harding in July, 1921, adding to it the foes' plan.

In this pamphlet on page 6 I explained that England "could not disobey the Hidden Hand and thus commit suicide."

We read in the New York World on April 12, 1925, that Great Britain is **"in a serious position,"** that she faces **"Grave Industrial Conflicts"** and is "stranded by ebb tides of Commerce," etc.

Great Britain was purposely put into this dangerous condition by the Hidden Hand, which thus can force its own wishes upon the British Lion, throwing this noble nation against any power, which is ordered to be destroyed, according to the Rothschild's scheme of the World Domination. My belief in CHRIST made me use all my efforts in 1919 and 1920 in order to prevent England from getting into the present awful situation.

The Financial News of London published my warning Manifesto on January 24, 1919, entitled "Essentials of Stable Peace," in which I pointed out the terrible blunders of Messrs. Woodrow Wilson, Lloyd George and Clemenceau, and offered them the "Way of Salvation." I took 10,000 reprints and spread them.

Then the Hidden Hand ordered that I be "silenced."

*The best weekly in English is the British Guardian of London (40, Great Ormond Street, London). In its issue of March 20, 1925) in the articles: "The Warburgs: International Crooks" and "International Bible Students' Association Financed by Jews," are confirmed Sen. Pettigrew's words.

14

However, in the same Financial News on November 12 and 25, on December 31, 1919, and February 17, 1920, appeared my vigorous letters entitled **"How to Save England"*** In the last letter I offered twenty "remedies" and "preventions," some of which were adopted.

My fourth and, alas, last message 'ended with the words:
"In my next letter I shall explain the science of foreseeing, indispensable also for all financiers and merchants, and how to pay all England's 8,000 million pounds sterling of debts without increasing taxes, without levies on capital. and without spending a penny from her Treasury."

This was too much for the Hidden Hand, which wishes to bend down England until she will consent to attack the United States. That is why my fifth letter has never been published and disappeared in the office of the Financial News, whose famous editor, Sir Ellis Powell, was "suddenly" dismissed and "suddenly" died. . .

And now we see England in the terrific position which I foretold to her and from which I sought to rescue her. I warned nearly all the officials of England, beginning with Mr. Lloyd George and his colleagues in 1919 about the situation in which she now finds herself. But he was a mere tool of the Hidden Hand and even according to Mr. John Spargo (the Independent of New York, April 9, 1921) he was **"following the policy of Disraeli,"** viz. **Rothschilds'**.

Only once, when he lost his majority in the House of Commons did he obey my **advice** to declare that England will **pay** her debts in thirty or forty years "without increasing taxes, without levies on capital and without spending a penny from her Treasury," which I suggested in my letters to him and to the Financial News.

This declaration of Mr. Lloyd George produced a sensation in the House of Commons. He received a majority of some 350 votes and maintained his power for many months   But his "secretary." Sir Philip Sassoon-Rothschild, who was "cornacking" Mr. Lloyd George forbade him to execute my "plan of salvation."

And we now see the results...

Many Americans rely upon a tacit "Anglo-American Secret Alliance." But it can be dismissed under the heavy pressure of the Hidden Hand, which, I repeat, is purposely crushing England's finances and commerce until England will accept the motto:

"To go to the dogs or to assault and plunder the United States."

No other way out will be left to the splendid Islanders.

And an Anglo-American war will be the end of the so-called "Christian" civilization, which ignores CHRIST.

*****The Hidden Hand influenced the proud Britishers to rebuke me, saying: "England goes very well and needs not to be saved" But facts prove that I was right!—(New York Times, April 8, 1925).

FOREIGN AND DOMESTIC DANGERS UNCHECKED.

"There are more Bolsheviks here than there are in Russia" (H. Ford).

Nobody here seriously fights Bolshevism, i. e. Judeo-Mongolism·

"Two thousand agitators between Chicago and the Rocky Mountains are preaching a gospel which will wreck the U. S. Constitution, unless intelligent citizens talk a constructive doctrine to overcome that tragical influence." "Organized labor's program is nationalization of all basic industries, as you will observe from the conduct of the present strikes. They are not strikes for money, but are steps toward Government ownership and operation of industry" (John B. Maling, "The Chicago Journal of Commerce," July 21, 1922).

"The Jews have always formed a rebellious element in every State, and not more in those where they were persecuted than in those where they were allowed to dwell at peace." (Mrs. Nesta Webster, "World Revolution," p. 163).

These agitators are hired by the Hidden Hand, Gompers said. Nobody dares to reveal it and warn the workers and youth.

"Our people don't understand these things (awful dangers). The people do not understand the situation" (Admiral Sims, N. Y. Times, Febr. 28, 1925).

Very few understand the possibility of a foreign assault.

"The American Navy is prepared to lose the next war. Our fleet, as it now exists, cannot defend itself against modern naval forces" (Admiral W. F. Fullam, The New York American, March 4, 1925).

"We have no air forces. Without a dominating air force, our armies and navies are merely organized for defeat in modern war" (Col. W. Mitchell, June 3, 1925).

Why such appalling blindness on the eve of disaster?

"History (a true, not "bunk") is the best Philosophy" (Napoleon).

The absence of an "History With Conscience," as is my "Unrevealed In History" produced lamentable results everywhere.

"The Washington Conference may be the last failure to stave off the disasters and destruction that gathers about our race" (H. G. Wells).

"Japan prepares for war, but the U. S. does not" (Admiral B. A. Fiske).

"There will be a war in 1925. There will be no declaration of War. It will start by a sudden aerial attack" (Gen. Branker, ex-Chief of Air Forces).

"Serious differences are brewing with England over shipping and other policies. These differences can be prevented from developing into a conflict only by a strong navy. England is resentful over the new status of the United States as World Power and over the fact that we no longer pay $300.000.000 a year to her merchantmen for transoceanic transportation" (Admiral W. W. Phelps, March 3, 1925).

"Britain and America are calmly preparing industrially, politically and militarily for the coming war" (McLean in "The Coming War with America").

"The war between England and America has commenced" (Sen. P. C. Knox).

The message of this book could alone avert such fratricide.

"THE DANGER IS WITHIN AMERICA AS WELL"

Such was the warning of the immortal Abraham Lincoln, recently repeated by Secretary C. E. Hughes.

The Hidden Hand can in due time start a tumult between the Protestants and the Catholics (tenfold increasing the Herrin fightings) when the general strike would be fomented, and at the same moment it will order its agents to create a financial panic, as R. F. Pettigrew foretold. which would cause confusion and a chaos here.

The Hidden Hand is "**Anglo-Sassoonizing**" this country instead of "Americanizing" it and this may disrupt the United States, as foreseen by "The Brooklyn Eagle," in May, 1921.

The Hidden Hand, according to the declaration of Paul Warburg, to the Senate, covertly financed simultaneously the elections of Mr. Roosevelt, Mr. Taft and Mr. Wilson. The Hidden Hand can help to envenom the Democratic-Republican duel in 1928, support a Third Party and finance the "Blue Laws" in order to increase the discontent and to breed revolution to the utmost.

"**America is a land of bondage. The people soon will revolt against the efforts of moralists.**"—(Rabbi A, Spitzer of New York, on July 18, 1921).

He knows his Jews well. And there are at least five million Judeo-Mongols in America and three or four million more of "secret" or "crypto" Jews, as Disraeli called them.

"The Jew never was a real true American. In this war **the Central Powers were financed by the Jews** with money from America, and this money was used to fight against our own homeland."—(The Rev D J Brouse, Pastor of the Grace Episcopal Church, The Jewish World, July 13, 1921).

"If 10.000 American Jews would go to Palestine, she would be revolutionized" (ex-Minister, Sir Alfred Mond, a Jew, Jewish Chron., Nov.9, 1924).

The Jews are so successfully making "red" America, that hardly any of them are willing to go to "bolshevize" Palestine.

As the 12,000,000 Negroes here are incited by the agents of the Hidden Hand, they will be ready to help the 8,000,000 Asiatics here (the Judeo-Mongols) to start any revolt. The newspaper of the colored people, "The Messenger," wrote (September, 1921):

"This country has 300 billions in wealth, with human beings existing on corn meal, while 2% of the people own 60% of the wealth."

"**The blacks in the U. S. are to look to Bolshevism for delivrance**" (the Editor of the Defender of Chicago in March, 1924).

Say only 2,000,000 men are unemployed; but 5,000,000 souls are suffering and urging a "change."

The German-Americans are also dissatisfied. Any pretext, created by the Hidden Hand, which is intoxicating the masses with a poisonous "moonshine," can provoke a riot, which the agents of the Hidden Hand will transform into plunder and murder.

All the 120,000 men in jails will be released, as was done in Russia and in France at every revolt.

17

THE WAR WITHOUT DECLARATION OF WAR

The beginning of all may be any strike which will be fanned by the Hidden Hand into a general strike, followed by all the above-mentioned conflicts, and a circular foreign attack.

Many persons are fooled by the famous "ratio" 5 to 3, as the American fleet is supposed to be superior to that of Japan. But nobody takes into consideration that an unexpected night attack by the Japanese could easily reverse this "ratio."

The Women's Peace Conference at Washington in January, 1925, enumerated twenty-four reasons which are provoking wars. They "forgot" the main: "the devil's lust of murder" of the Jews!

Of course, they work in great secrecy. However, we perceive them from time to time. Thus we read in the New York American:

"Geneva Protocol—a Direct Menace to America. Threatens War if We Don't Obey Super-State."—(Prof. Philip Marshall Brown, October 19, 1924).

The realization of this Protocol was postponed. But the "good intention" remains. But let us return to the eventual assault.

When the squadrons of foes are facing American ports, and their airships hovering above New York, Chicago, Washington and other towns, then an ultimatum will be issued:

"Consent to pay 100 billions in cash, bonds or shares and surrender the remaining ships and airships. Otherwise your harbors and plants will be blown up, towns poisoned and the Capitol and White House destroyed."

Gen. W. Mitchell, the Assistant Chief of American Air Forces, rightly stated that one bomb can annihilate a whole town.

"War between U. S. and Japan is quite inevitable," (Gen. Bernhardi).

"Japan's foreign minister K. Mutsui speaks with an irritation which this country cannot afford to ignore." (Chicago Tribune, Feb. 9, 1924).

"War between the United States and England is imminent before 1926," confessed Trotzky, the Jew ex-Dictator of Russia, who received directions from the Jew-Dictator of Germany, the late W. Rathenau, as the latter confessed.—(Plain English, June 11, 1921).

"In 1925 in Japan seventeen divisions in naval aviation will be ready," telegraphed Mr. Parry from Tokio.

"Defenseless is America," such is the title of Mr. Hudson Maxim's book. Yes! She is defenseless and facing certain disaster, unless she will regard the Jews, as described by CHRIST.

If the American fleets only were sunk or seized, and plants blown up, all the expense of an attack would be covered tenfold, and the United States weakened for many years, and even opened to a Judeo-Japano-Mexican Mongol overt mass-invasion!

"Mexico gives Russia a good base to develop further contact with America" (Chicherin, the Soviet Foreign Minister, N. Y. Times, March 6, 1925).

As a consequence of finding a good base in Mexico: "A Revolution in Mexico Impending" (N. Y. Herald, June 13, 1925). And also: "A cloud has appeared on the horizon of Mexican-American relations" (N. Y. Times, June 15, 1925).

"Our conflict with Mexico is irrepressible" (Chicago Tribune, Editor)

PREVENT THE EDUCATION OF "INCURABLE IMBECILES"

Every Jew or his hireling, who disdains CHRIST (as the "Rationalists" founded by a Jew Spinoza, are doing) is helped by the Hidden Hand here, but truth about it is strictly forbidden. Churchmen, professors, writers and politicians hide the truth or ignore it and thus foster "Incurable Imbeciles."*

The thousands of authors, who have written the history of the last 150 years, seemed to be blind and to be nothing but reporters "en grand". They never go to the roots, but just glance at the surface and then offer their dead pictures, without conscience.

Why are they doing it? Because they have been bribed or "for fear of the Jews," as St. John (VII.13) and also Cicero mentioned or because of their ignorance! In either case the result is the same.

The readers obtain quite a false view of history and politics, and become mere politicians, even "real incurable imbeciles."*

By saying "bribed," I do not mean that thousands of authors received money, positions, or publicity for their harmful writings.

Contemplating the mountains of gold on which the Rothschilds are seated, these authors, politicians, preachers, professors unvoluntarily felt their mouths water. Most of them practically "sold themselves" to Satan, and to the Jews, inspired by him and led by the Rothschilds, but were never compensated.

The notorious Otto Kahn, partner in every sense of the "Anglo-German-American" bankers, who according to Mr. S. Gompers, wish to drown his country in an ocean of blood, also partner of the Warburgs mentioned by The British Guardian in the article "Warburgs: International Crooks" proves how right CHRIST is.

Otto Kahn gave a tip of $25,000 to one clergyman. Then some 100,000 other clergymen began to think: "If reverend so and so received $25,000, why could I not have the same reward, if I would never denounce the Jewish crimes."

And the 100,000 clergymen became "pro-Jewish". . . .

The sympathy of each of them cost but 25 cents. Cheap! . . . .

"The World became safe only for D-n-Hog-race-y" (Garstin Smith).
"The Jew has persistently shown himself ungrateful" (N. Webster).

The negative opinion of the famous Thomas Edison about the defects of the American instruction, which is here constantly confused with education, is well known. Instruction is not education.

To make mental cripples of youth is a crime. . . .

Did not CHRIST warn us (St. Matthew XVIII, 6):

"But whoso shall offend one of these little ones which believes in ME (Who is Truth Itself) it were better for him that a millstone were hanged about his neck, and that he were drowned in the depth of the sea."
* "The Incurable Imbeciles," according to Urbain Gohier, are those, who pretend not to know what is this World Government, which according to Hon. Marshall, is making abortive all efforts of peace-lovers.

19

NO OTHER BOOK TELLS THE WHOLE TRUTH

Nobody speaks about the leaders of the Hidden Hand, the Rothschilds—the real "World Assassins of the Peoples" (as the "Foreign Affairs" of Oxford called them) and the Autocrats of the World. And how they misrule the World!

Books written about them were bought up at once and disappeared like "The Rothschilds" by Mr. John Reeves, published by McClurg in Chicago, "Les Rothschilds" by Demachy, etc.

These books constitute a rarity, though they do not describe the political phase in the life of this sinister and fatal famliy, to which could be attributed at least one half of all the bloodshed and calamities that have befallen the White Race since 1770.

The excellent "The International Jew"* is the clever and undeniable exposure of the Jewish Power, but only as exercised here. Perhaps, because the Rothschilds and their "Invisible Government" are in Europe (except a score of members, who are here) these four books, so masterfully written, do not explain their satanic work of the last 150 years; a role absolutely unequalled by contemporary rulers, but hidden with the utmost care.

"The French Revolution," "World Revolution, The Plot Against Civilization," and "The Secret Societies," by the most talented Mrs. Nesta Webster of London, the best historian of today, are so important, that I will refer to them later. No student of history, no politician or preacher, especially no woman should miss reading them. Among the thousands of historians Mrs. Webster stands as a colossus endowed with a rare erudition and courage.

"The Cause of World Unrest," by the "Morning Post" in London, is tremendously useful. But it does not mention the Rothschilds.

"The Secrets of the Rothschilds," by Mrs. Mary Hobart. has also disappeared, though there is nothing about them in it.

But the Press, controlled by them, prevents the real facts from being known, as Mr. W. J. Bryan rightly said.

The professors, clergymen, politicians and writers would die of fear rather than speak the truth.

Furthermore, 99% of Americans do not know the A, B, C of foreign politics, and much less do they understand its so-called "mysteries," which puzzled even the greatest statesmen since, according even to Mr. Lothrop Stoddard, "something happened," (which he does not explain)which endangered our 1900 old Christian civilization. What is the result of such "mass lying"?

"96% of the people of the U. S. are below the accepted standard of intelligence and only 4,000.000 are above the standard" (Pres. of the Southern California University. Dr. Kleinmichel, Chicago D. News, July 30, 1923).

*By "The Dearborn Independent," 4 volumes, 25 cents each.

TRANSFORM POLITICIANS INTO STATESMEN

What is the result of constantly hiding the Truth?

"Never has Congress been at lower ebb than it is today," confessed Secretary of War Mr. Weeks (The Chicago Tribune of June 16, 1922). And Sen. Borah has no better opinion, saying:

"It is just plain man failure on the part of the politicians to run their jobs" (Collier's Magazine, Nov, 1922).

"American foreign policy has come to its lowest ebb since the founding of the Republic. We come to complete stagnation due to incapacity for individual action and to terror of concerted action. No such low estate of American courage has ever been recorded in American History" (The Editor of The Daily New of Chicago, on Dec. 6, 1922).

"To step blithely into the deep torrent, equipped only with moral truisms and easy formulae without a clear knowledge of the deep seated Forces, which control policy, is to invite costly commitments and unexpected sacrifices" (The Editor of the Chicago Tribune, Sept. 9, 1922).

"Our statesmen are children compared with theirs (European). **A foremost place in world affairs is offered us time and again. It is thrown into our lap, and through our plain stupidity we reject it"** (Chicago Herald, July 22, 1923).

Roy K. Moulton wrote (The New York American, May 24, 1924):

"So far as diplomacy of our country just now is concerned, there is nothing the matter with it for the reason that we don't seem to have any. **We do not grow diplomats.** We raise politicians. The lack of sharp diplomats is one phase of our national life which makes us shudder at the mere thought of any diplomatic passage or entanglement with Europe. **We** should be at a tremendous disadvantage in any conference or in any World Court **We are a nation in its infancy.**"

Mr. Wilson confessed his blindness in World Affairs thus:

"Diplomacy works always in the dense thicket of ancient feuds, rooted, entangled, and entwined. It is difficult to see the path. It is not possible to see the light of day. **I did not realize it until the Peace Conference.**"

"Wilson was not quite enough of a statesman to win out against allied diplomacy at Paris" (Ambassador Bernstorff, Chicago Tribune, Feb. 5, 1924).

"America has no foreign politics" ("The World Work").

"Americans know nothing about what is going on overseas" (Mr. Shaw Desmond, The Chicago Daily News, March 1, 1924).

"The United States is just about 40 years behind the times in political thinking, compared with the rest of the world" (Oswald Garrison Villard, Editor of The Nation, Chicago Tribune, March 8, 1924).

"Your (Europeans') superior knowledge will take the initiative" (General Dawes).

"A blunder in politics is worse than a crime" (Talleyrand).

"If we blunder, there may be no America tomorrow" (Copeland)

"League will never prevent wars" (Major A. Hamilton Gibbs in 1925).

"America is in that diplomatic position where war may come to it through slogans such as 'The War to End All wars' and 'Making the World Safe for Democracy'" (Gov. John J. Blaine on Oct. 20, 1923).

Yes! The "sons of the devil" will invent any such slogan.

"The U. S. is passing through a critical period in its History" (Gen. H. C. Hale, Commanding the 6-th Area Corps, Chicago).

"The Soviet Ambassador to China, Kara-Kahn is a dangerous and mischievous adviser." (Ambassador Schurman, N. Y. Times, March 6, 1925).

All this is most dangerous . Why not create a "School of Foreign Affairs" and teach my "Science of Polit. Foresight?"

"An ounce of prevention is worth a pound of cure!"

21

WOMEN COULD PREVENT WARS

Nine national women's organizations with a membership of about 5,000,000 women held a Conference on the Cause and Cure of War, in Washington in January, 1925.

The meeting was rendered abortive before it began, because of the failure of the president to state the real causes of war.

None of the members had the courage to proclaim, that, first of all, in order to prevent wars we ought to point out who is staging them. This was foretold by CHRIST Himself:

"Ye, Jews, will do the devil's lust of murder."

As war is but a "legalized mass murder," He clearly said:

"Ye, Jews, will organize wars and revolts."

Those who took part in the above Conference thought that they "knew better" than CHRIST, and even insulted HIM by inviting an arch-enemy of the PRINCE OF PEACE, Rabbi Stephen S. Wise, to explain how to avert wars. To avert wars is just the reverse of what his Talmud is dictating to him. He proved to be more honest and clever than his audience, and openly confessed that "being a Jew he was in trouble" to solve the problem!...

What could a rabbi answer to the imbeciles or hypocrites, who invited him to devitalize his own Talmud?

"Corral the 50 wealthiest Jews and there will be no wars" (H. Ford).

"Wars are the Jews' harvests" (Werner Zombart, a Jewish Professor).

How right is the brilliant Field Marshall Lord Haig, in saying:

"The Gospel of CHRIST is the world's only social hope and the sole promise of world peace. It is a crusade to which I urge you—a crusade not having for its object the redemption of a single city, however holy, but a freeing of the whole world from the devastating scourge of war" (New York Times, Febr. 22, 1925).

The above Conference proved once more, how true are the following opinions about women.

"American women delude themselves when they think they are advanced politically. They are behind the women of many other countries" (Miss Alice Paul, Vice-President of the National Women's Party, Chicago Tribune, Nov. 10, 1922).

"The trouble with you women is, you are too ignorant. Unless you get out of this ignorance, you are a positive menace" (The British Ambassador, Sir A. Geddes, Chicago Tribune, May 1, 1922).

"The almost total eclipse of the United States Delegates (women) under the shadow of the oratory of the foreign women was astonishing" (Mrs. O. D. Oliphant, Nat. Pres. of the American Legion Auxiliary, May 13, 1925).

The want of faith in OUR SAVIOUR among the women is one of the potent causes of the wavering morals of today and recalls the following. A newspaper, commenting the data of a statistician that there are 536,000,000 Christians exclaimed:

"We are depressed when we wonder where they live."

"Many are ashamed to acknowledge CHRIST. England and the U. S. in spite of their self-confidence and their ability to produce wealth, are in the greatest moral danger of all" (Miss Christabel Pankhurst).

The scorning of CHRIST is conducive to catastrophe.

WATCH AND EXPOSE THE WORK OF SATANISTS

A famous Russian, A. Kryloff, has told the story of a country-man who travelled to the Capital to see the Zoological Museum. Returning home he narrated how he had been roaming in the Museum and had seen all there—even to the insects.

"And how does the elephant look?", asked a child.

"I did not notice the elephant," answered the peasant.

This fable reminds me of all historians and authors who have written about the French Revolution and Napoleon I, and on other periods of History. Thus there appeared a book, "The French Revolution," by Mr. G. P. Gooch ("Helps for Students of History.")

Mr. Gooch and the 100 authors on the French Revolution, whom he quotes, have studied all the "insects" which brought it about, except the chief one, the Hidden Hand. This "Elephant" of the Political Zoo, or more aptly, this "Tiger," is responsible for the French and for all the other revolutions, wars, and for all the "World Unrest" and bloodshed.

These authors and professors describe the birds, sheep and goats of the political zoo and say to their pupils:

"Now you know all the animals. You can go into the jungles and hunt, but beware of the goats and monkeys; they are dangerous; and may even upset you."

Such is the political preparation in the schools. It can produce but "incurable imbeciles".

As Mr. Gooch's book is published by the "Society for Promoting Christian Knowledge," one assumes that the author is a Christian. Satan offered CHRIST "all the kingdoms of the world". And having failed to thus destroy CHRIST, Satan inspired the Jews to kill HIM, while all the people shouted:

"His blood be on us and on our children!"

And 300 of the worst Jews, satanists, compose the Hidden Hand.

The Invisible Judeo-Mongol World Government is headed since 1770 by the dynasty of Rothschild . I shall throw complete light on their demoniacally sinister activity. Such revelations for "unknown and independent" reasons have always been interrupted, though in order to foresee ("to govern means to foresee," otherwise "without foreseeing one could not successfully govern") everybody ought to watch these Jews. Why is it kept secret?

"I have glimpsed into hell (Russia). The Jews are in control. Lenin spent his last days crawling on all-fours round the room and shouting repeatedly: 'GOD save Russia and kill the Jews.' 90% of the important posts in the Soviet Government are held by Jews" (Sir Percival Phillips, Daily Mail, London).

"The Jews are the cause of nearly all the ills of the World" (the Kaiser).

"The benefits brought to the Russian people by Bolshevism exist only on paper painted in glowing colours by bolshevist propaganda" (Emma Goldman, a Communist Jewess).

29

The Jews bequeath to their posterity the same hatred and destruction of the heritage of CHRIST.

"The Jew is the Anti-Christ; was in St. John's day; is to-day and will be" (Rev. Meryon Smith, a Jew).

"The strongest supporters of Judaism cannot deny that Judaism is anti-Christian" (The Jewish World, March 15, 1924).

"The Jews detest the spirit of the nations in the midst of which they live" (a Jew, Bernard Lazare, "Antisemitism").

WELL, how does it happen that students of history are invited to study the work and influence of the Church and yet are told nothing about the work of CHRIST'S foes—the Jews, the heirs of Satan? Why this constant conspiracy of silence?

They have kept their government and their Executives—the Hidden Hand—secret, with the object of ruling "all the kingdoms" offered by Satan to CHRIST, and which the former would grant to the Jews, should they accomplish the destruction of everything sown by CHRIST. Their program is exposed in the "Protocols."

Everybody must take into consideration what is being done, not only by the Church and the State, but also by the Anti-Church or the executors of Satan's will—the Jews.

Note also the fact that they have always brought as their sacrifice not **one** scapegoat, but two: one for Jehovah and one for Satan. Whosoever forgets or omits the Jewish question, be it through ignorance, or fear, is unfit to be a preacher, teacher or official.

Books in which, because of ignorance, cowardice or bribery or "mouth-watering," the chief satanists—the Rothschilds, are not mentioned, are worse than useless. They are even harmful, by reason of the light which they fail to kindle.

Numberless authors like Mr. Fr. Neilson in his "How Diplomats Make War" (which is not true); Dr. P. S. Reinsch in his "Secret Diplomacy" (the diplomacy which he describes is not "secret" but he does not speak about that which is really secret); and Prof. J. Holland Rose of Cambridge University, have written about the "Origin of the War". They exposed 99 causes of the war, except the main one: the "lust of murder" of the Jews.

A war is a "legalized" murder. Who is the Chief Murderer? CHRIST said: "The devil (Satan) is a murderer and the Jews will do his lusts of murder and lying". Simple, but how infinitely true. And History proves this with appalling accuracy!

My readers will pardon repetitions; they occur because the above words seem to be **entirely unknown to the nation.**

It looks as if I was the **only** man, who proved in my Gentiles Review that **a pagan could not be a statesman!**

"No man, unless he is drunk with optimism, can deny that the world is very sick, and it may be the sickness unto death" (Sir Ph. Gibbs).

"CONSCIENCE" MUST BE GIVEN TO HISTORY

The famous Al. Lamartine, Dictator of France in 1848, in his "Essay on the Manner of Writing History for the People," said:

"If you desire to mold the opinion of the masses, to rescue them from the **immoral doctrine of success,** do what has never been done before—GIVE A CONSCIENCE TO HISTORY. By treating your theme in this spirit, you will win **less popularity;** * you will not fire the passions** or the imaginations of the people, but you will render a **thousand times better service** to their cause, their interests and their reason. Teach them by facts, by events, by the hidden meaning of those great historic dramas (of which we perceive only the scenery and the actors, while their plots are contrived by a HIDDEN HAND) to know, to judge, and to moderate themselves. Make them capable of distinguishing those, who serve them from those, who mislead them, those who dazzle from those who enlighten them. Point to every great man and great event, and say: Weigh them for yourselves, not with the false weights of your transient passions, your prejudices, your anger, your national vanity, your narrow patriotism, but by the Universal Conscience of the human race, and by the utility of each act for the cause of civilization."

Even before I had read the above lines, I had already tried to give a Conscience to History and to rescue the readers from the "immoral doctrine of success," by proving to them, that the "marvelous successes" of the so-called "great men" (in reality great mischief-makers), were due to the support of Satan's delegates. I explained the "hidden" meaning of those great historic dramas, like the dethronement of the three well meaning ancient dynasties recently upset, because hundred years ago (in 1815) they had the courage to sign the "Holy Alliance", i.e. a League of Nations with CHRIST as the Supreme LEADER.

"Suppress a truth of which we have good evidence, and, like the stone of stumbling and rock of offence, it may fall upon us by and by and grind us to powder." (Henry W. Rankin).

"The most unpleasant truth in the long run is the far safer traveling companion than the most agreeable falsehood" (Emerson).

"The truth about demons, not ignorance, shall make us free from their subtle deceptions. As all truth makes free, we are, in a sense, free in proportion to the truth which we apprehend." (Evangelist Arthur C. Zepp).

The Truth in History and about the demons composing the Hidden Hand was suppressed. What are the results of such crime?

The famous defender of criminals, Clarence Darrow, stated:

"An intelligence test (in the army) of 2.000,000 men between 20 and 30 shows that of our intelligent men in America, 70% run below 14 years of age. That is better than the average, because there are left out of that all the real imbeciles that have been discovered; all the insane; all the criminals that have been captured-all of those have been left out-and 70% average 14 years of age or less. Only 4% up to an ordinary standard in the most self-satisfied country on earth. Only 1% go to College."

"Present day young people are as ignorant of the Bible as the heathen," (Rev. Herbert L. Willett, Professor of the University of Chicago).

*Because the Jew controlled press will try to kill a truthful History through silence, as it will this very volume.

**Lamartine is advising the reverse of what Lionel Rothschild (Sidonia in "Coningsby") taught Disraeli.

25

CURE COWARDICE, IMBECILITY AND TREACHERY

Think of the father of a girl 5 years old, who, during a fire in his house, would discuss the danger of her being married to a crook some day. Yet The New Age Magazine, The Protestant, etc., are thus distracting our attention from the world's fire, which is the Judeo-Mongol satanic Bolshevism.

Thus The Protestant of June, 1922, assures us:

"A rapidly growing number of men are fully alert to the peril of Romanism and are helping to arouse the people to a realization of that peril in order that it may be resisted."

If there exist a "danger of Romanism" it is like the famous "poison"—coffee: it takes a century to feel its "harmful" effects. If "Romanism" were permitted to do what it likes in America, which is not easy to conceive, in a 100 years perhaps there might be some change. But to accomplish it, it would be necessary to put both this country and "Romanism" under a glass cover beyond the influences of all Satanic forces. But this country already is watched by the Judeo-Mongol Hidden Hand, which is working to blow up the Vatican and also to smash the United States.

"Romanism" is itself in terrific danger, menaced by the same fierce wholesale assault of Satan's agencies upon all Churches.

Only very ignorant people (or crooks, hired by the Hidden Hand in order to split the Christians still more) pay no attention to the universal attack of the devil's sons upon CHRIST.

Thus, since 1917, when the Jews Kerensky (Kirbis Adler) and later on Leiba Bronstein (Trotzky) seized power in Russia, they did all they could to disunite, split and degrade her Church.

A Jew, Rev. Hecker went to Russia and organized the so-called "Living Church". He belonged to the Y. M. C. A. of New York.

A Jew, Mustapha-Kemal, Dictator of Turkey, cast out the Oecumenical Patriarch from Constantinople, where the Patriarchs of the Eastern Catholic Church have lived for a thousand years.

A Jew, Masaryk, President for life (though this is against the Law) is preparing to drive out from Prague the Envoy of the Pope.

A Jew, H. Gluck, ejected the Russian Metropolitan of America.

The Jews in France, headed by E. Rothschild Vth, are urging their "French" free-masonry to bring about the severance of all diplomatic relations with the Holy Father, against the will of nearly the entire French nation. The Hidden Hand is not touched by the dove talk of General Dawes and all the "pacifists". It wishes to "do the lust of murder".

A Protestant-Catholic clash is the Hidden Hand's chief aim!

"Do the reverse of what your foe wishes." (Napoleon, a genius).

Only the reconciliation and co-operation of all the Christians could prevent the, otherwise, imminent catastrophe.

26

THE CATHOLIC CHURCH AND THE JEWS

"Let the Roman and Anglican Churches be united" (Lord Halifax).

Thus, the Anti Vatican move is doubly profitable to the Hidden Hand: it lowers the Church and it can also provoke a Civil War everywhere, as the brilliant General Castelnau warns us. And a fratricidal war would mean a new attack by Germany, which is again ready and again inflamed by her "sons of the devil."

What are the relations between the great Christian Church, called Roman Catholic and the Jews?

"At the last Secret Consistory the Holy Father called upon all right thinking men to combine in fighting the threat of socialism and communism. His words are considered the severest condemnation of a foreign government" (The New York Times, Dec. 19, 1924).

But what is Bolshevism? It is the Jewish mask of Communism.[*]

"Bolshevism is militant Judaism; the extermination of the White races and the substitution of Asiatic parasites for the Aryans. It is the work of Jewish assassins for the purpose of causing a new domination of the World by a criminal sect" (Sir Patrick Hamilton).

"The communists are Jews, and Russia is being entirely administered by them. They are in every government office, bureau and newspaper. They are driving out the Russians and are responsible for the anti-Semitic feeling which is increasing." (Mrs. Clare Sheridan, friend of Bronstein-Trotzky, in the The New York World, Dec. 15, 1923).

"**I am prepared to prove that Bolshevism (which is merely a modern word for Judaism)**, the vicious manipulations of foreign exchanges, and the general 'world unrest' prevailing today, may be summed up in two words, namely, 'Jew Finance'" (President of the best English patriotic society "The Britons," the famous patriot H. H. Beamish, author of the "Jews' Who's Who.")

Thundering at Bolshevism, the Roman Pontif hits Judaism.

"Rome is the greatest enemy of Bolshevism," pointed out a Jew, Sir Alfred Mond in his own "English Review" in an article—"The World Battle of the Jews", in which the Christians are shown between the Jewish anvil—Capitalism—and the Jewish hammer—Bolshevism. Thus Rome was designated to the Jews as the chief target at which they must strike. . . .

Mr. York Steiner, a known Zionist, quotes the words of the Cardinal Merry del Val, then Papal Secretary of State:

"We meet the Jews in every camp, hostile to us, Christians. As soon as a dirty book appears, or a journal, which shocks us, we find behind them the Jew" ("Ritual Crime. Jewish Treason," at La Renaissance Francaise)

The Jews Apfelbaum ("Zinoviev"), Rosenfeld ("Kamenev") etc., the "Czars" of Russia would throw all the Russian troops into Central Europe in order to stage the bloody World Revolution, as Frunse confessed (The New York World, Febr. 21, 1925).

"Should some new catastrophe overtake Europe the U. S. would be irresistibly drawn into the maelstrom ere the conflict ended" (Sen. Oscar Underwood).

[*]In his "Jews In Russia" (at "The Britons," London) Mr. Victor E. Marsden, correspondent of The Morning Post, published the names of all the 545 Soviet Commissars. Of them 447 are Jews, 34 Letts, 30 Russians, etc. But even many of these Letts and Russians are in reality Jews or married to Jewesses.

27

"WILL EUROPE FALL INTO THE HANDS OF JEWS"?

In his book "The Dawn of Day" Nietsche wrote:

"One of the spectacles which the next century (the XX-th) will invite us to witness is the decision regarding the fate of the Jews. It is quite obvious now that they have cast their die and crossed the Rubicon; the only thing that remains for them is either to become masters of Europe or to lose Europe, as they once centuries ago lost Egypt, where they were confronted by similar alternatives... Europe may some day fall into their hands like ripe fruit, if they do not clutch it too eagerly."

"The British Guardian" of London, rightly states:

"Now this is exactly what the Jews have done, and so have saved Europe: they have been too eager. The first clutch was the Boer War which put the World's chief gold supply into their hands The Great War was their next eager clutch. The Bolshevizing of Russia followed. Then came the clutch at Hungary, under Bela Kun, which lasted 100 days, then the clutch at Bavaria, which lasted three weeks. By this time the world is beginning to awake and the fiat of the White Race has gone forth: 'The Jews must lose Europe, as centuries ago they lost Egypt.' They are on trek to Zion once more. They are Zionists this time, as they were when they trekked out of Egypt."*

When one has read the predictions of Dostoiewsky, of Nietsche, of the Jew J. Lemann (who 30 years before this war and Bolshevism exposed the "Plan of Hell" and foretold "The Funereal Lines"); and the recent confessions of the prominent Jews: Dr. Oscar Levy of London, and Rene Groos of Paris, how absurd, if not criminal, seem all those naive or hypocritcal persons, who despite all the above are willing to deceive their readers into the belief, that the above "funereal lines" happen just through the "inability of the diplomats," or "because of the corruption of the Czar's regime", as Lloyd George, Bernard Shaw, Guglielmo Ferrero and other "lickers" of the Jewish boots are falsely saying. No, all that has happened since 1914, and is still happening—is the logical consequence of a deliberate Judeo-Mongol satanic "Plan of Hell" traced out in the "Protocols of the Learned Elders of Zion."

All the efforts of the Jews and of their valets to prove the forgery of the "Protocols" fall flat: we daily see them realized!

In his clever book: "The Truth About the Protocols Of Zion" a brilliant Slav author Gregory Bostunich pictured the symbolical satanic "Serpent", having surrounded all Europe, with his head in Odessa looking to the South on Constantinople. The Oecumenic Patriarch has been, "blown out" from Constantinople after a sojourn of 1,000 years. This move of the satanic "Serpent," succeeded, not because Turkey is ruled by Ottomans but because a Jew-Mongol, Mustapha-Kemal, is its virtual Dictator.

"Alas, Satan is not done with Europe" (Mr. Lloyd George).

"America's prosperity hinges on Europe" (Secretary Herbert Hoover).
*Note that these lines are from the pen of Dr. John H. Clarke, a great scientist, known as the most successful homeopath on earth. In The Bolshevists in Ancient History "by Aplonus" (at The Britons, London) is proved that the Jews staged Bolshevism in Egypt and, therefore, were expelled.

SAVE CHRISTIAN ARYAN CIVILIZATION

The First World War brought to Edw. Rothschild and to his 300 Jews, composing the "Hidden Hand", more than 100 billion dollars. Why not repeat it? They are the executors of Satan.

The First World War caused 40,000,000 casualties. And the Jewish Revolution in Russia cost her some 30,000,000 lives. This only increased the "lust of murder" of the satanists and now they are staging a revolt in the United States, if possible a new Civil War, (inflaming Protestants, who are the employers—against the Catholics, 95% of whom are hard workers) and then cause America to be attacked by a whole Foreign Circular Coalition.

My object is to explain what has really happened in history, all that will happen, if we still continue to be frightened by a band of criminals, who should be arrested, tried and made harmless, to rid the world of this unspeakably shameful fear, which paralyzes our defense and which will cause our destruction.

I shall reveal all the "mysteries", show the way to become a statesman, expose the plan of our Satanic foes, and the way to save this wonderful country, Christendom and the White Race.

My "Theory of the Satanic Forces" gives the key to all the most complicated problems. As every second counts, if Christendom is to be saved, I did not waste time in trying to improve my foreign style of English. My readers will understand the gravity of today's situation and will magnanimously forgive this.

Many deficiencies of this book could have been remedied but for the lack of civic courage and patriotism of American publishers, and my own depleted resources, which compelled me to abridge the material, and arrange it, not in the best, but in the most economical manner, and to have it printed by foreigners, like myself; hence its telegraphic, often stilted style, and lack of proper sequence.

My prime purpose has been to corral the facts and bring them before the public as speedily as possible.

I expect the Hidden Hand to seek my life for disclosing their diabolical deeds and sinister plans; but "we cannot attempt to save the world and repose in a realm of safety". Aside from the fact that nobility and rank impose grave obligations upon my conscience, Christian duty and racial concern impel me to publish this book, demand that you read it, and urge others to do likewise.

"The world will never again seem the same to you." (H. Vikingson).

Respectfully,

New York City, September, 1925.   THE AUTHOR.

THE INVISIBLE WORLD GOVERNMENT

PROOFS OF ITS EXISTENCE

To prove to my readers, how indispensable this book is, and also to make clear the existence of the Judeo-Mongol Invisible World Government, known as the Hidden Hand, I shall mention the most vital declarations of the great political leaders.

All that amazed the brainiest heads of humanity will be an "open secret" to my readers.

Why France and Russia went to war in 1812 has been a puzzle It was the Hidden Hand, that organized it.

Disraeli-Lord Beaconsfield, wrote (1844, "Coningsby," p. 252):

"The World is governed by very ''different'' personages from what is imagined by those who are not behind the scenes," i. e., not by Kings and Ministers. Disraeli said not "others," but "different", which means "not the kings, ministers or other similar men", but absolutely "different", possibly even of a different race. Who they are must be known first of all and only then can we control them and establish peace! Not before.

Bismarck, the Iron Chancellor, perceived the existence of invisible forces, but could not or did not wish to formulate them, and called them "imponderabilia" (Powers which no one could fathom).

The existence of the Hidden Hand was stated by Lamartine.
"We wish to break every kind of yoke, yet there is one that is unseen, yet that weighs on us. Whence comes it? Where is it? No one knows, or, at least, no one tells. The association is secret, even for us, the veterans of secret societies" (Mazzini to Dr. Breidenstein).

What imbeciles or criminals are the Gentiles, who are upseting the Christian Monarchs in order to serve the Jewish.
"Beyond the Masons and unknown to them, though formed generally from them, lay the deadly secret conclave, which nevertheless used and directed them for the ruin of the world and their own selves." (Mr. George F. Dillon in his "The War of Anti-Christ with the Christian Civilization," p. 72).

But who is the head and of whom consists the secret conclave, which leads these misled Masons? It is the Hidden Hand.
"The French provinces complained that they had to receive their revolutions by mail from Paris" (Robert Mackenzie in his "The 19th Century").
"The 'popular' revolution was only the camouflage of foreign conspiracies" (Saint Just, the terrible companion of Robespierre, the only man of his gang who kept his courage till his head fell under the guillotine).

Yes! All the revolutions were prepared by the Hidden Hand, with criminals freed from jails, and by all kinds of bribed agents and adventurers headed by provocators of foreign powers, interested in checking the then strongest powers: France and Russia.

Today Great-Britain and the United States are the strongest.

30

"Casimir Perrier (President of the Council of Ministers and practically the Dictator of France in 1832) talked of the 'mysterious' vexations, that filled his political life. He had often been forced to bend beneath a power superior to his own" (Louis Blanc in his "History of Ten Years," 1830-1840, p. 611).

What was this "superior and mysterious power?" It was not the King, who was C. Perrier's friend. Was it not the same Hidden Hand, that humiliated and overthrew his grandson 60 years later, when in turn he became President of France?

"History does not recollect another instance of such unparalleled success, of such immense fortunes won in such a short time by. sheer force of intellect rising superior to all adverse circumstances. The firm (of the Rothschilds) startled the world like the flash of a meteor. . . . The more one considers the marvellous manner in which it won its way to fame and fortune, the more incredible the story seems. . . . From being dealers in old coins, the founder of the family and his sons rose to be "friends" of the government of every nation" (Mr. John Reeves in his "The Rothschilds," p. 2-3).

But he explains nothing, as nobody does, except myself.

"In times of revolution, authority remains with the greatest scoundrels" (Danton, leader of one of the worst revolutions, "French Revolution," by Mrs. Nesta Webster, p. 390).

"This mighty revolution, which is at this moment preparing in Germany and of which so little is as yet known, is developing ehtirely under the auspices of Jews, who almost monopolize the professorial chairs of Germany" (Disraeli in 1844, in "Coningsby," p. 250, of the revolution of 1848.)

"In the movement of Vienna in the month of March, 1848, the people played no part" (Blaze de Bury in "Germany as it is," p. 122).

"Other than Gambetta, no man has less deserved the high role, that the HAZARD of the popular revolutions made him play, to the misfortune of France," (Henri Dutrait Crozon in his "Defense Nationale," see "L'Action Francaise," November 11, 1920).

Nothing is left to HAZARD in the revolutions and there are no "popular" revolutions, but all the revolutions of the past, as of the future (also in the United States) are prepared and precipitated by the same HIDDEN HAND, unfortunately ignored here.

"Wherever revolution breaks out, it is managed by the Jews" (Ch. Wibley).

G. Hannotaux, French Minister for Foreign Affairs, confessed that"mysterious forces" were ruling politics and "muddling the cards of diplomacy," ("L'Europe et les Balkans").

Count A. de Mun, French Academician, member of the Chamber of Deputies, after fifty years of study asked:

"What are those mysterious X-es, which are creating all the events?"

Sazonoff, the Russian Minister for Foreign Affairs, has stated that many events (foretold by me) were quite "unexpected" to the diplomatists (such as the declaration of the First Balkan War).

THE "MYSTERY" OF 5 GREAT HISTORIANS.

"In the Middle Ages there was the Asefah or Synod to unify Jews under Judaism. From the middle of the 16th to the **middle of the 18th century,** the Waad or Council of Four Lands legislated autonomously" (Israel Zangwill in his "The Problem of the Jewish Race").

What happened in the middle of the 18-th century, which made superfluous or which replaced the Waad?

"The modern social revolutionary movement dates from the **middle of the 18th century.** Ever since that time there has been flowing a continuous stream of subersive agitation, assuming many forms, but essentially the same, and ever broading and deepening until it became a veritable flood which has submerged Russia and which threatens to engulf our civilization," wrote, in 1922, Mr. Lothrop Stoddard, in his excellent book "The Revolt Against Civilization." Yes. But what gave such sudden impetus to the "Forces of Unrest?"

"From the **end of the 18th century,** revolution and war had become, in western civilization, a kind of inebriating sport, with the governing classes. Poets, philosophers, statesmen, journalists and parties exalted wars and revolts, sometimes both, thanks to extraordinary (?) concourse of favorable circumstances" (G. Ferrero, Italy's historian, Chicago Herald, July 30, 1922).

Why did these men drive humanity into an ocean of blood, as the Gadarene swine were driven into the sea?

The explanation is that murder became the "inebriating sport," when the Jews invaded Masonry and became the "governing class."

"The great revolutionary movement began at **the end of the 18th century**" (Mrs. Nesta Webster, the best British historian, in her famous "World Revolution—The Plot Against Civilization").

H. G. Wells stated that the mental and moral progress of the human race ended with the 18-th century (New York American, July 27, 1924). Bernard Shaw in a debate with H. Bellock implied that "something" enormous happened in 1790 (N. Y. Times).

That is why also Rev. J. Roach Straton of New York rightly stated, that "we are every day in every way becoming sillier and sillier."

But all the above very best Jewish, American, Italian and English historians are all wrong in data·

The 5 excellent authors (except Mrs. Webster) would die from fear rather than reveal this "Mystery."

The great revolutionary movement began **between the middle and the end of the 18-th ccentury,** when in 1770 Amschel Rothschild became the manager of the Landgrave of Hesse Cassel. Amschel hired all the "Miliukovs," "Kerenskies," "Lenins" et al. of the 18th century to start their subversive agitation, just as E. Rothschild hired those of the 20th century in order to stage bloodshed, as was foretold by OUR SAVIOUR.

THE "MYSTERIOUS" X-ES WHICH CREATE THE EVENTS.

A "prophet", Abdul Baha, said certain "scorpions and wolves" should be kept apart. But he does not say who they are.

"The limitation of armaments is not peace. The causes of war lie deeper," (Mr. Samuel Gompers, Chicago Journal, Oct. 19, 1921).

And one "very limited" bomb could blow up or poison all New York or Chicago, as Gen. W. Mitchell confirmed.

The Bishop of Michigan, Senator La Follette, the Bishop of New York, Mayor J. F. Hylan and the New York Times have spoken vaguely about an "Invisible Government."

Miss Jane Adams, "foremost woman of America," simply refused to answer certain questions after her talks. She said:

"The women will save the League of Nations." *

"This League is Israel's mission", declared Mr. Israel Zangwill. Would it not be better that women save Christian civilization and leave to Israel the task of "saving" their "Kosher" League of Nations, which, according to the Editor of "Plain English," the talented Lord Alfred Douglas, was destined to be the Jewish Central Government for obtaining World domination.

"The League of Nations is a Jewish idea. We created it after a fight of 25 years" (Nahum Sokolow, Zionist leader, Aug.27,1922 at Carlsbad Congress).

Facts confirm that events following 1897 (the Zionist Congress at Bale) were the result of the above "Jewish fight"...

"Remove the misconceptions produced by well organized propaganda," appeals Mr. Joseph Daniels on Nov. 6, 1921. But he does not say where it is, and why is it not revealed and forbidden?

"This improvement of Europe comes from below and not from above. Her rulers and her leaders are still viewing the men of her nations as hostile tribes" amazingly exclaims G. H. Lorimer, Editor of The Saturday Evening Post. on July 8, 1922. Yes! But who are those rulers, who hate their people? Surely, they are not the Christian Monarchs.

"Can the powder magazine of Europe be guarded from the danger that would come from the sparks of a Viennese revolution? Can the danger of lightning and the flames of another war be avoided? If Europe is to be saved from this catastrophe, (and I believe it to be immediately imminent), some formula must be found." (F. A. Vanderlip, Chicago D. News).

Yes! And I give this formula, as efficient as it is simple.

It is the trial of Ed. Rothschild V. and of his "300."

*The League of Nations is entirely run by the Jews: Paul Hymans (Pres. of the Council); Sir. J .Eric Drummond (Secr. General); Paul Mantoux (Chief of the most important Political Section); Major Abraham (Assist. Chief of this Section); Mrs. N. Spiller (Secretary of this Section); etc., etc. The Jews' valet, Albert Thomas, who helped with French millions to enthrone the Judeo-Mongol bolsheviks in Russia, is the Chief of the Labor Section. He receives a fabulous salary (see "Le Peril Juif. Le Regne d'Israel chez les Anglo-Saxons," at B. Grasset, 61 rue des Saints Peres, Paris).

SATAN VERSUS CHRIST

Satan offered "all the kingdoms of the world" to CHRIST in order to prevent HIM from spreading HIS teachings.

Having failed in this, Satan readily found Jews willing to kill CHRIST and, this being insufficient, to annihilate HIS DOGMA!

These efforts of the Jews which can be traced step by step from the death of our Saviour until to-day were and are backed by Satan, his followers and their agents.

In order to succeed more easily and to exercise their power in all its magnitude, i. e. to establish "Israel Above All", the Jews have kept their Government **secret** and "**invisible**".

In order to dissimulate their purpose, they organized, thousands of years ago, their numberless executive committees under the name of Free-Masonic lodges.   Those Lodges bribed or attracted by deception the most influential and unscrupulous Christians and made them (some of them unconsciously) further their Satanic plan.

Immense libraries of books, confirming that Free-Masonry is an entirely Jewish organization, may be found in Paris at "La Renaissance Francaise" (3 Rue Solferino); at the "Revue Internationale des Societes Secretes" (96 Boul. Malesherbes); at "La Vieille France" (5 Rue du Pre-aux Clercs) written by such authors: as Jouin, Gohier, Copin-Albancelli, Daste, et al. It is a real disgrace that these books have not yet been translated into English.

"Facts of world importance are known to too few men, and we need more facts, Humanity cannot find the light, unless it has facts" (The Editor of the Chicago Daily News.)

The chief (and perhaps the only) object of the Free-Masons, (except a few Lodges, which are "mock Masonic") and especially the Grand Orient of France, is to ruin the Christian Church and every State (which is not yet governed by a Vice-Roy of the Jewish Supreme World Government) and bring about Anarchy as foretold by the famous Russian philosopher Dostoiewsky (1880), which will compel the people to recognize "Israel Above All"

Mrs. Nesta Webster in her 3 excellent books, The Morning Post in its "Cause of World Unrest" and numberless authors exposed in detail the history of the creation of Free-Masonry by the Jews, and also how the Jews later invaded or re - educated nearly all the Free-Masonic Lodges, opened by the Christians.

To be a free-mason means to "hob-nob" freely with hell. Nearly all the masonic lodges became "laymen's synagogues." As soon as the Jews joined Gentiles' Masonry murders began· "The Jews supply 50% of the criminals" (Chief Police, Gen, Binghan).* *Add to this figure numerous criminal Jews, camouflaged as "Russians,"

34

"THE PLAN OF HELL"

A Jew, Abbe Joseph Lemann, wrote in 1886:*

"There is a plan 'of hell' to disorganize at one blow Christian society and the beliefs of the Jews, then with this double organization to bring about a state of things where, religiously speaking, there will be neither Christian nor Jew, but only men stripped of divinity, and where, politically speaking, the Christian will become, if not the slave, at least the inferior of the Jew, the MASTER. . . At the hour in which we hold the pen, we see this plan unrolling itself in sombre horizons and great funereal lines"

Thus the Jews knew in 1886 what would happen in 1914-1918!

It is true, that there is a plan of "hell", i.e., of Satan, but it is not true, that it would destroy "the beliefs of the Jews." No! According to CHRIST the Jews are the sons of Satan, and faithful to Satan the Jews will remain.

Quoting the above words of a Jewish patriot, the author of "The Cause of World Unrest," warns:

"This passage suggests, that there is some terrible sect, controlled by the Jews for destruction of our present social order,"(p. 87).

Yes! But why not reveal this Jewish organization and its known leaders and thus disarm them? How would it be possible for Americans to avoid fatal political blunders, worse than crimes, if nobody could solve the mystery of these hidden forces. It is always the same Hidden Hand. A prominent Jew, Rene Groos, wrote:

"There is a Jewish Conspiracy against all Nations, but first of all against France, and the principle of order which she represents in the world. This conspiracy occupies almost everywhere the avenues of power; in France it is at present the actual reigning power. For observe that there all intelligent men see the danger: all those who think French thoughts, those who have any care for the future of France are getting ready for the struggle. The only people who appear not to know it are the very people who have no excuse for not knowing it—THE MEN IN THE GOVERNMENT. I not only say it was the duty of these men to see the plot which is being woven against France; I say these men were in the best position for seeing it. They alone, however, showed no reaction against this double assault of Jewish Revolution and Jewish Finance. They have been domesticated by the latter. They have bowed before the former. Am I wrong in speaking of a Jewish reign? If it is less apparent than in Russia and Bolshevik Hungary, it is none the less real. And it is against the interest of France that it exercises its rule over it. Whoever observes and thinks, sees the peril. At the same time we see, parallel with it, and consequent upon the progress of the universal Jewish conspiracy a recrudescence of anti-Semitism. . . The Universal Jewish Conspiracy must be disrupted or France will perish as did Russia. The evidence presses on all minds. Even political passion is not strong enough to mask it. The life of France is at stake. We must take sides either for France or against her." ("Le Nouveau Mercure," June, 1922).

"A few imperialists make the sinister proposal (new French ships); they are not French people." (Repr. Cooper, Chicago Tribune, Dec. 18, 1921.)
*In his book "L'Entree des Israelites dans la Societe, Francaise."

35

THE MOST FORMIDABLE SECT IN THE WORLD

"The Curse of the Romanovs." Thus a Jew, Angelo Rappoport, entitled his huge book, but did not reveal, who cursed them

"The appalling thing is not the tumult but the design. Through all the fire and smoke (of the "French" Revolution) we perceive the evidence of calculating organization. The managers (?) remain studiously concealed or masked, but there is no doubt about their presence from the first" (Lord Acton, the famous Cambridge Professor in his "Essays on the French Revolution").

But he does not reveal, who these "managers" were.

Mrs. N. Webster suggested several answers (which practically means none) and confessed, that she wandered into a "blind alley."

Everybody fears to speak of the **Hidden power**, the mischief maker. The Jews maintain the greatest secrecy about their Occult Government, but hundreds of writers, even Jewish, have confirmed its existence. A repetition interposes itself:

"In the Middle Ages there was the Asefah or Synod to unify Jews under Judaism. From the middle of the 16th to the middle of the 18th century, the Waad or Council of Four lands legislated autonomously"

testifies Mr. Zangwill in his "The Problem of the Jewish Race."

The Waad was no longer needed since Rothschild I· granted the countries, which were formerly ruled by the Waad to his 5 sons. Thus all these "mysteries" are simply explained. Since the Jews became the "governing classes," murder became the "inebriating sport." Yes! But CHRIST proclaimed this 2000 years ago. There are numberless proofs, that the Jews never sought the improvement of any nation, but that their aims were to murder and de-Christianize.

The same is now true of Russia, lulled by the Jew-bolsheviki.

"Lenin was the chief of the most formidable sect in the world," Secretary of War, Winston Churchill, wrongly declared in the House of Commons on Nov. 5th, 1919.

No! It was this "sect," which chose Lenin and sent him as a mere agent, though its ablest. Warburg gave him $10,000,000.

"Lenin (or Oulianov by adoption, originally Zederbaum, a Kalmuck Jew, married a Jewess, and whose children speak Yiddish) is no more. The press assures us, women fainted and leaders wept. Such is the report published by the press. Who purveys such 'gup' to swallow and what is its object? The Hidden Hand wangles it into our press" (The Patriot, Jan. 31, 1924, Capt. A. Proctor).

"What is this 'formidable sect' of which Abbe Barruel speaks in the 18th century. and Churchill in the 20th? Upon the answer may rest the safety of Christianity and of civilization based on Christianity. It was a power outside of Russia: it was a world-wide power, and it was strong enough to bring Russia down, and also the House of Hohenzollern. What was it?" (the author of the "Cause of World Unrest," p. 35).

Nobody ever answered, except I. It is the Hidden Hand.

"Once more we are in the cycle of revolution" (Mrs. Nesta Webster).

THE FINANCIAL OCTOPUS STRANGLING AMERICA.

The Secretary of the Treasury during the war Mr. William Gibbs McAdoo pointed out on June 22, 1924, the danger of the "Invisible Government" (the Hidden Hand) which he said is located in Wall Street, (in reality rather in Pine Street) and implied that the "newspapers do not give the facts," as did also Mr. W. J. Bryan:

"New York is the city of privilege. Here is the seat of that invisible power represented by the allied forces of finance and industry. This invisible Government is reactionary, sinister, unscrupulous, mercenary and sordid. It is wanting in national ideals and devoid of conscience... This kind of Government must be scourged and destroyed."

Yes! But this "Invisible Government" in Wall Street or Pine Street, is but a branch of the Judeo-Mongol World Government headed today by Edouard Rothschild V th in Paris.

Mayor J. F. Hylan of New York declared on June 24th, 1924:

"Wall Street is a hotbed of political and financial schemes and plots for the control of everything, from the food you eat to the clothes you wear. It is in Wall Street that the International bankers grind out gold and more gold for the favored few, move faithless party leaders, nominate candidates for public office and use the army and navy of the United States for their private purposes as relentlessly as does the hand of fate move the children of men."

Does not this most startling declaration prove that the "International bankers" (the Hidden Hand) could throw the United States into a war whenever they desire it for their own ends?

"War starts in the brains of a few-conquerors, financiers or autocrats — not in the mind of the dull mob" (Brisbane, The N. Y. American).

"Let the assassins first stop murdering" (French dictum).

"The real menace of our Republic is the Invisible Government, which like a giant octopus sprawls its slimy length over city, state and nation. At the head of this octopus is a small group of powerful banking houses, generally referred to as the 'International' bankers. This little coterie of powerful International bankers virtually runs our Government for their own selfish ends,"

declared Mr. John F. Hylan, on March 26, 1922, in Chicago.

All this is true, but Mr. Hylan purposely or unknowingly stated an untruth, when he added, that the octopus is headed by J. D. Rockefeller· The latter is not a banker, is not International but 100 % American and is not a "menace," because he would spend $100 millions to prevent what the Rothschilds would willingly spend 100 millions to attain, viz., that the Christians murder one another. And the Rothschilds and the "300" are 200 times richer and meaner, than are the Rockefellers. Misinforming the public as did Mayor Hylan is especially harmful on the eve of an assault upon the United States by the Hidden Hand.

"We speak loosely of the Morgans and Rockefellers, but can trace little evidence of their control"

wisely states the eminent Mr. Theodore H. Lunde of Chicago.

THE HIDDEN HAND IS AN ABSOLUTE MONARCHY.

Mr. Lloyd George, himself a "friend" of the "International bankers", however wrote:

"The international bankers dictated the Dawes reparation settlement. The Protocol which was signed between the Allied and Associated powers and Germany is the triumph of the International financier. Agreement would never have been reached without the brusque and brutal intervention of international bankers. They swept statesmen, politicians and journalists all on one side, and issued their orders with the imperiousness of absolute monarchs, who knew that there was no appeal from their ruthless decrees. The settlement is the joint ukase of King Dollar and King Sterling. Dawes report was theirs. They inspired and fashioned it. The Dawes report was fashioned by the Money Kings."

"The orders of German financiers to their politicians were just as peremptory as those of the allied bankers to their political representatives. Will this last? If the settlement brings peace, there are multitudes who have hitherto disliked and distrusted cosmopolitan finance, who will secretly bless it and feel that Providence has at last found good use for the International financier" (The New York American, June 24, 1924.)

All those "Allied" and "German Jews", members of the Hidden Hand are in reality Judeo-Mongols (according to History and the "Jewish Encyclopaedia") who are arousing all the Mongols!

On June 16, 1900, the Jew-owned newspapers in Europe published as news that the German Ambassador to China, Count Clemens von Ketteler, was killed, because he entered a district of Peking forbidden to the Whites.* But the murder occurred exactly two weeks later, and precisely when he came into this district. For this "Chinese" crime, the Chinese people were severely punished. in order to irritate the Asiatics against the Whites. Who did all this? Somebody in the entourage of the Kaiser persuaded him to be most drastic with the Asiatics. Who staged the crime in Peking and who acted simultaneously in Berlin, and who knew two weeks ahead that this would occur?

"By a combination of Big Capital and Bolshevism Judaism is getting ready to conquer the World" (Deutsche Tageszeitung).

"The Judeo-Masonry means constant wars" (The Universal Anti-Jewish Alliance, the Aryan Committee, 33, rue Gioffredo, Nice, France).

"Lloyd George said he did not believe any ruler or statesman caused the war. It may be a century before the world will know the full truth" (Sen. Copeland).

I state now: the Hidden Hand caused this and all the wars.

*"Incidentally," of course, in Peking, as in all the important towns of Asia, there are agencies of the Sassoon ·Rothschilds, as confirmed by The Saturday Evening Post of June 19, 1909. And Bleichroeders, the Berlin agents of the Rothschilds. were practically the tutors of Bismarck and of the other Chancellors of Germany, including Bethmann-Hollweg-Rothschild, a Jew, the "hero" of the "scrap of paper," who started the World War!

THE HIDDEN HAND FEARS TRUTH

When Mr. Lloyd George promised to hang the Kaiser, there appeared in the Financial News, on Feb. 17, 1920, my prediction:

NO TRIAL OF THE KAISER.

"The Unseen (Hidden Hand) will not allow the trial of the Kaiser, because he may reveal most of its crimes... Instead of signing the Peace Treaty, casting out Bolshevism (only 30,000 soldiers were needed in 1918, and only 300,000 from the ten Allied Powers in 1919); the Hidden Hand wishing to bleed Russia white, and to enslave Europe by ruin and starvation, has imposed a 'Covenant,' showing its non-Christian origin and objects," etc.

On July 3, 1922, in the Chicago Tribune was published an interview of Baron C. v. Radovitz - Nei with the Kaiser, in which the latter declared, that the **Jews were at the bottom of the world's every ill.** You see that I was right in foretelling, that the Kaiser would denounce the Hidden Hand, if he were tried. That is the reason he was not brought to trial, and Lloyd George, knowing this, deliberately lied.

"Lloyd George cannot be trusted" (Lord Rhonnda, Nov. 1921.)

How immeasurably far from the truth are the statesmen, who believe, as does Lord Parmoor that "all the worst wars of recent times have been due to economic isolation," as is Signor Tittoni, ex-ambassador of Italy, who declared in Milan, that a League of Nations would make war more difficult. No, Signor...

No! The only way to prevent wars, among the White nations at least, is to expose the chief cause of wars: The Judeo - Mongol World Government, the direct Legatees of Satan.

"If the Czar would hang 300 criminal Jews, he would save 30,000,000 innocent Russians and his family" (Urbain Gohier, a great Frenchman)

"The Jews who surrounded Lloyd George, Wilson and Clemanceau are to be blamed for having created a 'Jewish Peace'." says M. G. Batault ("Le Probleme Juif", p. 38.)** According to CHRIST, the Jews are the sons of the devil, who is a mankiller. Therefore, no real peace could be expected from the above "statesmen", guided, as they were, by the Jews. M. Batault wrongly believes, that at Paris "people" were in the entente of two 'Internationales': of Gold and of Blood." It is like stating that there is an entente between the War and Navy Departments of the United States Government. There is constant "entente" between the two departments of the Judeo-Mongol Government.

*"The International bankers are offering Germany $10.000.000, if she will withhold the note renouncing the war guilt" (N. Y. American, Sept. 15, 1924).

**As Mr. Wilson brought to Paris 117 Jews and 39 Gentiles (mostly valets) I thrice warned Mr. J. W. Davis, the Ambassador, that Peace could not be signed.

39

THERE ARE 8,000,000 JUDEO-MONGOLS IN U. S.

Every English speaking person ought to read the 4 wonderful volumes on "The International Jew," published by "The Dearborn Independent." They cost only 25 cents each, but they give a masterly, though appalling and undeniable picture of the Jewish activities in the United States. It is a colossal pity that Henry Ford, a real genius, did not extend his study of the Jews in Europe also, where at least 200 of the 300 Jews, comprising the Hidden Hand, are busy at mischief making. In Volume II. we read:

"How many Jews are there in the United States? No Gentile knows. . . It is with the utmost difficulty that even ONE person can secure permission to enter this country from Germany, Russia, etc. But the Jews from these countries enter by the thousand unhindered and in utter disregard of the laws. . . It is like a moving army, which having done duty in Europe for the subjugation of that continent, is now being transferred to America."

It took me — a Major - General of an allied power, and of the most friendly — 30 months of insistent requests to secure permission to enter the United States, which I had already visited in 1907 and 1908, and where I have a score of very prominent friends. But a visa for a Jew is given almost at once, or a passport is forged!

There are nearly 2,000,000 Jews in New York (called Jew-York), nearly 3,000,000 more in the United States and at least 3,000,000 so-called "secret" or "crypto" Jews here. This is confirmed by an expert on the Jewish question, Mr. Aristide Tsaconas.

"If a Jew from England would meet in Lisbon two competitors, an English-Christian and a Jew from Portugal, he would of course, help the Portuguese" stated Lord Palmerston, former British Prime - Minister.

The same could be said about the Jews enrolled by the American Government as its Ministers abroad, where any day they may face the alternative of whose interests to defend, America's or those of the Jewish Supreme World Government. And as the latter is now preparing to destroy the United States, the situation of the Jews, who represent it, will be most difficult· And America will surely be betrayed, if not in every case, at least in many. Lord Palmerston may prove a real prophet.

"The Jews are in the eyes of the law aliens in the highest degree" (Lord Chief Justice of Great Britain, Hon. Coke).

'Numberless disintegrants are active. Forces of evil, driven under cover during the war, are re-emerging, issuing from their hiding places in answer to an atmospheric murkiness produced by those whose business it was, and who should have known how to keep the air clear" (Mr. Edw. Price Bell in The Chicago Daily News, of October, 1922). He speaks like Rene Groos.

Yes! But why not say, who are behind the "Forces of evil"? E. Price Bell, like the above mentioned authors, does not grasp the "crime of unrevealed facts," "the responsibility of knowledge!"

"We, Jews, invented the 'chosen people myth' " (Dr. Oscar Levy).

ALL MASS MURDERS — BY THE HIDDEN HAND.

The study of History proves indisputably, that all the revolts and wars since 1770 were started by the Rothschild Jews, and that revolutions and murders were organized,not because the rulers were bad, but because they became too good. It proves that the nobility and the clergy of France were imbued with the most liberal intentions to unanimously grant freedom to the press, to workers, to religions and to renounce all their privileges, and that the workers should be exempt from taxation.* It is proved by the records prior to August 4th, 1789, that all this was granted.

But this was not the object of the Jews, and on Aug. 10, 1792 appeared 82 unknown men, who seized the City Hall and power. Even Robespierre and Danton did not at once follow them in their manner of mass murdering and obeyed only later. Thus everything needful for the French nation was obtained on Aug. 4, 1789 without any mass bloodshed. Likewise in Russia when Alexander II. prepared to sign the constitution; when Stolypin granted the lands to the peasants and wished to nationalize the banks; when Nicholas I. practically forbade wars by threatening to "fire on the first, who fires" and when Alexander I. wished to make CHRIST the SUPREME LEADER instead of the Monarchs. All those excellent men were murdered one by one by the Hidden Hand.

"Remember that the rulers of Russia (Nicholas II.) were the most charming and cultivated people in the world" (The Mirrors of Downing Street.")

In his "Helps for Students of History," G. P. Gooch mentions many of the best known historians, scientists and authors, who have written about the French Revolution, but all failed to explain why and how it occurred. This means, that having left their readers in ignorance of the causes of past revolutions, they have denied them the knowledge needed to prevent future upheavals; a most grievous omission. There is no doubt, that the White Race is facing a most terrific World Revolution staged by the Judeo - Mongol Hidden Hand which may put an end to civilization based on Christianity. The only means of salvation lies in a knowledge of the truth, by spreading this book, which reveals all the "mysteries."

"The order of Illuminati abjured Christianity; patriotism and loyalty were called narrow minded prejudices; it intended to root out all religion and ordinary morality, and even to break the bonds of domestic life, by destroying the veneration for marriage vows, and by taking the education of children out of the hands of the parents" (Robison, "Proofs of a Conspiracy," p. 106).

All this has already been accomplished in Russia by the Jew - bolsheviks and is now being attempted in the United States.

*Louis Daste, "Free-Masonry and Terror."

41

THE HIDDEN HAND

"Only 300 men, each of whom knows all the others, govern the fate of Europe. They elect their successors from their entourage. These German Jews have the means in their hands of putting an end to the form of any State which they find 'unreasonable.' " (Walter Rathenau, on Dec. 24, 1912, in the "Wiener Presse," see "Plain English," June 11, 1921).

This late Dictator of Germany declared, like Disraeli, that these "300" are not the visible rulers, because the Czar of Russia did not know these men. Thus according to Rathenau, the Czar was NOT among the persons, who governed Europe and thus the Czar was NOT guilty of making the war. When these revelations of Rathenau began to be repeated, he "suddenly" died, as perish "suddenly" all who expose the "300". Walter Rathenau's death was falsely attributed to the monarchists. But "suddenly" also the press stopped mentioning this "mystery".

"We, French, believe that we know all about the forces of our planet. But we know nothing about the most terrific of them. These are in the hands of 7 men, whose names our masses could not even rightly spell. These men, more powerful than Caesar or even Napoleon, rule the fate of the Globe. These men rule the Chiefs of States, control and subdue the governing personages, manipulate the exchanges and incite or suppress revolutions" (Stephane Lausanne, Editor of "Matin," Paris, on Jan. 6, 1923).

These 7 men are E. Rothschild V., his nephew Sassoon Rothschild, the heir presumptive to the World Throne, et al.

These Jews form the Supreme Council of the Hidden Hand.

"We are 300 men," shouted the conspirators of the "French" Revolution, when in 1770, a Jew, J. Balsamo-Cagliostro (the Rasputin of Queen Marie Antoinette) was adopted as their secret agent (read Al. Dumas) near Frankfort, this den of Rothschild.

These and the 300 men of Rathenau were "The Learned Elders of Zion." Since 1770 they have been led by a Rothschild·

"The phrase 'masters and men' is altogether out of date. Indeed, I begin to question, who are the masters," naively questioned Mr. J. H. Whitley, Member of the House of Commons ("The Daily Sketch" on October 27, 1920).

"Nominally we govern ourselves: actually, we are governed by an oligarchy of the American branch of the International Bankers' Plunderbund. The British Government is the camouflage behind which the money kings of the world have hitherto hid their economic warfare upon the masses of the world." (Philip Francis, ex-Editor of "The New York American" in his "The Poison in America's Cup", p. 45-59).

"Whoever is in power in Downing Street (British Foreign Office), whether Conservatives, Radicals, Coalitionists or pseudo-bolsheviks, the International Jew rules the roost. Here is the mystery of the Hidden Hand, of which there has been no intelligent explanation" (Leo Maxse, Editor Nat. Review, Aug. 1919).

* The Jewish New York Times of Sept. 8, 1924, quotes the protest of the Zionist Executive Committee against settling Jews in the countries (Mexico) over whose destiny they have no control. The same Jews help settling Jews in the U. S., which means they have control of its destiny."

42

Nobody explained the "mystery" of Robespierre. Nobody explained why he was shot and why "forgotten"? I will.

Dr. Dill Scott, President of the Northwestern University and the late Prof. Baron S. C. Korff of Georgetown University, both falsely declared at Evanston, in 1922, that there were many "inexplicable" and "un-understandable" events in the French Revolution of 1789 and in the Russian Revolutions of 1905 and 1917. Whether they were ignorants or hypocrites, the students remained untutored in the use of History (a mere "fog" even to the teachers) and without knowledge of the "secrets" of revolutions, which are staged by the same evil Forces. These forces organized also the Revolution in Germany in 1848 and what is more vital to us, they are obviously preparing one in the United States and may, possibly, start it in a few months. When one does not know the causes of an illness, it is most difficult to cure it.

My criticism of Mrs. N. Webster's book, French Revolution (1920) in Plain English of Aug. 28 and Sept. 4, 1920, inspired her.

In her wonderful World Revolution (1921) she already dares to quote from Charles d'Hericault (La Revolution. p. 104):

"At Wilhelmsbad in 1782 it was decided to remove the headquarters of 'Illuminized' (i. e. re-judaized or re-satanized) Free-Masonry to Frankfurt-on-Main, which 'incidentally' was the stronghold of Jewish Finance, controlled by such leading members of the race as Rothschild, Mayer Amschel. At this head lodge of Frankfurt the gigantic plan of world revolution (practically murdering) was carried forward and it was there, that at a large Masonic Congress in 1786, the deaths of Louis XVI and Gustavus III of Sweden were definitely decreed." (And also of Emperor Joseph II. of Austria).

The absence of these eight lines in Mrs. Webster's book French Revolution most visibly detracts from its great value.

Wilhelmsbad was a palace of Landgrave Frederick of Hesse-Cassel, Grand Master of the Bavarian Free-Masonry, whose "alter ego" and practically Minister of Finances and Foreign Affairs was the same Amschel Mayer the future Rothschild I., the World Emperor and World Assassin.

Adam Weishaupt (a Jew), Mirabeau, Rousseau and numberless actors in the events at the end of the 18th century were nothing but hired agents of the Invisible Judeo-Mongol Supreme Government, (the Hidden Hand) as are the Miliukovs, Kerenskies, Trotzkies and other world traitors salaried by the Jews for the extermination of Christendom by any means. But instead of losing time over them, let us acquaint ourselves with the Rothschilds.

THEY WANT TO BLOW UP THE UNITED STATES

ROTHSCHILDS, THE FORCES OF EVIL

"What is the good of our being a wealthy nation, if the wealth is all in the hands of German Jews?" (W.Hughes, the great Premier of Australia). "The house of Rothschild was (and is) the ruling power in Europe, for all the political powers were willing to acknowledge the sway of the great financial DESPOT, and, like obedient vassals, pay their tribute without murmur." (J. Reeves, in his "The Rothschilds," p. 105).

All the above "mysteries" and "forces of evil" and this "something," which happened in the 18th century, and which L. Stoddard, Ferrero, Webster, Zangwill, B. Shaw and Wells mention, but do not reveal — will be uncovered in this book, and I shall also explain the "mysteries", which puzzled the press concerning Northcliffe, Rathenau, Venizelos and others.

All is understandable, when one knows that this war, as every bloodshed since 1770, was organized by the Rothschilds; and as they control 90 % of the press, it was ordered to keep silent about their nefarious deeds.

A Jew, Sir Alfred Mond, the ex-Minister of Health of England, in his English Review, in "The World Battle of the Jews," proved, that the stupid Gentiles are between the Jewish anvil, Capitalism, and the Jewish hammer, Bolshevism, well co-ordinated.

"Nothing would constitute a more needless and base betrayal of civilization than the recognition of the bolshevik tyranny. The policy of the American-Anglo-German bankers is the most dangerous element in the whole chain of pro-bolshevist efforts. The bolshevist funds amount to millions." (Mr. S. Gompers, in The Chicago Tribune, of May 1, 1922.)

Not one single American asked him to explain, who are those "American-Anglo-German" bankers and why they are allowed to basely undermine the American Government? However, the three above enlightening statements prove, that the 300 men of the Hidden Hand are controlling the assault of both Jewish Finance and of Jewish Bolshevism against Christendom.

"Bolshevism (is) the Jewish attack on Civilization" (The patriotic Society of Great Britain, "The Britons," in a manifesto).

As all these "American-Anglo-German" bankers are autocratically ruled by the Hidden Hand, headed by Ed. Rothschild V in Paris, it is clear that he is the real chief of Bolshevism, the actual curse of the world, and also the head of the Financial "Octopus", which according to "Common Sense" (Monte Ne, Arkansas) is ruining the farmers and business men of America?

"Thanks" to the "help" of the Jews B. Baruch, Eug. Meyer, A.Shapiro, etc.,the farmers lost $32 billions (Gentiles' Review, №3).

"This system of banking (causing the ultimate ruin of all those who cultivate the soil) was the invention of Lord Overstone, with the assistance of the acute minds of the Rothschilds, bankers of Europe." (R.F.Pettigrew).*

*"An Internat.Crook" (see the British Guardian),Warburg brought it here.

ROTHSCHILDS RECOGNIZED AS MONARCHS.

As was proved for the 1.000th time at the Great Convention of Free-Masons (Nantes, France) on April 23, 1883, Weishaupt enunciated the same doctrine as that preached by the Jew-bolsheviks of to-day, viz. the "Hatred of Fatherland and of Patriotism"

When a man ceases to love his country, a Jew can buy him cheaper for any crime. Patriotism unites the nation and this makes it more difficult to enslave it.

"The Jewish influence has led the Russian revolution into the by-paths of wholesale murder, torture and rapine" (New Witness, London, Aug. 1, 1919)

"Coningsby (Disraeli) perceived, that all yielded to him, (Sidonia L. Rothschild), appealed to him, listened to him, were guided by him. What was the secret of his influence?"

asks Disraeli in his "Coningsby," page 258, and in the same book he reveals, that practically all wars and revolutions were then financed by the same Sidonia L. Rothschild (p. 218-219).

"Rothschild could be King of France, if he desired," (Mazzini, July 27, 1844, "The Birth of Modern Italy," p. 62, by Jessie White Mario.)

"The Kaiser and Bethmann-Hollweg were quite optimistic in believing that the conflict (Austro-Serbian, July, 1914) could be localized and that the solution could be left to Austria and Serbia" (Dr. Paul S. Reinsch in his "Secret Diplomacy," on p. 104).

No! The Kaiser was deceived, but Bethmann-Hollweg-Rothschild knew perfectly well, that he was deliberately pushing events towards war and ruin.* As a Rothschild he was one of the "300."

The Saturday Evening Post of June 19, 1909 revealed:

"The Montefiores have taken Australia for their own, and there is not a gold field or sheep run from Tasmania to New South Wales that does not pay them heavy tribute. They are the real owners of the great antipodean continent, and when the day comes, as it doubtless will, when the Commonwealth decides to overthrow British rule, it will be of the Montefiores and their associates of the Unseen Empire that it will ask permission."

How can the Americans expect Australia's help against Japan?

The secret of Montefiores' power and wealth lies in the marriage of Abraham Montefiore with Henriette, daughter of Amschel Rothschild, and in the marriage of his grandson Lord Anthony Rothschild with his cousin Montefiore.

"The league against Napoleon I, which was instrumental in shattering his dream of universal empire, was a Jewish organization" (Walter Hurt, "Truth About The Jews," p. 323).

"The principal 'loan floaters' of the world, the Rothschilds, were later the first railway kings. The period of 1820 onwards became the 'Age of the Rothschilds', so that at the middle of the century it was a common dictum: There is only ONE power in Europe, and that is Rothschild " (Prof. Werner Sombart in "The Jews and Modern Capitalism.")

*Read The Gentiles' Review, NN-2-8 in which are revealed the "Origin of the World War" and the "mysteries" of Bethmann-Hollweg-Rothschild, of the Crown Prince and numerous others.

UNDISPUTED AUTOCRACY OF THE ROTHSCHILDS.

"King Rothschild (James, III.). Emperor Nicholas," is what the first "Russian" bolshevik Al. Herzen (the Jew Herz) entitled a story of the 150 years assault by the Rothschilds upon the Romanovs. (Fortnightly Review, April, 1911, by a Jew, Rappoport).

"I sold myself to Satan (Rothschild) but he is German," (i. e. from Frankfort) Bismarck often repeated. Everybody knows, that Clemenceau was led by Mandel-Rothschild and Mr. Lloyd George by Sir Ph. Sassoon-Rothschild. E. Mandel House led Mr. Wilson.

Rothschild of London, discussing in Berlin a loan of 2 billion with the Jews, Rosen and Rathenau, German Ministers, said:
'If I decide it, no state on earth would dare to oppose it" (The Daily Express of London, 1921).

"Make Rothschild pay all France's war losses," recently pleaded one of the most esteemed Senators, M. Gaudin de Villaine, in the French Senate. Numberless proofs of the leading role in nefarious politics continuously played by the Rothschilds were adduced in the weekly, "La Vieille France," Paris.

"Rothschilds are everywhere masters of the financial situation," wrote a Rabbi in his book "A Rabbi on Goym (Gentiles) " read by the Czeck Deputy Bresnowsky in the Parliament of Austria in 1901 ("Luch Sweta" by P. Shabelski-Bork, p. 128).

"There is but ONE power in Europe, and that is Rothschild. He no longer needs the State, but the State still has need of him," (M. Weill).

"Its (the Bank of Rothschild) influence was so all-powerful that it was a saying, no war could be undertaken without the assistance of the Rothschilds"... "They rose to a position of such power in the political and commercial world that they became the Dictators of Europe." (J. Reeves).

"Bismarck, Beaconsfield, Gambetta, et. al., all these as a force are a mere mirage. It is the Jew their master who is the real force. He will proffer one word and Bismarck will fall." (Dostoiewsky in 1880).

And so it happened. He also meant Rothschild.

The same is said by the very best authors and patriots of Europe about the Rothschilds, who by one word, can cause the down-fall of a Lloyd George, to say nothing of the sinister Jew Dictators: of Russia (Trotzky; of France (Millerand-Kahn); of Italy (Shanzer); of Germany (Rathenau); of Czecho-Slovakia (Masaryk); of Turkey (Mustapha); of Central Asia (Enver Pasha) of Greece (E. Venizelos) and others.

"The World Government leaders are pagans" (Rev. C. F. Wishart).

'So well do they (the Jews) understand the power of money, that we seldom if ever see a Jew, who is a pauper. Acting upon this ancient knowledge, the House of Rothschild with a few co-religionists conspire to own the world.' (Mrs. Mary E. Hobart in her book "The Secret of the Rothschilds.")

Unfortunately, there is nothing concerning the Rothschilds in it.

ROTHSCHILDS REAL "SATANIZERS — MANKILLERS."

"What Hidden Hand is protecting the purveyors of pornography? Why does not the Censor act?" (The Patriot, June 11,1925, Dr. Stuart Holden).

Even the cautious New York Evening Post confirmed:

"The Kaiser had to consult Rothschild to find out whether he could declare war. Another Rothschild carried the whole burden of the conflict which overthrew Napoleon" (July 22, 1924).

The Jewish "Humanite" in Paris admitted (September, 1924):

"The revolt in Georgia (Caucasus) was staged by Rothschild."

The Hearst's Chicago Evening American stated:

"The Rothschilds can start or prevent wars. Their word could make or break Empires" (December 3, 1923).

"In the Imperial archives in Berlin was found a letter from Rothschild to Wilhelm II, dated 1911, urging against war" (Walter Hurt, "Truth About The Jews," p. 324).

As the war was quite ready, with Morocco as pretext, why did Rothschild postpone it?

Because he wished previously to murder the Prime Minister of Russia P. Stolypin and also to irritate all the world against Russia by staging the ritual murder of Andrew Iuschinski, which as Rothschild thought, would provoke "pogroms" and these would serve as a pretext for starting a world wide campaign against Russia, just as was most successfully exploited the Kishineff "pogrom," staged by the Jews before inciting Japan against Russia!

The Editor of The New York Evening Post stated:

"Somewhere behind the fog-bank of propaganda, sinister UNSEEN HANDS are seeking to destroy the peaceful relations between this Nation and Japan. Japan does not want war... Certainly America does not want war. Why then, this perennial clamor that Japan is an enemy to be watched, distrusted, dreaded, armed against and finely fought?" (December 9, 1924).

Yes! Japan does not want war and America still less. However, the war is practically imminent. Why? Because, as the Editor recognizes, there is an Unseen Hand or as it is called the Hidden Hand, which desires war. And war and disaster will surely come, may be in 1926, unless the Americans open their eyes and spread the message of this book, thereby arresting the Hidden Hand!

"Have we, straining every fibre of our national body escaped Pax Germanica only to fall into Pax Judaica?" (The Times, London, May 8, 1920).

The World War caused the United States alone, a direct expense of some $40 billion which passed through the hands of the satanic Rothschilds. And the next war, which may annihilate this country possibly within a few months, will be decided and started by the same Rothschilds... And what do Americans know about those Super-Arbiters of America's fate? Nothing!

"Alphonse Rothschild consented to pay all the indemnity of France to Germany, if France would elect him King" (Comte d'Herrisson in his "Journal d'un Officier d'Ordonnance").

"Lloyd George is adapting British policy to suit the wishes of 'foreign' financiers, interested in the increase of munition industry."(W.Guiness, M.P.)

At the last decisive council of the British Cabinet on July 3, 1914, Mr. Lloyd George invited Lord Rothschild to listen to and guide the debate. This Prime Minister played his demoniacal game on behalf of the Rothschilds, whose mere tool he has always been and still is. If England had then honestly declared that she would, stand by Russia and France, there would have been NO WAR, because the Kaiser would never have permitted it, notwithstanding the 10 Jews, who closely surrounded him: Bethman-Hollweg-Rothschild, Rathenau, Ballin, Dernburg, Ambassadors E.Goschen, Schoen, et al.

The Rothschilds, through Mr. Lloyd George, prevented such declaration by England, and thus made certain the most bloody, senseless and disastrous war in all history.

The presence of Lord Rothschild at the Imperial Council of the British Cabinet is revealed in the 6th volume of Mermeix's "Le Combat des Trois" (The Combat of the Three: Wilson, Lloyd George and Clemenceau).*

But the title of this book is wrong, because the three "great" men were merely the tools of "Col." E. Mandel House, Sassoon-Rothschild and Mandel-Rothschild according to a great French contemporary—Urbain Gohier. And these three in turn received their orders from Edouard Rothschild.

Baron Edouard A. Rothschild V. is today the "Uncrowned Ruler of the World." He controls the 300 men of the Hidden Hand, $300,000,000.000 and 90% of the World's press·

Most of the "statesmen" are his obedient valets!...

Now the Rothschilds are the Dictators and Assassins of the World. If they could upset Napoleon I. as Walter Hurt asserts; or if the Kaiser had to ask their permission to start this war, as the Editor of the Evening Post observes; or could make or break Empires, as the Editor of the Chicago Evening American asserts, how is it that in no History can we find even one line about their most mischievous satanic activity?

Thus my "Unrevealed In History" is the first effort to infuse Conscience into history and to show the most despicable role played by the Rothschilds. I hope that there will be found other honest and courageous historians, who will continue my work of "rescuing the masses of the people", as the glorious Lamartine has already suggested and strongly advocated!

*These volumes are published by the Jew, Ollendorff.

THE FIRST ROTHSCHILD (1743-1812)

The founders of the Dynasty of the Occult Supreme World Emperors and World Assassins were Amschel Mayer, a Jew, and his wife, Gutta Schnapper, a Jewess, in Frankfort —on—Main in Southern Germany.

The house on the Judengasse (Jewish Street) in which they lived, was a wooden hut, imitating a gothic design. The husband and his wife occupied the first floor and had a shop, where they bought and sold wares. Outside on the pavement lay all kinds of second hand objects. This miserable shop remains historic as the birth place of to-day's proud "barons" — rulers of the world. On the shop was placed a red ensign or a "red schield", in German "rothschild". All the children of Amschel adopted the name of Rothschild.

Born in 1743 at Frankfort, Amschel was destined to become a rabbi and entered a school, in which a good dose of Talmudic poisonous hatred against everything Christian was instilled into him. This done, he was sent to the bank of Oppenheim at Hanover, where he remained three years as an apprentice.

There he made the acquaintance of Lieutenant-General baron von Estorff the man nearest to Landgrave Frederick II. of Hesse Cassel (1760-1785).

In 1770 Amschel returned to Frankfort and was married to Gutta Shnapper. They had 5 sons and 5 daughters. They started very modestly; the wife took care of the shop and the husband went around the town with a trunk full of goods, but especially to visit the Jewish patriots and to inform himself.

Soon baron von Estorff, to whom Amschel rendered some services at the expense of Oppenheim, introduced the young Jew to the Landgrave Frederic II, whose fortune was then evalued at 70-100 million florins, an unheard of figure in those times. As this prince was very greedy and stingy, he did not care much concerning the means through which his fortune, left to him by his father Wilhelm VIII (the brother of the King of Sweden) was increased...

Frederic II, hearing from baron von Estorff about the ability and the unscrupulousness of Amschel, became interested in procuring a "cursed soul" a "man of straw" for all his doubtful operations.

THE SELLING OF HUMAN "GUN-FODDER"

The first Rothschild started on a gigantic scale the enrolling of young men, intoxicating them with liquors and with the glamor of fame, equipping them for the role assigned them, then selling their services to whatever powers anxious to make wars. This applied especially to England, then fighting France and the future United States, against whom sixteen thousand and eight hundred young Hessians were brought by Rothschild for the service of George III, the German born sovereign of England.

All the financial deals were arranged by Amschel. At first he tried to get the confidence of the Landgrave by remitting to him all the dividends from their Satanic operations, which caused so much bloodshed. Amschel soon changed his father's sordid shop into a banking house. His chief object was to obey the teaching of the Talmud, being thoroughly inculcated with the ideas, taught by the Judaic religion that "All the people whom Jehovah delivers into Your (Jews') hands must be exterminated." It can be briefly formulated as: "Down with CHRIST and with all the Christians" and "Jews the Masters of all".

Upon the pretext of fabulous gains, if the bloodshed was increased and of political advantages for the German nations, Amschel induced the Landgrave to make him his "alter-ego". Through the Landgrave's influence, and, always working hand in hand with the Secret World Jewish Government, located in Frankfort, Amschel began to control all the Lodges of the Free Masons and to guide them.

France then was the most Christian country and the venomous hatred of the Jews (satanists, according to CHRIST HIMSELF) turned against her first of all. Amschel co-ordinated the hostility of England and Germany against France, (because she helped the United States and because of their jealousy) with the Satan's legacy to the Jews—to destroy the Christians. Thus Pan—Judaism gripped once more the necks of Pan-Britanism and of Pan-Germanism for its own ends and our destruction.

"To the public the archives of the family, which could throw so much light upon history are a profound secret, a sealed book, kept hidden" (J. Reeves, "The Rothschilds. The Financial Rulers of Nations," p. 59).

Of course, if the archives were revealed, the Rothschilds would be torn to pieces by the most merciful of men, so dreadful and numberless are their crimes, perceived even by the watching of events.

The archives would prove, how boundlessly right is CHRIST.

Amschel was clever enough to simulate modesty publicly and to conceal his tremendous income and boundless influence upon the Synagogue, and upon the old Landgrave, to whom he pictured a gain of numberless millions as well as the political success of the Germans, and thereby excited his greedy passions. Amschel's grand son, Lionel Rothschild in London, revealed to his puppet-Disraeli — this immoral doctrine of success, viz. "The end justifies the means" ("Coningsby", p. 240) which was introduced by the Jews-Jesuits into their order, as the Jews assert.

Since 1770 when Amschel became a kind of Minister of Finance and of Foreign Affairs of the wealthiest man on earth, the Land-grave of Hesse Cassel, it appeared as if devils had entered into the Europeans, as they did into the notorious Gadareen swine

The Jews, practically intoxicated by such elevation of Amschel, increased their satanic efforts ten fold, and obtained enormous successes in Austria and Prussia, where reigned 2 Jewesses-Izig.

Frederick II was succeeded in 1785 by his son Wilhelm IX, who became Elector Wilhelm I. He was born in 1743, the same year as Amschel, and died in 1821, the same year as Napoleon. The Jew with the Langrave's money destroyed the Corsican genius.

Wilhelm was entirely under the guidance of Amschel, who prac-tically "judaised" and hypnotized him through every possible means. In this Amschel was helped by all the Jews and by the Free-Masonic organizations controlled by them. Being of the same age as Wilhelm, and as Amschel knew all the secrets of the Landgrave's family, they were like two shoes of the same pair.

Amschel however, dressed very simply in order to deceive the Landgrave as to his real income and fortune, and never changed his clothes and underwear, until they fell into pieces. From the time that Amschel became the all powerful manager of the tremendous fortune of Wilhelm, it ceased to increase, while the wealth of Amschel grew day by day, and at his death in September, 1812, he left to his sons ONE BILLION FRANKS, some authors say.

In 1794, the famous French General Hoche took Coblentz. The Elector of Hesse Cassel was frightened, because of the crimes committed by Amschel, and fled, leaving his fortune to Rothschild.

Many writers later went to the antichambers of the Rothschilds' palaces, begging tips and stories about the origin and beginnings of the "Dynasty," and there appeared in print all kinds of invented fairy tales about the genius and integrity of Amschel's sons.

LAMARTINE AND DOSTOIEWSKY

Obeying the great Lamartine, I shall teach my readers "by facts, by events and by the hidden meaning of those great historic dramas of which we perceive only the scenery and the actors, while their plot is contrived by a hidden HAND". And I shall prove what a wonderful prophet F. M. Dostoiewski, this independent Russian philosopher, was when he warned Christendom as early as 1880:

"Bismarck, Beaconsfield, the French Republic, Gambetta, etc. all this as a force are nothing, a mere mirage. It is the Jew alone with his Bank, who is their master and who rules all Europe (is it only Europe?). The Jew will suddenly profer: VETO and Bismarck will fall as grass cut by a scythe. The Jew with his Bank is the master of Education, of Civilization, of Socialism above all, by means of which the Jew is going to TEAR UP Christianity by its roots and destroy its Civilization. And when nothing but Anarchy remains, the Jew will put himself at the head of All. For, while propagating Socialism among all the Nations, the Jews will remain united among themselves; and when the wealth of Europe is dissipated, the Jew's Bank will remain".

Nothing but anarchy now remains in Russia...

Dostoiewsky's words would be more listened to, if he were more precise: instead of saying the Jew, he ought to say "Rothschild" which is right. The "Hidden Hand" of Lamartine and the "Jew" of Dostoyevsky, it is always the same Rothschild: to-day it is Edouard Rothschild in Paris.

I shall not repeat the fallacies of many people, although not all are bribed, who assure us, that the Rothschilds were and are geniuses and they imply: "The Rothschilds were geniuses, therefore, let us obey them".

Remember, that the Jewish Secret Supreme Government has existed for thousands of years that it was located in 1770 precisely in Frankfort-on-Main, and that two Jewesses, daughters of Izig, ruled the Monarchs or Austria and of Prussia. Thus Amschel was not the originator at all. He had no need to be a genius. It was the Supreme Government itself, which was daily and nightly watching the able men, and especially the most devilish Jews and Jewesses to enroll the first into the rabbinic schools, which inspired them with most dreadful, destructive, Satanic hatred against the Gentiles, these "animals", according to the Talmud. The Jewesses were encouraged to become the mistresses of men of high standing or, at least, to be their secretaries. Thus Senator Borah has as his secretary a Jewess Rubin Cora, who "corroborates" his desire to "recognize" the Jewish Soviets.

When these young Jews were "instructed," they were promoted through numerous channels, in order to further the Jewish Satanic idea of World Domination—through the destruction of all true Christians and the enslavement of other Gentiles. Scores of Miliukoffs, Kerenskys, Trotzkys of the XVIII-th Century were hired. Therefore, the Jewish Government or the Hidden Hand invaded through its agents all the secret societies, like the Free-Masons and even the Jesuits, as revealed by Disraeli himself and by the fact that one of the leading Jesuits, the terrible Torquemada, was a Jew. He tortured only the Jews, who deceived the Government of Spain through simulating to become Christians, but who continued to visit the Synagogues. Thus these false Catholics obtained high posts and could greatly harm the country, which according even to a Jew, Dr. Max Nordau, offered them the most cordial hospitality. Torquemada did this only to irritate all the Jews everywhere against the Christians and to prevent their eventual assimilation.

"If the Jewish Peril is so extremely powerful, then is there no salvation?", many readers may ask. There is, and a very simple one. It was offered by OUR SAVIOUR HIMSELF, (St. John, viii 44). It would be sufficient if many Christians would remember this and act accordingly. Is it not wonderful, that my "Science of Political Foresight," the rules of which I spent 42 years in establishing and which enabled me to accurately foretell events as if I were a prophet, is all confirmed in the above statement of OUR BELOVED SAVIOUR.

Only after you know that the Jews are satanists, can you become a real statesman, and then you cease to ask foolish or misleading questions of the scores of "leaders of men", as I mentioned.

Everything becomes clear to you and there is "nothing hidden, which will not be revealed." Only then can you expect to prevent all the calamities, which are being prepared for the years 1926 and 1927 by the Jewish Secret Supreme World Government, headed to-day by Edouard Rothschild V, in Paris. According to an old wise proverb, the Rothschilds and their 300 Jewish Vice-roys are "as mean and treacherous as cats and as cowardly as rabbits."

A Jew painter, Maurice Oppenheim, was engaged in 1861 to paint a double picture, showing the Elector transferring his fortune to Amschel, and his 5 sons returning the money with 5% interest, which seemed so extraordinary to them, that they wished to com - memorate this "unusual" act.

S. GOMPERS CONDEMNS THE "ROTHSCHILDIANS"

IN AMERICA AS "STATE TRAITORS"

The Rothschilds were and are involved in the dirtiest and bloodiest acts dating from 1770 till to-day· Did not even Mr. Samuel Gompers denounce them, when he declared (The Chicago Tribune, May 1, 1922):

"Nothing would constitute a more needless and base betrayal of civilization than the recognition of the bolshevik tyranny. The policy of the American-Anglo-German bankers is the most dangerous element in the whole chain of pro-bolshevist efforts. The bolshevist funds amount to millions."

Mr. Gompers is too old to lie and he risked too much by revealing the most treacherous activity of those "American-Anglo-German" bankers. Does he refer to Otto Kahn alone, because he was "German", then "English" and finally "American"? It could not be Mr. J. P. Morgan, who is only American. These "American-Anglo-German" bankers are the same Jews: Otto Kahn, Mortimer Shiff, Warburgs, etc. But even an infant in politics would never believe that these bankers would commit that which is veritable treason against the United States without an order from the Supreme Jewish World Government, led to-day by E. Rothschild V.

This is proved by the amazing fact that no Senator or Congressman demands an explanation. The newspapers announced, that Mr. Otto Kahn's bank "Kuhn, Loeb and Co." received $600 millions gold in deposits· And as a result:

"Is there any doubt, that there is a political revolution going on in this country?" (Senator Borah, Chicago Tribune, July 7, 1922).

This is so much more important because Sen. Borah is advocating the recognition of the Soviets, which would facilitate the introduction here of numberless bolshevist agitators, camouflaged as "travelling salesman", who would do the same as in Bulgaria

Thus Mr. Gompers practically declared recently, that the Rothschilds have remained the instigators of all the bloodshed up to the present day just as they were in "the middle of the 18-th century" and as they were in 1830-1840 when L. Rothschild made his satanic confessions to his clerk Disraeli.

The Rothschilds wish to whitewash themselves as much as possible· They fear that the so called "Christians" might cease to be unheard of imbeciles,cowards and boot lickers. Therefore, the Rothschilds pretend or claim their motto is "Concordia, Industria, Integritas", while no family has done more to cause bloody discords and murders and has less integrity than these satanists!

54

ROTHSCHILDS NEVER USEFUL TO HUMANITY

The Rothschilds never invented anything useful to humanity; never created an industry from the first. They started work with enormous capital and they kept for themselves all the benefits. Any means were good for them, if they were materially advantageous.

The Rothschilds have been the backbone of all political and finan cial happenings since 1770. Their name ought to be mentioned on each page of the history of every country. The authors, teachers, lecturers and politicians, who do not speak of them, must be con sidered dupes, hypocrites or criminally ignorant.

Henceforth men of intellect must have the courage and patriotism to demand of the professors and teachers in the schools and colleges, as well as of the statesmen, that they tell us the real facts concern ing the causes of the world's unrest, and cease feeding us, the people such adaptations of the truth that render us docile and inert, while these biped vultures devour us. Bid them tell us the truth about the criminal machinations which have brought about all the calamities of Christendom for the last 150 years.

The histories of the nineteenth century, that omit the record of these crimes of the Rothschilds against civilization, should be condemned and all confiscated as unworthy of a place in our educational system. Our men and women of the future must not be handicapped by being schooled in lies, that an alien people should be spared the records of their crimes against us and our religion. Let us be done with lies!

Most of the archives, containing details about the Rothschilds were purposely burned in Paris during the Commune in 1871, of which A. Rothschild IV was the financier.* It is significant, that the principal barricade was built just to cover the chief palace of Rothschild, where the rue de Rivoli joins the Place de la Concorde. The palace, which belonged formerly to Talleyrand Perigord and now is Rothschild's home, was never even visited in 1871 by the Communists, who appeared in Paris, only in order to frighten the French Government and to compel it to appeal to Rothschild in order to pay the heavy indemnity to the Germans. Thus the Communists guarded the 250 town houses of A. Rothschild, and Bismark was in his country palace La Ferrieres. Between the anvil (Bismark) and the hammer (Communists)—both governed by the same A. Rothschild, France was compelled to surrender and pay whatever sums and such terms as her foes demanded.

*) "La Libre Parole," May 27th, 1905.

55

REAL FREE-MASONRY IS ANTI-CHRISTIAN, I.E. SATANIC

I speak only about the Free-Masonry of Euro-Asia, but nevertheless American Free-Masonry was created by Jews Stephen Morin (in 1761) etc. and directed here by the followers of the Assassins of Asia Minor. There is no doubt that the soul of Free-Masonry is entirely Jewish and utterly anti-Christian, as numberless authors have proved most convincingly. To those, who have not been attracted to Free-Masonry, I would most emphatically recommend— "do not join it!" It is absolutely "Hobb-Nobbing with Hell" and does not even pay. It is selling one self most shamelessly and gratis.

The striking resemblance between the Jewish ritual and of Free-Masonry is exposed in the "Cause of the World Unrest" and in the "World Revolution," which ought to be read by every intelligent man, as also Mrs. Webster's "Secret Societies".

Again I repeat that all of these references to Free Masonry apply only to the European Lodges and practices, which are not recognized by Free Masons in America.

M. Copin d'Albancelli confirms that the occult power which moves behind Free-Masonry is the secret Government of the Jewish nation. This has been proved thousands of times and it would be useless to repeat it here. The masonic cry: "Nekum" ("revenge" in Hebrew) and numerous Hebrew names (Temple of Solomon, Hebrew Captivity, Murder of Hiram, etc.) in their ritual prove it sufficiently.

In the 18th degree the Free-Masons are told, that Christ "was no more than a common Jew, crucified for his crimes." The Knight Templars (27th Degree) "must deny Christ and defile the cross."

In the 30th degree are admitted only those, who consent to upset the Church and the State.

The revolutionist Louis Blanc states that even above those high degrees there exist some "shadowy sanctuaries." And those are only Jewish. It is the Jewish Supreme World Government. I knew the chiefs and the Secretary General of the Masonic Lodge of Paris—"The Grand Orient", the notorious Vadecard.

Many Masonic lodges have been created by the Occult Jewish Government ad hoc, i.e. for a certain period or for a certain act. As soon as this period has passed or the act was performed or failed, the secret society was dissolved and its leaders even annihilated, in order, that the Christians would never learn or guess, who was behind it. The "best" men (from the Jewish point of view) were gathered into the next superior lodge, or a secret Masonry.

56

THE ROTHSCHILDS ARE RULING FREE-MASONRY.

"The Morning Post" in its excellent book "The Cause of World Unrest" has dared to describe only some of the agents (not the heads) hired or attracted by the Rothschilds through their Central Executive—the "Universal Israelite Alliance"—in Paris, rue Bruyere, its branches and the Free Masonic Lodges. Not only did this newspaper lack courage to write anything about the "Rothschild Dynasty," but it also said almost nothing about its chief valets of to-day (except about Lenin, Trotzky and a few others) for whom the Occult Emperor provided the highest situations in many countries, and later on, however, executed some of them...

Mr. John Albion in his remarkable article—"If Lenin came to London," in "The Sunday Pictorial," Sept. 5, 1920, confirmed, that Lenin, Trotzky, etc., etc., are merely the agents of the Occult World Jewish Empire.

The Hidden Hand is its Executive and it is the power, which Mr. Winston Churchill denounced on Nov. 5th, 1919, in the House of Commons, as "the most formidable sect."

"The Morning Post," July 12, 1920, wrote about it:

"It was (and it is to-day) a power outside Germany, a power outside Russia; it was a world-wide power, strong enough to bring down Russia, strong enough to bring down the Imperial House of Hohenzollern. Ludendorff seems to suggest that the German Government handled this power clumsily, so that they were also brought down by it."

We shall reveal all "the mysteries" and all that "The Morning Post"; that talented historian of the French Revolution and World Revolution, Mrs. Nesta Webster; that which the boldest of British statesmen—Mr. Winston Churchill and the cleverest of the German Generals—Ludendorff—ignored, or did not have the courage to expose.

Yes! This "most formidable sect," which amazed the above eminent persons and also Lord Acton, who only felt that it existed, but could not answer the question as to what it was—is the Occult Supreme Jewish Empire, which has been led by the Rothschilds since 1770, also known as the **HIDDEN HAND**.

If my readers wish to have a 1001 proof, that Free Masonry and Judaism are one and the same, see the "Rappel" of Paris, which published on August 1, 1922, a most impudent letter of the Jew, B. Wellhoff, Grand Master of the Grand Lodge of France, insolently demanding M. Poincare, the then President of the Cabinet to free a convicted State traitor, Marty.

The fact that millions of Christians will know through this book, the plan of destruction, engineered by the Satanists, is sufficient to at least make them postpone it, if not abandon it, and thus give us time to enlighten more people. Then their fell plan would become simply unfeasable.

Truth! Truth! Truth! Nothing else is needed to check Satan and his delegates. The "Jewish Peril" is the "acid test" of intelligence for every Christian. Who does not recognise the Jews as Satanists, as CHRIST HIMSELF declared, is not a wise Christian. This said, I would recommend that my readers peruse the books, mentioned in the Introduction and especially the books of Mrs. Nesta Webster and "The Cause of World Unrest" (Grant Richards, London) by the "Morning Post," of London, England, one of only a dozen publications in the whole world, which are not yet compelled to lie by the satanists.

A whole library of lies was and is being written about Bolshevism, which adopted the mask of Communism, but in reality, is a genuine agency of the satanic Hidden Hand with the sole object of bleeding white, de-Christianizing and enslaving Russia, then the United States, then England, and so on. Therefore, it is an imbecility to affirm, that the bolsheviks "failed" in Russia. No! They succeeded, because most of the true Christians there are destroyed and the Orthodox Church received an almost mortal blow. The news that the bolsheviks became rich by plundering the Christian Churches (not one synagogue was robbed) made many politicians and writers "mouth-water." And we read again about the pathetic and fiery appeals to "recognise" the Soviet Government. Poor imdeciles, or bribed by the Hidden Hand's money *.

"Forgive them, for they know not what they do"

Numberless authors, like J. Holland Rose of Cambridge University have written about "The Origin of the War." They exposed 99 causes of the war, except the main one which they could find in the words of CHRIST (St. John, viii, 44). War is a "legalized" murder. Who is the Chief murderer? CHRIST said: "The devil (Satan) was a murderer from the beginning and the Jews are of the devil and will do his lusts." How simple and how infinitely true! And the "History with Conscience" proves this with certainty!

I need not repeat the anecdotes about the Rothschilds, which they circulated, but will state only undeniable historical facts.

*) Read the appeals of Arthur Brisbane in the "New York American."

ROTHSCHILD ATTEMPTS TO CRUSH AMERICA.

"The first to attract attention (of A. M. Rothschild) was the outbreak of the War of Independence in America," confessed Mr. John Reeves in his "**The Rothschilds. The Financial Rulers of Nations**," published by A. McClurg of Chicago (which has "disappeared") The numberless details, given by the author, prove that he received his information from the Rothschilds.

According to my "Science of Political Foresight"—the Hidden Hand could not fail to take part in a revolution and being "satanic," it ought to help both sides and thus murder as many Christians as possible. A. Rothschild I. sent here 16,800 Hessian youngsters to murder the Americans, yet through his Jewish agents (Franks, Haim Solomon etc.) he plundered both combatants.

"To the Rothschilds nothing could have occurred more propitiously than the outbreak of the American revolt and that of the French Revolution, as the two enabled them to lay the foundation of the immense wealth they have since acquired" (J. Reeves, p. 86).

Is that the reason that no historian has ever mentioned them? And why do we forget the wise dictum of the ancient seers: "Is feci cui prodest", which teaches that the one guilty of a crime is the man to whom it was "propitious".

"A stupid friend is more dangerous than a foe," wrote the famous Russian Kryloff. This is once more justified by an adept of Rationalism (invented by the Jew, Spinoza, according to Israel Zangwill) a Percy Ward. In his lecture "The Story of the Jew," delivered in Chicago, he confessed:

"When Robert Morris was making his appeal for funds to finance the American Revolution, a Jew, Haim Solomon responded. He immediately subscribed $300,000, and in all furnished over $600,000. He sacrificed almost his entire fortune to the cause of American Independence."

A 1002nd confirmation of the words of Disraeli, that all the revolts and bloodshed were financed by a Rothschild. And even in this effort to blandish the Jews, Percy Ward cannot fail to lie because, though "Haim sacrificed almost his entire fortune," he, according to the "American Jewish Historical Society," remained immensely wealthy.

Why? He simply gave in his name the money of Rothschild, who demanded not "one pound, of human flesh," like Shylock, but mountains of human corpses. Yes! Rothschild financed the American revolution, but P. Ward failed to prove, that this revolt or any other, served any nation, except the Jewish.

Everything unpleasant about the Jews' satanic work is always thrown out of the histories, written for the Christians, and the most important details must be reproduced from private diaries.

Thus "The Dearborn Independent" found many facts in the Jewish archives of the American Jewish Historical Society, Vol. 6, about the activity of the Jews of the Franks family in the United States. The glorious review of Mr. Henry Ford, a genius, on October 8, 15 and 22, 1921, described, how the Jews, the Franks, induced even a brave General, Benedict Arnold, to become a traitor. The 4 Franks in the U. S. acted just as the 4 branches of the Rothschilds are now acting on a large scale in Europe.

Mr. Israel Zangwill confessed that until the "middle of the 18th century the Waad or Council of 4 Lands legislated autonomously in those Central European regions, where the mass of the Jews of the world was then congregated" (p.15, "The problem of the Jewish race") After 1770 the Waad was replaced by the Occult Jewish Government in Frankfort with Amschel Rothschild I. as the Occult Jewish and World Emperor and Assassin. Thus the Jews Franks were working under the command of Amschel.

How the 4 Franks offered the "30 silver coins" to Benedict Arnold in order to prolong the bloodshed, is so masterfully described in "The Dearborn Independent", that it would be a literary sacrilege of me to repeat it. Every parent should buy the 4 volumes of "The International Jew" (25 cents each). This fact is one of a million, which prove, how criminal, base and stupid are the Christians, when they neglect the warning of CHRIST (St. John viii 44):"Jews are satanist-murderers" (moral, mental and physical)

Many seemingly intelligent Gentiles are lulling their minds to sleep by such platitudes as "there are many good Jews," so, lest we harm one of them, let the tribe destroy us. So did Arnold.

David Franks wished to remain a spy and send information to the royalists. "Arnold took D. Franks, an army contractor of the British army as his aid-de-camps." "In Jan. 1778, David Franks' letter to Moses Franks in London was intercepted and found inimical to the safety and liberty of the United States. Arnold was ordered to arrest David." But the Jew, Haym Salomon was credited with having the "fathers" in his books. Briefly, David was dismissed. Again, upon the establishment of Arnold's treason, the two Jews the Franks were arrested. But as Salomon had still the "fathers" in his pocket, both Franks were released."

THE PANDORA BOX OF THE AMERICAN REVOLUTIONS

Trying in vain to deny Mrs. Webster's correct statements, in her magnificent "Secret Societies", Mr. Silas Bent wrote:

"But it is not so easy, even if one takes Mrs. Webster's side of the disputed statement, that Mirabeau was a freemason and concedes that Adam Weisshaupt was as wicked as Cagliostro, to conclude therefrom that Freemasonry was the hothouse of the French Revolution. From what Pandora's box, we begin to wonder, did our Colonial Revolution leap forth?"

There is **no dispute** that Mirabeau was a freemason, member of lodge"Les Amis Reunis", where his partner was Talleyrand, who with Robespierre "discovered" Napoleon, and thus became the "missing link" between him and Amschel.

Mirabeau was introduced to the freemasons "Illuminati" by his mistress a Jewess Henriette Herz in the house of a Jew Moses Mendelson in Berlin. Mirabeau was present at the Freemasonic Congress in Wilhelmsbad, which was then a Landgrave's palace, managed by Amschel, who headed the **"deadly secret conclave beyond the masons and unknown to them"**, mentioned by George F. Dillon, by Robespierre and others.

Weisshaupt and Cagliostro (Joseph Balsamo) were Jews. They and Mirabeau, Talleyrand etc. were mere agents of Amschel.

"From what Pandora's box did the American Colonial revolution leap forth?" Mr. S. Bent is asking. Our Saviour foretold:

"Ye, Jews, will do the devil's lust of murder."

A revolution is a mass murder and Haim Solomon, a Jew, "gave" $600.000 to start it in America. It was Amschel's money. And it was he, who sent 16,800 Hessians to "bleed her white." Bent adds:

"Mrs. Nesta Webster cannot escape the conclusion that international financiers put up the money.* More it is Jewish financiers who supply the **funds; it is Jews who have been the agents - provocateur of revolution for** the last two thousand years *. It is the Jews who are the secret inner council of the five principal organized horrendous movements at work in the world with which organized government has to contend:

"1) Grand Orient Freemasonry (centre in Paris); 2) Theosophy with its innumerable ramifications; 3) Nationalism of an aggressive kind, now represented by Pan-Germanism **; 4) International Finance; 5) Social Revolution".

"Taking these up in turn, to see where the money grows, Mrs. Webster concludes that it is indigenous to international finance which is synonymous with Jews. She agrees with Henry Ford: **Put under control the fifty most wealthy Jewish financiers, who produce wars for their own profit, and wars will cease."** (The New York Times, March 8, 1925).

*) Mr. S. Gompers confirmed it on May 1, 1922 (Chicago Tribune).

**) My "Science of Political Foresight" confirms this.

Mr. Angelo Rappoport has written a book the "Curse of the Romanovs." But who cursed them, when and why, he does not explain because, as a Jew, he is a satanist.

Never before has a light been turned on this "mystery."

This "curse" began when Empress Elisabeth of Russia (1741-1762), answered to all the "temptations" offered by the Jews:

"No! We want no profits from the foes of CHRIST" (1743)

This glorious Christian was a daughter of Peter the Great. She crushed the "Prussianism" of Frederick II. and her reign was very prosperous which denies the false idea that the Jews make "good." Her declaration was an open challenge to the Hidden Hand, which then cursed all the Romanovs. Her successor was the illegitimate daughter of Frederick II. of Prussia, Catherine II., who even forbade the Jews to pour into Russia.

Mr. Samuel Maunder in his "The Treasury of History," p. 683, described her reign as "most prosperous," because both great Empresses considered the Jews as "satanists" and avoided their nefarious work.

The Jews cursed the Romanovs for their loving CHRIST and honesty. Catherine II was well inclined toward the Jews, but their dominant role in the French Revolution revealed by Robespierre, frightened her.

On Sept. 27, 1793, the French National Assembly decreed the emancipation of the Jews. Catherine issued an Ukase on June 23, 1794, by which the boundaries of the Jewish Pale of Settlement were fixed. (A S. Rappoport, "The Fortnightly Review," April, 1911)

Why was she not killed? Because her illegitimate father (not uncle, as the "bunk" historians are telling us) was the Grand Master of the Free Masonry of Germany.

Modern History must be looked at as a mortal implacable assault of the Judeo-Mongol Invisible Government (headed by a Rothschild since 1770) against CHRIST, Christendom, Christian ideals and Monarchs. The most idealistic of the last were the Romanovs, whose ancestor was Prus, brother of the Roman Emperor August.

Since 1770 the Rothschilds have turned much of their attention time and weans in order to dethrone the Romanovs, and all the Czars were murdered by the Hidden Hand.

Every Romanov was the sincerest peace-lover and this quality, and their devotion to the SAVIOUR made them absolutely intolerable to the Rothschilds, the Vicars of Satan on Earth.

ROTHSCHILD AND THE FRENCH REVOLUTION

In 1770 Amschel, became manager of the 70 or 100 millions of the Landgrave of Hesse-Cassel and the Treasurer of the then secret Universal Jewish Alliance and soon its Autocrat. He hired a crowd of Weishaupts, Mirabeaus, etc., who were the prototypes of the Miliukovs of today. In 1778 Weisshaupt, a Jew* founded in Bavaria the "Illuminati" a secret society and instructed the "Central Committee" of the Grand Orient of France to be ready for a revolt.

In 1782, Amschel R. I., summoned in Frankfort, the poor scoundrel, Adam Weisshaupt, (born in 1748) the official "leader" of the "Illuminati", who before he was hired, was unable to borrow 50 marks in order to pay for an illegal operation to be performed on his sister-in-law. Thereafter he miraculously developed his bandit work, covered Germany with Secret dens and poured thousands of cut-throats, mostly Jews, into Paris.

Weisshaupt went to Paris with endless means to bribe able men, to unite all the parties against the Monarch (as Gambetta afterwards did in 1870), to organise a revolt and to upset him in order to free the throne for Rothschild, to shed an ocean of Christian blood and provoke all Europe to attack France and "bleed her white," giving Amschel the opportunity to finance all the fighters.

The Lodge of the Coq Heron alone had $4,500,000 - at that time an enormous sum, but not for Amschel who had rallied all the Jewish bankers. Besides alone they were also able to create a "fictitious famine," as they afterwards did in Paris in 1847-48, in Petrograd in February 1917, etc.

But the Bavarian Government captured the "Protocols" of the "Illuminati" and forbade this Free-Masonic Lodge in 1786. Officially dissolved, this organization only changed its name and continued to work, because it was supported by the H. H. New organisations ("Enraged", etc.) were created with butchers** Danton, Marat, Robespierre, etc. When all was ready, the Red (Roth) flag (Schield) was hoisted in Paris in 1789. The "French," but in reality Jewish revolution broke out and the best men of France were killed in order to place France under Jewish rule.

"It was a royalist assembly which proclaimed a republic in France" (Aulard — "Histoire Politique de la Revolution Francaise", p. 37 and p. 175).

* Pouget de Saint-Andre, "Le Auteurs Caches de la Revolution Francaise," p. 16.

**) Many authors stated that Marat was a Jew—Mosesohn. M. Louis Marchand wrote in 1895 that Robespierre was also a Jew from Alsace called Ruban and Danton was a Polish Jew. This seemed incredible in 1895. But did not all the Soviet Jews change their names into Russian!

THE "MYSTERIES" OF THE FRENCH REVOLUTION.

"The more one studies the history of the French Revolution, the more one encounters enigmas" ("Les Auteurs Caches De La Revolution Francaise" by Pouget de Saint Andre, p. 1).

"Why were the reforms bought for 4 billion francs and 50,000 heads, when Louis XVI was offering them free?" Granier de Cassagnac.-"Causes de la Revolution Francaise").

"Why did the Convention shed so much blood? They say that bloodshed was caused by the hartred of the people against the privileged class *. How could the small percentage of executed aristocrats be explained; only 5% of all condemned" (Pouget de Saint Andre — "Les Auteurs de la Revolution Francaise", p. 3).

"All the French people are against us, said Robespierre at the Jacobins' Club. Our only hope is based upon the citizens of Paris. No! answered Desfieux: even in Paris we would be in a minority, if the vothing were secret." (Buchez et Roux — "Histoire Parlementaire", vol. XX, p. 300).

"The murder of King Louis XVI. was an act of the most hideous materialism the most shameful profession of ingratitude and baseness, of most roturiere villainy and of forgetfulness of the past" (Ernest Renan in his "La Monarchie Constitutionelle en France").

All the Revolutions and World unrest have been and will be organized by the same Jewish Occult World Government. That is why they ought to be studied carefully, without falling into fantastic hypothesis, as the "hundred blind authors," quoted by Mr. Gooch in his "Helps For Students Of History" have done.

Practically the only author in England, who honestly tried to throw real light on the French and World Revolutions is the talented and learned Mrs. Nesta Webster. It may be that by her woman's intuition she opened the door where male historians faltered. An immense amount of credit is due to her, because of her courage, and erudition. My articles ("Plain English", 1920) "created" her!

All the books of the "Hundred Blind Authors" on the French Revolution **ought to be abandoned,** or kept in libraries as examples of how History ought not to be written.

Herder says the French Revolution was as big an event as the rise of Christianity. No! It can be compared only with the other less important successes of Satan: The detachment of the Orthodox Church and that of the Protestant from the Mother Church, Herder's intuition suggested to him that the French, like any other Revolution, was not a mere political and economical event! It must be considered as the beginning of the substitution of Christian Monarchies by the Jewish.

* I do not think that Queen Marie Antoinette ever once missed an opportunity of saying an agreeable thing to those who had the honor of approaching her." (Mrs. Vigee-Lebrun in her "Memoirs").

The future authors must take into consideration not only the "jackals," which helped the Revolutions, but first of all, the "Tigers," who have prepared the main roads to it and who have broken the chief obstacles against all bloodshed - the Christian feelings. According to my "Science of Political Foresight" each author must ask himself:- "Where is, or will be the Hidden Hand?"

In his "Helps For Students of History. The French Revolution" Mr. G. P. Gooch, recommends "The Lectures on the French Revolution"—(there have been no French, Russian or German, etc. revolutions, but only Jewish revolutions, in France, in Russia, etc.) of Lord Acton, who like a horse in blinders, points out just what the Jews wished to prove through their agents—Cagliostro in Paris and Rasputin in Petrograd, that the "worst of advisers was the Queen,"

She and Queen Amelia of Portugal prior to the revolution there; and the Empress of Russia, were all discredited by the Jews and made the scape-goats by them for events with which they had no connection.

Lord Acton attributes the failure of the moderate reformers to the intrigues of the Court (as was done in Russia). He says:

"The Declaration of the Rights of Man—is the triumphal proclamation. This simple page of print outweighs libraries, and is stronger than all the armies of Napoleon. It had one cardinal fault: it sacrifices liberty to equality, and the absolutism of the King is succeeded by the absolutism of the Assembly. The attack on the Church was a needless and fatal blunder."

He "overlooks" the "Tigers"—the Hidden Hand. Yes! They "sacrificed liberty" but did not establish equality. "The King was succeded by the absolutism of the Assembly," but the Assembly was itself obeying the absolutism of the Jewish Occult Emperor.

The attack on the Church was not "a needless blunder"; it was and is the main object of each revolution, because it is a Jewish means to destroy Christendom.

Mr. John Reeves insists that the American "revolt" and the "French" revolution enabled Rothschild to lay the foundation of the immense wealth he has since acquired. He forgets the ancient dictum: "Is feci cui prodest", and neither he nor any other author exposed the role of Amschel in the above capital events.

One can understand that Amschel financed both sides in the American bloodshed. But what "side" did he finance in the French?

ALL REVOLUTIONS WERE JEWISH - SATANIC.

Of course, Prussia and England intensely desired the destruction of France even by beheading her through the murder of Louis XVI. All the dirty and bloody work, however was introduced into the Revolution by the Jewish World Government, or "The Hidden Hand," then headed by Amschel Rothschild I. For those who ignore it everything is a "mystery."

"It (the revolution) brought on the stage, forces which have moulded the actions of men ever since, and have taken a permanent place among the formative influence of civilisation" (Mr. G. P. Gooch).

It brought the Jewish World Empire, and each Revolution surrenders a country to its yoke! The "equality" remained a dream. The "liberty" excludes the "equality".

"Despite its horrors, the Revolution was a great effort towards the emancipation of the common man," states Mr. Gooch. The common man was "emancipated" from his Christian King, who defended him, only in order to become more terribly enslaved by the Jewish rulers, who hate and despise the common men, as proved in the case of Gambetta, a Jew, et al.

Mr. Gooch believes, that "No man has done so much to expound the history of the Revolution as Aulard." Aulard was bought by the Rothschild who offered him the well-paid "Chair of History," in Paris in 1886, if he would put more fog on the "Cause of World Unrest." And he did it.

My "Science of Political Foresight," or the "Theory of Satanic Forces," which rule the World with its advice: In each event watch for the Hidden Hand, will do more to reveal the truth than the 100 blind or bribed authors, quoted by Mr. G. P. Gooch.

"Are any of you sorry for the French Revolution? Liberty was enthroned, the old order was destroyed and a new France was born," childishly wrote Mr. Clarence Darrow of Chicago in his "Arguments in Defense of the Communists". By saving the two Jewish murderers Leopold and Loeb, and now potentially having freed them, Darrow proved, that the Jews are "Above all Law" here.

For 10 years I lived in Paris. There is no liberty, but a slavery of the French under the Rothschilds' autocracy. All that made France famous was accomplished by the Monarchies. She is only eating this inheritance, incapable of producing anything grand. The utter failure of the "III-rd French Republic" is well described by M. Joseph Santo in his book "La Faillite de la Republique" and was proved by M. Urbain Gohier, the greatest Frenchman of to-day.

"MYSTERY" OF ROBESPIERRE REVEALED

On the following pages I shall quote numerous "mysteries" which puzzled the "historians", but are clear for my readers.

From whence came the influence of Robespierre upon persons far more intelligent and talented? Michelet, a progressive historian describes Robespierre, as a small lawyer with a poor figure, endowed with but mediocre intelligence and colorless capacities.

"One can imagine a tyrant surrounded by an army, not a tyrant alone and without soldiers" (G. Lebon, — "La Revolution Francaise", p. 231).

The greatest Frenchman of today M. Urbain Gohier, and a famous French Historian, commented in his "La Vieille France," N-261 (Febr. 2, 1922) about the strange fact, that while Danton has a monument and a fine street dedicated to him in Paris, there is nothing to remind one of Robespierre. M.Gohier explains this by the fact, that Robespierre was incorruptible, while Danton was a dishonest immoral rogue and sold himself to everybody. Yes! to the H. H. But it was not, because of his honesty, that Robespierre received no reward from the "French" Republic. It was because of his last speech, in which he revealed that the French Revolution like all the others, was **NOT** run by the French, but by the foreign agents. What angered them in 1794, continues to displease them today. Robespierre then said imprudently:

"I distrust all these foreigners, whose faces are covered with masks of patriotism and who are trying to appear more republican and energetic, than we, ourselves . . . They are agents of foreign powers, because I know well, that our enemies did not fail to say: 'our emissaries must simulate the most warm patriotism, the most exaggerated' in order to be installed into our assemblies. These agents must be crushed despite their perfidious art and the masks, which they always assume."

Mr. J. Goldworth Alger even asks in his "Paris in 1789-94":

"Was he (Robespierre) afterwards a monarchist" (p.447).

Why did Robespierre's two hours speech on July 26, 1794 cost him his life? And why on the Sabbath, was the Tribunal closed,* though it was destined to meet on that day to order the execution of Robespierre?" (Alger. p.463).

Why was Robespierre badly wounded and not killed, by a Meda, whom people nicknamed "Merda" and whose brother was Meng? The "French" Revolution, as the others have been was organised and financed by the Rothschilds in order to murder the Christians, to plunder them and to obtain "all the kingdoms."

* Why did the Tribunal rest on Saturday—inference is they were in the Synagogues those "French" leaders of the "French" revolution:

The supposed "leader" Robespierre was Amschel's tool.

"It seems to me, that we are pushed by a 'Hidden Hand' above our will. Every day the Committee of the Public Salvation is doing what it decided a day before not to do. There is a faction conducted in order to ruin it whose directors we have not been able to discover". (Robespierre to Amar, Memoirs de Mallet du Pan, vol. II, p. 60).

Robespierre lost his life, because he dared to express his disgust, that the Aliens (Jews) introduced by Weisshaupt and by other agents of Amschel, had become the real rulers in Paris. He was not killed by Meng (not a Frenchman), but only badly wounded in the jaw, in order to cause him most awful suffering, prolong his agony as long as possible and by depriving him of the power of speech to prevent him from revealing, that it was not a revolution, but the grabbing of France by Jews.

It was mere "kosher-butchering"!!! This confirms, that the "French" revolution was Jewish.

"It was not reason that created the French Revolution" (Lionel Rothschild" Sidonia. "Coningsby", p. 240).

And Mr. Alger's implying, that since Robespierre revealed the Jewish plots, he must be a monarchist, clearly reminds one of the same Jewish methods of today to class as a monarchist everyone, who believes CHRIST's warning, that the Jews are murderers and liars!

Because Mr. Henry Ford boldly, patriotically and honestly revealed the Jewish crimes, the Hidden Hand induced "Hearst's International Review" through every possible means to insinuate, that Mr. Ford has become a "pro-monarchist"

Does not this prove, that the Hidden Hand, which set fire to France, is doing the same here through the same system by pouring her Jews into the U. S.?* Thousands of rascals and cut-throats were brought into Paris by the agents of Amschel R. I., as the bolsheviks-Jews are brought into the U. S. daily** camouflaged as Frenchmen, Prussian, Poles even Irish ("Plain English"). They were helped by the stupid, greedy mob, which understood nothing, and had nothing to lose. And when the U. S. is drowned in an ocean of blood, may be, some American Robespierre will make the same discovery, that all revolutions are Jewish.

* Please read "Reds In American" by Mr. R. M. Whitney; "The Red Conspiracy" by Joseph J. Mereto; "Underground With The Reds" by Fred P. Marvin and especially Mr. B. L. Brasol's clever books.

** The Secretary of Labor J. J. Davis confessed that hundreds of thousands of aliens are coming to America clandestinely. Two thirds of those are Jews, of whom 99 per cent are bolsheviks or pro-bolsheviks.

68

THE "MYSTERIES" OF THE "FRENCH" REVOLUTION.

Robespierre did not become a monarchist, but he understood, that the supposed "French" revolution was simply a "Jewish" acquisition of France and had nothing to do with welfare, freedom equality and other shibboleths.

If Free Masonry was chiefly guilty for the ocean of blood in the "French" Revolution why then were its lodges closed in 1793 and why were so many free masons executed?

It is true that many free masons claimed that the "French" (and the other) Revolution was staged by them. Thus Sicard de Plauzoles declared at the Convention of 1913:

"The Free Masonry can with pride consider the Revolution as its own deed" (Tourmentin — "La Franc-Maconnerie Demasquee")

This was also affirmed by the free mason Louis Blanc in his "History of the French Revolution". But the claim was especially set forth at the International Masonic Congress in 1889 by the free masons Amiable and Colfavru at a lecture on July 16 at the Grand Orient. They asserted that all the work had been done by the masons and that the plan of the Revolution had been elaborated by them before 1778. It is also significant that the Masonic Congress was held in 1889, exactly 100 years after the outbreak of the Revolution of 1789...

Yes! But, however, all the leading (seemingly) masons: Robespierre, Danton, et al. were later on executed, after having accomplished the "dirty work"... Who can explain why such a powerful organization could not save its members from being assassinated?

Outside of France two monarchs proved to be opposed to the Revolution: the King of Sweden Gustavus III and the Emperor of Austria Joseph II. When Gustavus decided to interfere against the French Revolution, he was stabbed at a court ball by the free masons. Joseph, also at a court ball, took some candy from a masked woman and died the next day (February 20, 1790).

When Mirabeau could have prevented the murders, by taking the side of the King, he was given coffee and "suddenly" died, while his two companions, who drank some of it with him (Pellenc and Frochot) became gravely ill.*)

Mirabeau died in great, but well deserved suffering...

By murdering King Louis XVI., the Free-Masons were revenged for the execution in 1314, by King Phillipe le Bel of their satanic, "judaized" Grand Master, Jacques Molai.

*) "La Revolution, La Terreure, Le Directoire", by Despatys.

THE "MYSTERIES" OF THE "FRENCH" REVOLUTION.

"The party that pushed the Revolution to violence was directed by a Hidden Hand,* which until today could not be surmised". (Alexis Dumesnil, — "Preface aux Memoirs de Senat").

"There has been an Invisible Motor which spread all kinds of false rumors in order to perpetuate trouble. This centre must have a great many agents, and in order to pursue such an abominable plan ,it must be guided by a subtle brain and have plenty of money. Some day the world will know this infernal genius and the provider of funds" ('Memoires de Bailly' vol. II, p. 33)

Now this infernal genius and provider of enormous funds is revealed by me. It was Amschel Rothschild I, who used the immense fortune of the Landgrave of Hesse Cassel for the destruction of Christendom; just as the Jews bolsheviks are using all the money they can find to destroy Russia, to "blow up" the U. S. and then all Christendom. Even a Jew, Gompers, asserted that the Jewish bankers are helping bolshevism with millions.

"An Invisible Hand rules the mob" (wrote Lafayette on July 24, 1789). "The more one is near the instruments and the actors of this catastrophe the more one is in darkness and in mystery; this will only increase with time" ("Memorial of Ste-Helene", vol. II. p. 32).

Joseph de Maistre, a famous Frenchman, attributed the Revolution to Satan. "Satan is the legitimate father of the revolution", said brilliant George Sand. Gustave Bord in his book "Le complot maconnique" wrote that the Revolution was staged by the Free Masonry. Yes! The Free Masonry did much abominable work. But who gave the money? Who wished the spilling of so much blood, which was unanimously disapproved of by the whole French nation? Who is "doing the lust of murder?" CHRIST pointed it out!

Cagliostro (the "Rasputin" of Marie Antoinette) learned that the secret society to which he was then attached, and the members of which shouted at his admission: "We are 300" (The Hidden Hand) — had deep roots and a great "Treasury of War". This was still the fortune of the Landgrave of Hesse-Cassel, who confided it to Amschel Rothschild I and which the latter used to destroy Christendom.

* Haugwitz, former mason and a stateman, and many other masons confirmed that the murders of the most kindhearted King Louis XVI. and of King Gustavus III. and the French Revolution had been decided 4-5 years ahead by the free-masonic conventions at Wilhelmsbad, Ingolstadt and Frankfort. But the palace of Wilhelmsbad was managed by Amshèl Rothschild, who lived and ruled in Frankfort. And his mere valet Weisshaupt, also a Jew, was from Ingolstadt. Thus all the murders attributed rightly to the free-masons, were decided by Amschel!!!

THE "MYSTERIES" OF THE "FRENCH" REVOLUTION.

"The first blows of the conspiracy against the thrones should be struck against France. After its downfall, Rome (Papacy) ought to be dethroned" (Confessions of Cagliostro, a Jew).

"Cagliostro obtained huge sums for propaganda; received the instruction from the sect, ("Illuminati") and went to Strassburg in France" (Louis Blanc — "La Revolution Francaise", vol. II, ch. 2).

"Why not suppose that our (French) monarchy was disliked by the Jew Weishaupt? It was he who sent his coreligionist Cagliostro to prepare the French freemasonry to accept the leadership of the German Illuminati. He it was who organized the international federation of the lodges." (Pouget de Saint Andre — "Les Auteurs Caches", p. 16)

One of the rules of the "Illuminati" was to spread the rumor, that a foe whom it was imprudent to kill, was an imbecile or insane. Mirabeau was lured into the "Illuminati" gang by a Jewess Henriette Herz, (Karl Rothschild was married with Adelaide Herz and the first "Russian" bolshevik was Herz-en) who introduced him into the house of Mendelssohn.

The masonic lodge of "Les Amis Reunis", ("United Friends") to which Mirabeau introduced the "German" delegates, was directed by a secret Committee composed of Mirabeau, Talleyrand and Chappe de la Heuziere, the deputy of the Martinists, at the Congress of Wilhelmsbad. This committee convoked on Febr. 15, 1785 an International Masonic Congress at which were also present Cagliostro, St. Martin and Talleyrand, who "discovered" Napoleon I and through Talleyrand Napoleon was made the instrument to overthrow the Christian Church. Among other members of the Congress were also three Princes of Hesse, relatives of the Landgrave of Hesse, whose "alter ego" and the "damned soul" was Amschel Rothschild I.

It was the lodge of "Amis Reunis" that schemed the affair of the necklace in order to defame the Queen Marie Antoinette, as Rasputin subsequently was to stigmatize the Empress of Russia.

Most Americans do not believe, that a bloody revolt is possible here. At least now, through this book, they will know, who is staging it.

"The Judeo-masonic peril is a question of life or death for all the nations" (Jouin, the famous editor "Revue Internat. Des Societes Secretes," Paris).

"Remember the French Revolution, to which it was we who gave the name of "great", The secrets of its preparations are known to us, for it was wholly the work of our hands" (Protocols of The Learned Elders of Zion, 3)

"We, Jews, are still here, our last word is not yet spoken, our last deed is not yet done, our last revolution is not yet made" (Dr. Oscar Levy, London)

71

THE "MYSTERY" OF THE "CURSE OF THE ROMANOVS"

This "curse" was started by the Hidden Hand located in Frankfort-on-Main and spread by means of numberless Synagogues to all the Jews. Amschell adopted it as his own and since then it was constantly renewed. Whosoever desires to grasp History must know that the Romanovs were the personification of Christian Monarchs with all the best qualities and that the Rothschilds were the worst "satanists."

Since 1770 there has been an uninterrupted assault of the Rothschilds, with all the numberless secret, Masonic and other organisations, their world press and their billions, against the Romanovs' (the "Fair Angels," as they were called) until all the press came under the control of the Rothschilds.

מה חליפתי. זה תמורתי. זה כפרתי.

Die hebräischen Buchstaben heissen: „sä chaliphati, sä femurati, sä kaporati". Die Uebersetzung lautet: „Dies sei meine Loslösung, Dies sei mein Tausch, Dies sei mein Sühneopfer"! Postkarten dieser Art wurden bereits 1914 in jüdischen Kaufläden verkauft. Das Golgatha Kaiser Nikolaus II. ist ein Werk jüdischer Hände.

The Romanovs were all too good and never took the offensive, while the Rothschilds never missed a single occasion to harm the Tsars morally, politically, financially or physically.

The Hebrew letters read:

The translation is: "This must be my belief. This must be my substitute. This must be my sacrifice!." Postal cards of this kind already in 1914 were sold in Jewish shops. "The Golgotha of the Czar Nicholas II, is the work of Jewish hands," says the German publisher of these cards.

72

AMSCHEL CHOSE NAPOLEON CHIEF "MANKILLER."

Like Weisshaupt, Kerensky and Trotzky, (who began his career by stealing from his school mates) Napoleon was so poor that he could not pay his laundry bill, though he had one shirt. Napoleon was knocking at the doors of all the officials searching for work, suggesting all kinds of plans. At the same time the "Great Assas sin" Amschel, disgusted with the inability of his Weisshaupt to continue wholesale murders, was searching for a talented fighter, and Talleyrand found him Napoleon.

His fiery Corsican temperament and the declaration of his readiness to shoot down any number of people during peace or war, made him the favorite champion of the newly born Jewish Dynasty, So much the more so because the population began to be tired of killing one another. Mass-murdering ought to be done on some other pretext besides "Liberty, Equality, Fraternity".

Even the very shrewd Amschel, from his centre in Frankfort's ghetto, could not foresee that the hungry officer, whose chief ambition was to obtain some stuff gratis for his uniform thru Josephine Beauharnais, might later on become a powerful monarch.

The possibility of executing Satan's legacy, i. e. to murder millions of Christians through Napoleon's talent and also the satanic desire to upset the Christian Church, simply inebriated Amschel. In the 5 great powers later granted to Amschel to his sons, he ordered the Jewish bankers and all the Secret Societies to help Napoleon in every way.

So much so that Bonaparte showed himself, or was considered by his supporters to be agnostic and very anti-Catholic. He simulated this to please the Free-Masons.

To ruin the Universal Christian Church, to humiliate the Holy Father through Napoleon, became the most ardent desire of all the Jews in all countries as "conditio sine qua non" for obtaining "all the kingdoms" from Satan. This explains why Napoleon's successes seemed "miraculous" and as if he were super-human. Have not many men supposed that Napoleon was the anti-Christ?

"It was claimed that war was the First Consul's sole element", the famous Minister of Police confirmed in his "Memoirs relating to Fouche," p. 151   This reputation gave to the young Corsican the support of Amschel.   Thousands of writers have tried to guess the real reason why Napoleon had such brilliant career, and they have all failed. Why? Because they all ignored the A. B. C. of politics, i.e. that which my "Science of Political Foresight" explains.

THE "MYSTERY" OF NAPOLEON'S SUCCESSES.

In the "Financial News", Feb. 17,1920 I wrote: "To understand what was going on, experts for centuries advised "Find the Woman." But today in order to understand all, one must watch the Hidden Hand".And no author or politician has connected Napoleon I with the Hidden Hand, which "created" and ruined him.

"In the whole range of history no one has aroused emotions so opposite and intense or has claimed so much of the admiration, the fear, and the hatred of mankind" (Mr. Herbert Fisher in his "Napoleon").

In 1786 Napoleon was a sub-lieutenant in Paris, where the Jews concentrated their Free-Masonic Lodges and all efforts. Did this Corsican avoid this secret, tempting den for every youth, which promised everything to its fellow members? No! He was the friend of Augustine Robespierre, the fiery adept of Free-Masonry.

"In 1790 Bonaparte succeeded by means, even then judged to be unscrupulous, in securing his election as second in command of a battalion" (Mr. H. Fischer).

"Augustine Robespierre, the younger brother of the terrible Dictator, had become acquainted with Bonaparte at the taking of Toulon (1793). The fact is indisputable that he contracted an intimacy, having all the appearance of warm friendship, with Augustine, who was to be fully as pitiless as his elder brother" (Charles Macfarlane, "The Life of Napoleon Bonaparte", p. 28).

The Robespierres, according to Louis Marchand were Jews from Alsace. They might be the "envoys" of Amschel. They were the "Trozkies" and the "Zinovievs" of today dispatched to Russia in 1917 by Paul Warburg, one of the Hidden Hand.. In any case the reputation of being pitiless helped Napoleon later on to be chosen by Amschel.

Do not many Jewish writers call Trozky— a "Napoleon"?
For his murders Trozky was made a 33-d degree Mason.
Napoleon's "pitilessness" made him a Masonic idol.

"Bonaparte was too shrewd to uncover all his means and assets. But he told me enough to persuade me that the destinies of France were in his hands" (Fouche, p .51).

If the best informed, cleverest detective found "mysteries", though he was at the bottom of all the secret dens, it is because these "means of executions" of Bonaparte were given to him by Amschel, through Talleyrand and his Free Masonry, because "war was Bonaparte's sole element", and he could destroy the Church.

Paris, Lyons and Avignon were nests of Free-Masonry.

"Bonaparte (fleeing from Egypt) aroused the wildest enthusiasm on his passage through Avignon and at Lyons. There was something fictitious, a SECRET impetus." (Fouche, p. 50).

Mr. H. G. Wells and Mr. Green wrongly refer to Napoleon as a "wrecker, hard, compact, capable, possessing initiative, and neatly vulgar". Knowing the unlimited wealth of Amschel and Co., the cowardly servility of the masses and the readiness of the leaders to be corrupted, we do not marvel, that

"A man, (Napoleon) born without any advantage of wealth or high descent, made himself master of the world before he was 35, and finished his career of unparalled romantic impossibility when he was 46." (Mr. Sidney Dark in his book, "How Great Was Napoleon").

Mr. Wells blames Napoleon for having "wrecked" the work of the Revolution and having failed to use the great opportunity that was his, when he was elected First Consul by an "overwhelming vote". Napoleon obtained this just as the Jews: Gambetta obtained it in 1870 and Kerensky and Trotsky in 1917. Those "overwhelming votes" were paid by a Rothschild. Wells childishly says:

"Now surely here was opportunity such as never came to man before. Here was a position in which a man might well bow himself in fear (!) of himself and search his heart and serve God to the utmost."

How could a Weisshaupt, Napoleon, Gambetta, Disraeli, Bismarck, Kerensky, Trotsky, Poincare, Lloyd George, W. Rathenau, et al, "serve God and man", when they were selected, bribed and supported by the satanist who wished them to "bore God," as Victor Hugo said, and to murder the Christians.

Napoleon's marriage to Josephine, the mistress of Barras, was arranged by Barras in order to quit with her amiably and, as dower, Napoleon received the command of the French army in Italy, which meant not so much fighting as plundering. And all the Free-Masonry in Italy was supporting the invaders. Amschel and Free-Masonry had one chief aim-to destroy the Church at Rome. All this helped Napoleon to develop his military genius and to acquire the fame of "invincible," which aided him later on. Even foes helped him.

What is the "mystery"? Why does H. G. Wells, and many others unjustly attack the Corsican genius?

It is because Napoleon soon grasped how awfully harmful were the Jews and became, what is called an "anti-semite". To please the Jew controlled press Wells is compelled to write untruths.

ON THE EDGE OF THE XIX. CENTURY.

Let us glance upon the glory of the end of the 18th Century and the first years of the 19th. J. Reeves wrote ("Rothschilds"):

"At the beginning of 19th century Great Britain, owing to false principles of government, to the ignorant and blind cultivation of trade and industries had the appearance of a State driven to the most opposite and contradictory extremes. Priding itself on the possession of the freest constitution in Europe, England yet concealed the greatest tyranny; possessing unbounded riches, it yet allowed the poor peasantry in Ireland to die of hunger, whilst tne privation and distress prevalent among the labouring classes was so great and indescribable as to threaten to end in riot and rebellion. The hardships endured by the poorer classes were aggravated by the disgraceful condition of our political system. Morality was at a discount; bribery and intrigue were the order of the day. The thoughts of all were turned to the complete forgetfulness of the sufferings of others. Corruption was so wide spread, that the independence of the Crown and that of the constituencies were threatened." (p. 136).

"In 1797 the English banks found themselves deeply embarassed, mainly in consequence of the demands of the Government, which borrowed millions every year for the war, and for the support by subsidies of half of the Continental Powers." (p. 162).

Such was the situation when Amschel found the moment was ripe and sent his third son Nathan to conquer England.

As Sir Thomas Buxton narrates, many English manufacturers sent in 1798 a man to Frankfort to offer their goods. The Rothschild trick consisted of keeping him a long time, and later giving him the hugest orders for Germany. In the meantime, Nathan was sent to Manchester, where he bought all the available cotton and dye stuffs. When the representative returned to Manchester with orders, the manufacturers had to apply to Nathan for these materials and he made them pay treble the price and even refused to sell the stuff, thus making them pay his father enormous "damages" Then he took the cotton and dyes to some manufacturers and they manufactured the stuff for him at the lowest price. This base trick of Nathan's ruined many people in Manchester. But it was the application of the Rothschildian motto:

"All for us — Rothschilds — nothing for anybody else."

This legal robbery was repeated many times by them.

This plundering made Manchester very indignant.

"None of the members of the London Stock Exchange could boast like Nathan, of having multiplied his capital 2,500 times in the course of five years". (p. 167).

NATHAN HASTENS TO CONQUER ENGLAND

Nathan was frightened and fled to London, where the Exchange was larger field for his exploitations. The reason also was that Wilhelm IX. of Hesse-Cassel (1785-1821) was persuaded by Amschel to transfer all his affairs in London, from the bank of Van Notten into the hands of Nathan. Of course, "accidentally" a whole gang of those Frankfort "Illuminati" went with Nathan in 1798 to London to try and do the same thing there, but the British were too clever to be deceived. When Napoleon I. invaded Germany, Wilhelm IX (since 1803 called Elector Wilhelm I) gave $3,000,000 to Amschel, which he sent to Nathan in London. Just at the moment the Company of India had $4,000,000 in gold. Nathan bought it and increased its price. He "cornered" gold in London. He knew the Duke of Wellington needed it. Nathan also bought the Duke's bills at a large discount. The Government asked Nathan for the loan of his gold and he transferred it to Portugal. Nathan loaned and had his gold returned but compelled the repayment of the bills of the Duke at their full value. Thus he made 50%. Then he again loaned his gold at 15% and received it back to be transported to Portugal with a huge commission.

The Duke needed this gold to pay the outfitters of his Army, who were all Portuguese, Spanish and Dutch Jews. Thus not a single pound of gold was sent. Wellington received only orders to these Jews in Portugal, who were paid by Rothschild, Chief and Treasurer of the Jewish World Government in Frankfort later on. This operation netted Nathan 100%. Thus the Rothschilds made colossal profits with the money of the Landgrave, but took all the profits for themselves.

Meanwhile, in Russia reigned, since 1796, Tsar Paul I.

"Poroshin (Paul's tutor) was learned and accomplished, a sound mathematician and a fine linguist. He became passionately attached to Grand Duke Paul . . . Paul's religious instruction was not neglected. French and German were taught him thoroughly, besides Russian and he was given knowledge of Italian and Latin. The Grand Duke regarded his instructors with great respect. Voltaire's works held a prominent place in the Tsarevich's Library." ("The Curse of Romanovs" by a Jew, Rappoport, p. 49).

"Paul's figure is well set and his face attractive. He is pleasant in his speech and manners, unassuming, polite and of lively disposition." (Solms to Asseburg).

"The Grand Duke has grown talkative and cheerful, as well as very tactful." (J. Harris, the Ambassador of England).

TSAR PAUL I. DESCRIBED BY FOREIGNERS.

The Emperor of Austria, Joseph II, paid a visit to St. Petersbourg in 1780 and wrote to his mother:

"The Grand Duke is far more entitled to consideration than is generally thought. He is clever, lively, extremely well educated, exceedingly upright, frank; the happiness of his fellow creatures is to him of higher worth than all the riches of the world." (Arneth, "Maria Theresa and Joseph II." Vol. III. p. 266).

The Landgravine of Hesse Darmstadt found Paul amiable, very polite, a good talker, and cheerful.

The Princess of Wirtemberg, wrote to Baroness d'Oberkirch ("Memoirs de D'Oberkirch" p.74);

"No one could be more lovable than the Grand Duke Paul. He is the most adorable of husbands, he is an angel and I love him to distraction".

A. Rappoport continues his description of the Tsar:

"When he was 7 years old, he was discussing politics with statesmen."

"Paul is reported to have been very handsome in his early youth:"

"The Grand Duke wrote to Rasumovsky: "I have imposed it as a duty on myself to live in as cordial relations as is possible, with everyone."

Paul I. never forgot anyone to whom he felt indebted.

When Paul travelled across Poland in 1781 with his wife, they were met by King Stanislaus and were so delightfully agreeable that they turned the heads of the King and his suite, Paul and his wife were a great success in Paris. Everybody raved about them and everything they said or did was greatly admired; also throughout Italy.

"Paul's figure is well set and his face attractive. He is pleasant"

Catherine II died in 1796, leaving him the throne.

"The Czar treated the Ministers and all the friends of his mother generously and loaded them with favours. He confirmed Zoubov in his office. Every hour, every moment announced some wise change, or some merited favour. Paul was a benevolent autocrat. The wise and beneficent regulations of his mother were confirmed, while ukases which caused discontent among the people were annuled." p. 186.

Paul annulled the command to levy recruits, sent a courier to end war in Persia and announced to diplomats that he "had not inherited his mother's quarrels." Paul visited the famous Polish hero, Kosciuszko, a State prisoner, and liberated not only him, but all the imprisoned Poles. He handed over a sum of money to them and enabled them to go to America, for which Paul was enthusiastic as were all the Romanovs, ("Russkayia Starina," 1882).

THE "MYSTERY" OF CZAR PAUL

"Stedingk, the Swedish Envoy in St. Petersburg, was full of praise, and informed the King, that the Emperor is employing every moment of his reign for some act of justice, order or benevolence."

But Paul I received a demoralised army from Catherine II. As the grandson of Frederick of Prussia, how could Paul I. look placidly at officers going about in pelisses and furs and muffs, and officials in fur nightgowns! He began to drill his army, forbade furs during parades and wore a light overcoat himself. This was considered cruel. But this rule is in effect today.

"You shall march to Siberia, if it is needed to teach you to do it," the Tsar shouted. And he ordered a regiment to begin such a task. After a good march of some 10 miles he ordered the regiment back and all was forgotten. The Czar demanded from his soldiers the same speed, as they are giving today in every army. But as Paul saved the Catholic Church everything he did was misrepresented by the Hidden Hand.

Paul's mother, the Prussian Catherine II., had many lovers. He could not have had much esteem for them and they insulted him. He disliked the last two, the Zubov brothers, and they were the only Russians, who joined the plot against him though Paul was most magnanimous even to them.

What were the "crimes of the Reign of Terror" as Rappoport described the rule of Paul I? He denies them himself; "Paul was peacefully inclined, Paul's early policy had therefore been one of peace. He withdrew his forces from Persia and, leaving Georgia to her own levies, discontinued the recruiting ordained by his mother." "He declared, that humanity did not allow him to refuse his beloved subjects the peace for which they sighed" (p.220) Please note the constant desire of the Romanovs to keep peace Paul offered hospitality to Louis XVIII. in Mitau (Kurland).

The French, having taken possession of the Malta, the Knights of the Maltese Order conceived the idea of offering the Grand Mastership of the Order to the Emperor Paul. Fond of ceremonies and wishing to pose as a hero of chivalry before the Princess Gagarina, Paul accepted with joy this honor so famous in history.

"This title—the Grand Master of so many Knights-errant,—says Sablukov— at the very moment, when a romantic love for the Princess Gagarina was inflaming his tender heart, set the poor man quite beside himself" (p. 221).

Paul knew, that he was deceived by his German wife!

79

"MYSTERY" OF "ROMA NOVA" AND ROMA III.

The more I study the real "Cause of the World Unrest," the more I believe that when Paul I. became Grand Master of the Catholic Order of the Knights of Malta and thus accomplished the impossible, i.e., the first steps towards the re-uniting of the Eastern (Orthodox) Church with the Universal Church,—the Dynasty of the Romanovs became hated still more by the Jews and by their Emperors, the Rothschilds.

"There has been no friendship between the Court of St. Petersburgh and my family," declared Lionel Rothschild to Disraeli ("Coningsby," p. 251).

And six Tsars Romanovs were thereafter murdered . . .

Why did the Rothschild, who praised Monarchy so much, ("Coningsby," p. 303) and found it even "divine," wish to annihilate the Monarchies? Was it for the welfare of the people? No! His aim was to substitute himself in the place of monarchs.

This is the only thing that has interested the Jews!

The chief reason was, that Autocracy might with one stroke of the pen re-unite the Mother Church and thus uniting at least two-thirds of the Christians, and thereby give the hardest blow to Satan.

Paul I took the first step and perished by assassins.

It seems that there was some mystic union between the Roma— the Ancient and Roma-novs (Roma Nova).

And Moscow has often been called Rome the Third.

Rome I and III were disunited by Rome II—Byzantium.

All the Tsars Romanovs were the best of Christians.

The Rothschilds have always been most anti-Christian.

Both Dynasties could not simultaneously exist.

The first Roma-nov(a) was the Roman prince Prus, brother of the Roman Emperor August. His descendents settled in the land, now called Prussia, and became princes Russingen. One of them Glanda Cambilla came to Novgorod in Russia in 1287 and took the name of Cabila.

His son Andrew settled in Moscow and became the adviser of the Grand Duke John (nicknamed Calita or Collector) and of his son Simeon the Proud. Andrew's son Theodore, nicknamed Coshka, (Cat) became the Regent of Russia in 1380. His daughter married the Grand Duke of Tver. His great grandson Theodore became Patriarch of Russia and his son Michael was elected in 1613 — Czar of Russia.

THE POLITICS OF PAUL I.

Let us read the "Curse of the Romanovs" by Rappoport:

"Paul abandoned his peaceful policy and joined England, Austria and Naples in coalition against Bonaparte (French Republic). Paul appointed Souvarov chief-commander. Souvarov achieved victories on the river Adda, Trebbia and at Novi. He crossed the Alps by the St. Gothard and entered Switzerland, buth the second Russian general, Korsakov, had been defeated by Massena, (a Jew — Manasseh)and Souvarov was compelled to retreat and to lead his army back to Russia. The Tsar was disgusted with the treatment, which he had received from Austria and England. Paul, as Souvarov himself had done, accused Austria of treason. Bonaparte, therefore, whose 'despotic'* principles now reassured the Tsar, availed himself of Paul's indignation against Austria and managed to win him over to his cause. Napoleon began by sending back to Paul all the Russian prisoners clothed in new uniforms and well provisioned. This clever move at once gained him the Tsar's heart and Paul was the more touched by First Consul's action since Austria and England had refused to exchange the Russian soldiers for French soldiers" (p. 222).

England and Austria acted with Paul just as Bronstein (Trotzky) acts with England to-day. However, Rappoport thinks that it was the Czar, who ought to be destroyed. The Jew continues:

"Paul spoke of the First Consul's noble conduct. 'Napoleon,' said Paul 'had suppressed anarchy, and there was no reason why Russia should not come to an understanding with him.' Disturbed by the maritime tyranny of Great Britain, which had declared the ports of France under a state of siege, Paul renewed the famous act of armed neutrality. The Tsar of Russia and the First Consul then entered into an alliance." (p. 223).

Such were the political "crimes" of the Tsar Paul I.

Mr. Rappoport narrates concerning the Czar's "tyranny:"

"Mrs. Sagrianski (a nobody) having failed in some act of politeness towards the princess Lapouhine, mother of the Emperor's morganatic wife, received the orders to leave St. Petersburg. She, however, was able to secure some degree of clemency, and was graciously granted some months in which to settle her affairs in order."

The Tsar, was compelled by his mother Catherine II. to accept a wife, whom he did not love, and who betrayed him. He wished to protect his real love, princess Gagarine from unmerited insults and only threatened Mrs. Sagrianski. She never was exiled in reality. However, Mr. Rappoport seems to be ready to compare the Czar with the arch murderer Jew Bronstein ("Trotzky").

* According to the Jew Rappoport everything non-Bolshevik is despotic.

ROTHSCHILD ABOLISHES CATHOLIC CHURCH (1798)

Meanwhile Amschel Mayer was pursuing the chief aim of the satanist Hidden Hand, the abolition of the Christian Church through Bonaparte, chief Commander of the French troops in Italy. All Italian Free-Masonry betrayed Italy and helped the French .

The "Americanized Encyclopaedia Britannica states:

"Shortly after the Peace of Tolentino in February 1797, Pius VI. was seized with an illness. Napoleon gave instructions, that no successor to the Office, should be elected and that Papal Government should be abolished. The French Ambassador in Rome proceeded through his agents to foment an insurrection!!! The outbreak of it was immediately made the pretext for abolishing the existing Papal Rule and the Roman Republic was proclaimed. It was under the protection of the Emperor of Russia, that after the lapse of 8 months, Pius VII. was elected Pope at Venice. He (1800-1823) succeeded in gaining the good will of Bonaparte and his accession was shortly followed by the Concordat of 1801. Catholicism was reestablished as the State religion of France. Pius administration of his Office was exemplary and the same may be said of his successors: Leo XII. (1823-1829), Pius VIII. (1829-1830) and Gregory XVI (1831-1846). Ecclesiasticism itself—assumed another tone; its morality was pure; its zeal in the performance of its duties conspicuous" (p. 4889).

"Pope Pius VI. (1717-1799) was taken prisoner by general Berthier and carried away from Rome to Valence in France, where he died. How mean and pitiful of the French the sending of the unfortunate Pope to an hospital in France at 80, not to end his days in a convent in his own country" (Mr. Vere Fisher in his "The Two Duchesses", p. 162).

As Robespierre revealed in his last speech, which cost him his life, the aliens agents of Amschel, then were ruling France.

Having upset the throne and undermined the Church in France and having failed to start a revolution in England in 1798 through a branch of the "Illuminati," the Hidden Hand turned its attention to the Czar of Russia, Paul I., who might again give the Church new vigor, having restored the Pope, hated by the Jews.

In his book, "The Curse of the Romanovs," Mr. A. Rappoport, a Jew, displays a knowledge of the World Jewish Conspiracy of the Rothschilds to destroy all the Christian Monarchies and to establish Jewish Presidents. Let us see how the enemy of the too-Christian Romanovs explain the death of Emperor Paul I.

Of course, when the Hidden Hand resolves to murder anyone, it always begins by pouring on the victim an ocean of muddy calumnies. This custom is unmistakable evidence that the Hidden Hand is arranging the plot. "Calumniate, and then kill," is its rule. I shall have occasion to emphasize this point later on.

PAUL I. SAVES CATHOLIC CHURCH—KILLED.

"At the solicitation of Emperor Paul, and out of regard for his mediation, Bonaparte, who even then was contemplating the conquest of the Two Sicilies, stopped Murat's march on Naples and respected the Holy See." ("Memoirs" of Fouche, p. 146).

Such were the terrific "crimes" of Tsar Paul I.

The chief "crime" of the unfortunate Emperor in the eyes of Amschel and all the Free-Masonic, anti-Christian Lodges, was the restoration of the Catholic Church, abolished by them. Rappoport states, (p. 221):

"It was somewhat strange to see the Russian Emperor, the head and defender of the Orthodox Church, thus recognized as Grand Master of a Roman Catholic Order, and the Pope as his Chief."

Here is "where the dog is buried," as the saying goes. One may imagine why it became the greatest of "The Sorrows of Satan." (The name of Mrs. Coralli's book).

Amschel was ready to kill himself of grief!

Did Paul save the Roman Church, because he was a descendent of a Roman prince Prus? We shall explain the "mystery" of the "Roma Nova" (New Rome): it was the Czars' esteem of Rome!

Now after eighteen centuries of merciless attack upon the Catholic Church by all the Satanic forces through the Free-Masonic Lodges, the Holy Father might yet be recognized as Chief of the Church by the Russian Empire! Every good Jew, especially Angelo Rappoport, and even more so the leading Jew, Amschel, would naturally be lashed to fury by such an unheard of "crime" as that of Tsar Paul. Mr. Rappoport states:

"Paul I. was brutally murdered by a drunken band of officers," (p. 19), and that his last words were, "What have I done?" Mr. Rappoport could not advance a single fact which might explain, what the unfortunate Emperor had done to merit such a death!

I explain the only reason: Paul I. had frightened Satan's agents at Frankfort by the possibility of the Orthodox (Eastern) Church combining with the Mother (Universal) Church (at Rome). Such a reinforcement of CHRIST'S work on Earth would be the greatest sorrow for Satan, since his failure with CHRIST Himself on the Mountain. No efforts should be too great to prevent this reunion!

A curious fact about Mr. Rappoport's book is the continous contradiction of his Jewish desire to blacken the Czar, at any cost, while the real facts, stated by himself, refute all his unjust opinions about the Romanovs. Many contemporaries of several nations prove this contradiction.

83

Therefore, all the mud which was thrown by the Jew Rappoport, in his devilish efforts to blacken Tsar Paul I., can be compared only with the panegyries of Mr. Buckle, lauding the traitor, the Jew — Disraeli; or of M. P. Deschanel's praise of the double-dyed traitor Jew — Gamberle (Gambetta).

The Rothschilds' politics in the XIX-th Century consisted of not allowing Russia to form an alliance either with England or with Rome, and the Russians were to be persuaded, that all the murders and all the calamities in Russia were committed by the "British" Government. The Hidden Hand before murdering Tsar Paul I., because he favored a reconciliation with the Holy Father, besmirched Paul's reputation by more or less fantastic calumnies, so that no one would help him, nor later on take the trouble to unveil the mystery of his murder, as I have done. The murderers were the agents of the Hidden Hand, or scoundrels, like the Zoubov brothers, the young ex-Alphonses of the old Empress. Even they were drunken.

Sir Robert Gunning relates, that a "plate of sausages was put before Paul and while eating, he came across some splinters of glass." Was that not sufficient to make him suspicious?

All these incidents were terribly exaggerated, the sole object being to discredit the all Too-Christian Tsar, and to facilitate his death, determined upon by the bloodthirsty Amschel Rothschild I. To render Paul perturbed, he was informed long before he was murdered, that he was doomed to death, and once he even asked:

"Will they really strangle me?" It is not surprising that feeling himself in a trap, he became irritated and anxious.

Paul's life until he became Tsar at the age of forty-two, was most miserable, and this would naturally make him irritable and suspicious. However, according to the Memoirs of De Sanglen (in the "Russkayia Starina," 1883) Paul I.

"had a warm, kind and feeling heart; he was endowered with noble sentiments, with a passionate love for justice and with a high sense of chivalry".

His wife, the Empress, was constantly being persuaded that she was a great woman, who could play the role of a new and even more famous Catherine II., and that, otherwise, she was in danger of an attempt on the part of the Tsar, to take her life.

"The Princess of Darmstadt (Paul's wife) was influenced by Count A. Razumovsky, her paramour." ("Diaries and Correspondence of James Harris," p. 212).

84

All the so-called "terrors" of Paul I. during his reign of five years, cost fewer lives than a single day during the rule of the Jew-Bolsheviks in Russia today.

The murder of the Tsar Paul was committed by foreign Free-Masons: Pahlen, Benigsen,* Admiral Ribas, Dr. Rogerson, etc. "Pahlen had been given his title by Paul, had been enriched with many earthly blessings and was being treated with the highest confidence by the Emperor" (p. 230). Who was the real murderer of Paul I.? I have explained all!

Paul was a danger to the anti-Christians and a most devilish plan was concocted by the Free-Masons. Many conspirators of the French Revolution came to St. Petersburg. All the men who surrounded Paul I. were bribed or estranged from him or sent away. Thus step by step one of the most demoniacal plots which Satan could formulate was brewed.

His own son, Alexander, was told that his father was jealous of his popularity and even wished to exile him, which was just the reverse of the truth. One of the chief villains, Pahlen, even revealed the plot to Paul and advised him to sign an order for the arrest of Alexander, who, Pahlen assured the Tsar was the chief conspirator. To save himself, Paul signed an order purely to prevent his son's crime. Then Alexander was shown this order and persuaded to consent to the abdication of his father from the throne, being assured that not one hair of Paul's head would be harmed.

Instead of being dethroned Paul I. was murdered. This was appallingly unjust.

"It is for history to clear up the secret of this tragic death, and to say what national policy was interested in provoking such a catastrophe," wrote Napoleon in the "Moniteur," when the news of the death of Paul I. reached him.

Rappoport says it was the "Perfide Albion":

"The British Ambassador, Witworth, had first conceived the idea of the conspiracy" (p. 235).

This version was first told by the German Jew Schliemann in his "Das Ermordung Paul's," p. 16.

*"A Hanoverian, of the name Benixin (Benigsen) was the man who conducted the whole murder plot" (Mr. Vere Fisher, who visited St. Petersburg next after the murder of Czar Paul, in his book "The Two Duchesses", p. 170).

Mr. Vere Fisher adds that it was a chief from Georgia (Caucasus) who assassinated the Czar, whose only "crime" was to save the Catholic Church annihilated by Rothschild's agents. Amschel passed 3 years in Hanover...

Amschel Mayer discovered Napoleon through Mirabeau and Talleyrand and supported him strongly, when he showed himself an agnostic, Anti-Catholic, even Mohammedan in Egypt, and an incomparable murderer of the Christians;* but Amschel was displeased when Napoleon, greatly impressed with the work of the Catholic orders in promoting the principle of authority, re-established the Catholic Church in France and began to "serve God and man."

After becoming Emperor Napoleon wished to treat the nation as his beloved children.

Until then the Jews had watched Napoleon's growing power without anxiety. Like Mr. H. G. Wells they, undervalued his genius.

The young Emperor of France soon understood, that his war against the Church would destroy his country. He even wished to transfer the Holy See to Paris and to make the Pope President of the Imperial Council, in order to bind all his conquests together. This enraged the Jewish Free-Masonry.

Every conspiracy, plot, and attempt became worthwhile in order to create a quarrel with Napoleon, first of all to embroil him with the Holy See; and even destroy the Franco-Italian genius, who alone could stop the successes of the Hidden Hand.

"The Maur has done his work, the Maur can go," thought the Frankfort spider, and La Sala was despatched from Germany to kill the Emperor. But the plot failed and the magnanimous Latin Lion granted La Sala his life. This is another example of the dangerous work of the Illuminati who, although officially dissolved, have remained as executors of the "Exterminator of Christians!"

In his early days Napoleon, influenced by Masonry, had promised to accomplish all the desires of the Jews and he became their well-beloved man. Later on Napoleon, becoming Emperor, thought he was a "Man of Destiny," and found it better to improve and assimilate the Jews. ("Le Juif, le Judaisme et la Judaisation" des Peuples Chretiens" by famous Gougenot des Mousseaux).

*) Only to please his "friend" Augustine Robespierre (younger brother of Maximilian—the dictator and arch-murderer (a Jew, Ruban, according to Louis Marchand) Napoleon was compelled to show himself most bloodthirsty, but he was an aristocrat, and bloodshed, except in battles, was distasteful to him. He was good hearted. "The stern soldier-emperor was always kindness and tenderness to all children." (Mrs. Agnes Carey, "Empress Eugenie In Exile", p. 273).

NAPOLEON CHALLENGES THE JEWS

Napoleon convoked on May 30, 1806 in Paris, the Jews of France and of Italy to a big convention, which became a Sanhedrin. In March 1808 Napoleon showed that he would no longer follow the anti-Christian advice of the Free-Masons, controlled by the Jews, but on the contrary, he required Jewish rabbis to become his agents, even to act as a kind of Police officials.

In the Council of the Empire he enumerated rudely the abominable crimes of the Jews. It was a challenge to the Hidden Hand, and the challenge was accepted. Napoleon said:

"We must look at the Jews not only as a distinct race, but as on aliens. It would be a most awful humiliation to be ruled by this, the most base race on earth." ("La Vieille France", N-305)

He wrote to his brother Jerome, King of Westphalia:

"Nothing more contemptible could be done than the reception of the Jews by you... I decided to improve the Jews. But I do not want more of them in my kingdom. Indeed, I have done all to prove my scorn of the most vile nation in the world" ("Letters of Napoleon," Lesestre, letter N-237, March 6, 1808).

Napoleon as all the World greatest geniuses, understood quickly, how boundlessly right is CHRIST in pointing out:

"Ye, Jews, are the sons of the devil, and his lusts ye will do."

Daily persuaded in this by facts, Napoleon often repeated:

"One cannot improve the character of the Jews by arguments. For them must be established special exclusive laws."

"Since the times of Moses the Jews were oppressors or usurers."

"All the talent of the Jews is concentrated on predatory acts."

"They have a creed which blesses their thievings and misdeeds."

"The Jews ought to be forbidden to make trade, as are forbidden the goldsmiths, who forge a lower kind of gold things, to continue their work."

"The Jews are locusts or caterpillars which are devouring France."

With all military genius Napoleon ignored my "Science of Political Foresight" and this lost him.

One hundred years after Napoleon's death a prominent Jew of London, Dr. Oscar Levy wrote:

"We, Jews, have made the World War! We, Jews, are nothing else than the world's seducers, its incediaries, its executioners! Our last revolution is not yet made! We, Jews, invented the myth of the 'Chosen people'."

Napoleon remembered that King Louis IX of France was called "Holy" and that he used to say:

"The best argument with a Jew — is to plunge your dagger into his stomach".

Why? Both of these great Monarchs read in the Talmud:

"Kill the most honest of the goym" (Talmud, Abod. Zar. 26 b.)

"He who sheds the blood of the goym (gentiles), is offering a sacrifice to God" (Talmud, Jalqut Simeoni).

HIDDEN HAND'S ATTEMPT TO KILL NAPOLEON

The agent of the "Illuminati" being found incompetent to remove Napoleon, a certain Stapps was despatched to kill the Emperor in 1809, when he was in Shoenbrunn. This plot failed, only because Gen. Rapp's vigilance stopped Stapps.

After a conversation with Stapps, the Emperor said:

"These are the effects of German (i.e. from Frankfort) "Illuminati". The rising generation are taught assassination as a virtue. Yet I still believe there is something more than appears in the affair."

Yes! The "Illuminati" were directed not only by the Weisshaupts but by the Hidden Hand, led by the 6 Rothschilds. It is obvious that the unjust and hostile opinion of the Emperor expressed by Mr. H. G. Wells, in his "The Adventure of Napoleon," is due to the same influence of the Hidden Hand and to Wells's ignorance of its activity. Despite his somewhat unscrupulous methods in politics, Napoleon remains in the eyes of the world a genius. And he even became peaceful.

How many times Napoleon gladly repeated, when he could enjoy peace, which so much annoyed the Rothschilds:

"Thank GOD, I am at peace with all the world."

But the "Tigers" constantly plotted new wars.

Mr. H. G. Wells and other critics of Napoleon ought to read pages 500-504 Vol. I of the "History of Napoleon," by Mr. G. Moir Bussey.

Through their numberless co-workers and Masons the Rothschilds, caused considerable difficulties and constant trouble to Napoleon, not only with the Holy Father but with all the Monarchs of Europe.* The Rothschilds spoiled the campaign of 1812 by disorganising Napoleon's supplies of food, and when his international army began to retreat from Moscow, the Jews on the way, were ordered to murder his wounded and freezing soldiers, which order was mercilessly executed. Hundred thousands of Christians were thus killed.

The dangers and plots and conspiracies began to handicap the genius of the Emperor. Lord Withworth reported to London how nervous Napoleon became. The Corsican could not grasp the fact, that the Hidden Hand which he had begun to neglect, was already against him. He had also under-estimated its strength, ignoring that it was backed by Satan, while he also, was not supported by the Vicar of CHRIST. Yes! Napoleon committed the hugest blunder in under-valuing also the influence of the Holy See.

*) "The league against Napoleon I, which was instrumental in shattering his dream of universal empire, was a jewish organization" (Walter Hurt, "Truth About The Jews", p. 323).

NAPOLEON EX-COMMUNICATED, LOSES THE SUPPORT OF THE CHURCH

In 1804 again began that coldness between the Imperial and Papal Courts, which afterwards ripened into dislike and ended in violence.

"Had the Pope before quitting his own capital but asked for the Italian Legations, they would have been restored; but it was another thing after the service had been rendered', wrote Napoleon's Secretary, Bourrienne" (Mr. George Moir Bussey's "History of Napoleon," y. 104).

This was very adroitly exploited by the Hidden Hand and Napoleon's General Radet was so influenced by its agents, that he dared to arrest the Pope without any order of the Emperor, who was really alarmed, but did not wish to chagrin his free Masonic colleagues and discredit his General, who as Napoleon thought. only did it because of too much zeal.

Then the Holy Father on June 11th, 1809 fulminated against Napoleon a Bull of Excommunication:

"By the authority of Almighty God, the blessed Apostles Peter and Paul, and our own. We declare that you, Napoleon, Emperor of the French, and all your abettors, have by the outrages you have committed, incurred the penalty of excommunication."

Napoleon wished to see the Pope Archbishop of Rome and Paris. But Pius VII. answered to all threats:

"Nothing on earth can induce me to retract.. I am ready to shed the last drop of my blood, to; lay down my life this instant rather than violate the oath which I have made before Heaven."

The ground began to tremble under Napoleon's feet, and later he confessed:

"The Pope, could he have been won, would have been an additional means of binding together the federated parts of the Empire. I should have had my religious, as well as my legislative sessions. My councils would have constituted the representation of Christianity, and the successor of St. Peter would have been the President."

But the Holy Father's unheard firmness prevented the "Gallicization" of the Catholic Church, which remained **Universal.**

"I was not so fortunate as Genghis-Khan, each of whose four sons rivalled the others in zeal for his service," complained Napoleon, but he should have said: "I was not so fortunate as Amschel, who had five sons and five daughters, who all attracted some support, to succeed him in ruling the World".

Nothing remained of the sons of Genghis Khan and of Napoleon, but a scion of Amschel—is the Autocrat of the World.

*) One of the Genghis-Khan descendants reached the rank of General in the Russian army during the reign of Nicholas II. He conserved the most typical Mongol face, awfully fierce looking and dark yellow.

NAPOLEON AMSCHEL'S "CHURCH BREAKER"

"Count Paul de Barras (1755-1829) appointed Napoleon Commander in Chief of the Army in Italy, and arranged the marriage of Napoleon with the widow Beauharnais" (Mr. Vere Fisher, "Two Dutchesses" p. 483).

Josephine was the mistress of Barras, who wished to get rid of Napoleon in this wedding and even promoted him, thus freeing her, but was fearful of her revenge. So he hurried to help himself of the fiery Creole.

Josephine Beauharnais was chosen for him also, because it was known, that she could not have an heir. Napoleon was an ideal "mankiller" of Christians, and the Hidden Hand was glad to allow him to continue his "pleasant occupation", of shattering thrones and the Church.

He was promoted First Consul for life. Amschel contemplated with almost indifference his pompous coronation as Emperor in 1804, though the arrival of the Pope was in his eyes already a bad omen. Amschel had taken the necessary steps in Paris and Rome to cool his eventual friendship . . . The Emperor's divorce from Josephine and his marriage with the Arch-Duchess Marie-Louisa in 1810 was a tremendous blow to the Rothschilds—"Tigers." But Napoleon's culminating "crimes" were his truthful and clever statements against the Jews and the birth on the 20th March 1811, of the King of Rome, who seemed destined to inherit the largest monarchy. Those who thought so were unaware that another monarchy—the Occult Jewish Empire, still greater, had already been established and the young Eaglet was destined to destruction. From the date of this birth James Rothschild was daily reminded by Amschel, to hurry to Paris and to ruin his rival.

Had the Occult Jewish Emperor spent so much money (not of his own, but of a Goy) and wasted so much effort in order to upset the Christian Monarchy in France, only to see another Christian Dynasty snatch the Throne which Amschel had predestined for his "Benjamin"—Jacob. And the last of Amschel's sons Jacob-James was despatched to Paris to give the "coup de grace" to Napoleon.

The "occult ruler of Italy" — Karl Rothschild — having done his best to envenom the relations between the Holy See and Napoleon, staged the arrest of the Holy Father without Napoleon's order, and then hurried to Paris to help his brother Jacob.

Ignoring the Hidden Hand, J. Reeves finds a "mystery":

"To establish a branch of their business in the leading state of Italy (Naples) when the political condition of the country was so disturbed, may appear to have been a rash move" (p. 253)

THE "MYSTERY" OF TSAR ALEXANDER I

His enemy a Jew Rappoport informs us about him:

"The right of conquest had no existance for him"...

"Paul gave him a republican Laharpe, as tutor."

„Alexander, born in 1777, was exceedingly good looking".

"He rejoiced at the establishment of the French Republic, and wished its success. The ideas of Alexander were those of 1789. He wished to see republics everywhere. Napoleon at Tilsit in 1807 had to use all his logic to prove to the Autocrat of all Russia, that hereditary monarchy was the sole guaranty of the peace and happiness of nations. The Tsar still maintained, that it was an abuse of sovereignty."

Thus it seemed to the noblest of the rulers.

He was compelled to sanction the conspiracy of 1801 in order "to protect his mother's life" because the free-masons the murderers of his father, deceived him into the belief that Paul I. wished to execute her: but Alexander never gave his consent to the assassination. The masons lied, saying it would only be an abdication, and a "bloodless" revolution, just as the Jew mason Kerensky lied.

Alexander's remorse and despair never left him:

"His grief, which he was continually reviving in his heart, was inexpressibly deep and touching, and his mental tortures never ceased". (Czartorysky)

"For hours he remained alone sitting in silence, with fixed and haggard looks" (Countess Edling).

"When he saw his dead father, Alexander overcome with grief, fell to the ground. On recovering his senses, he and his mother poured out their grief in a flood of tears" ("Fraser's Magazine", p. 324).

"The sensitive soul of Russia's Emperor will forever remain torn" (Empress Elisabeth, his wife).

"Those who were intimately acquainted with the Tsar could tell, how he would occasionally, in the midst of a brilliant reception, suddenly absent himself in order to pray and weep." (p. 361).

In June, 1814, Alexander visited England and the University of Oxford offered him the degree of Doctor of Law.

"The liberal minded Emperor of Russia played an exceptional part at the Vienna Congress in 1814".

"The power of that Emperor (Alexander I.) was great, assuredly, and formidable. He had led the march of peace from capital to capital; he had ruled the congresses supremely, and presided in the assemblies of kings; it was even granted him to see the fortunes of a greater man than Caesar grow pale before his own" (a revolutionary, Louis Blanc in his." The History of 10 Years").

Why France and Russia went to war in 1812 has been a puzzle to historians.

"Napoleon waged war upon me in a most odious fashion, and has deceived me in a most treacherous manner." (Alexander I.).

Both great Emperors fatally for them ignored the Hidden Hand!..

"I did not want to make war on Russia. Bassano and Champagny (French Ministers of Foreign Affairs) persuaded me that the note of Russia was meant for a declaration of war. I really thought, that Russian wanted war", repeated Napoleon... "What were the real motives of the campaign in Russia? I do not know; possibly the Emperor himself did not know any more than I did." (General Gourgaud in his "Talks of Napoleon at St. Helena," p. 154).

It was the Hidden Hand, which organised the war of 1812 *. The above remains a "Mystery" to all those, who have not read this book, which reveals all. The "Mystery" consisted of the fact, that the Hidden Hand was now against Napoleon, and Amschel had already inflamed all the Royalists to oppose the Emperor, as well as Pan-Judaism, Pan-Britannism, Pan-Germanism, etc., all to ruin one man, who was not aware of this conspiracy.

It is the same to-day with the splendid American nation, which seems doomed to perdition, because it ignores the World Government, which according to Hon. T. R. Marchall "will not permit peace". Otherwise, a war is to be expected, as confirmed by M. Mussolini in April 1925. And this war will be against the United States and will mean crushing of the Aryan race and its Christian civilization.

Europe and Mme. Kruedener got wind of it and were foreseeing the fall of the "dark Angel of battles" Napoleon—and the advent of the "fair angel" Alexander—destined by God to be the Savior of the World. For Amschel Napoleon became too "lazy".

Napoleon and his marshals did not wish to fight more.

Bonaparte had been found and exalted by the executors of Satan and began to "exterminate as many Christians, as possible" and to upset the Universal Christian Church headed by the Holy Father. As Satan wished to degrade CHRIST on the Mountain, Napoleon, eighteen centuries later, tried to lower the Holy Father and to make him descend to become his religious policeman.

"Napoleon in the might of his Caesarean temper believed in his star; he would point it out to convince the incredulous, that he was forced to walk in the ways that were appointed for his destiny".("Curse of Romanovs" p. 162)

But could Napoleon's Ministers disobey Satan's wish, transmitted through the Rothschilds, to "murder the Christians."

*) Exactly as it was foretold by CHRIST years ahead.

JAMES COMES TO "KNOCK OUT" NAPOLEON

There are documents in the National Archives in Paris, proving, that James, Karl and Nathan Rothschilds (from London) were over-busy with all sorts of plots and all kinds of smuggling. Prince d'Eckmuhl advised the Emperor to arrest all the Rothschilds, who crossed his frontiers.

This Minister of the Police had a huge correspondence about the activity of the Rothschilds, who in Germany exploited the influence of the Elector of Hesse-Cassel. It was a veritable conspiracy against Napoleon, who by a strange clemency (because he knew the cause of his brilliant career) did not wish to arrest and shoot the mischief-makers from Frankfort, as he did the Duke d'Enghien.

The misplaced, though real leniency of the late Tsar Nicholas II. towards 3 agents of the Hidden Hand, the 3 mischief makers and hangmen of Russia: Kerensky, (a Jew) Miliukoff, (paid by the Jews) and Guchkoff, (son of a Jewess) later caused the loss of lives of some 30.000.000 people and the murder of the Tsar and his family.

The same Hidden Hand which upset the Christian Empire in France, in 1815 and 1870, overturned the Christian Empires in Russia, Germany and Austria.

It was clear to me, that Russia was going "Toward the Debacle" (the title of my book in 1913), because her Government would not pay sufficient attention to the plots of the satanic Supreme Jewish Government.

In my last public warning to the Emperor, Nicholas II, in his own newspaper, "Zemstchina," 24 (11) August, 1916, I explained briefly my Theory of Satanic Forces, which rule the World, and proved that Russia had against her Pan-Judaism, Pan-Germanism, Pan-Asiatism, etc. united and that the catastrophe was approaching like a hurricane. As the only way of salvation I advised the recon-ciliation of the two Catholic Churches: Eastern and Western and the granting to the Catholic Slavs: Poles, Czechs, Croatians, etc. the same rights as the Orthodox Slavs: Bulgarians, Russians and Serbians had, by proclaming the All-Slav Union.

As my quite easy and sure "way of salvation" was ignored, the unheard of, but foretold by me, catastrophe to Russia followed exactly six months later. The same will happen with America, unless my readers open her eyes by putting this book in the hands of their respective Congressmen.

Since Elizabeth I. refused to grant Russia to the Jews, the Hidden Hand has done its best to kill and blacken the Romanovs.

THE FAMILY OF AMSCHEL ROTHSCHILD, I

Mayer Amschel had one sister, Gutesche, who married Salomon Daniel Goldschmidt, and two brothers: Salomon Amschel, dead in 1782, and Moise Amschel, who became the head of the Goldsmidts.

Mayer Amschel had five sons and five daughters:

a) Charlotte Mayer, born in 1770, and married to Benedict Moses Worms.

b) Anselm, born in 1773, died in 1855, married with Eva Hannau. He was chosen a member of the royal Prussian privy council of commerce, Bavarian Consul and Court banker.

c) Salomon, born in 1774, married to Caroline Stern; died in 1855. He entered into "intimate relations" with the prince Metternich, the "dictator" of Austria.

d) Nathan born in 1777 (as Alexander I, whom he poisoned); he married Johanna Levi Barnet Cohen; died in 1836.

e) Isabelle, born in 1781 and married to Bernhard Juda Sishel.

f) Babette, born in 1784; married to Leopold Beyfuss.

g) Karl, born in 1788; married with Adelaide Hertz and died in 1855. After the annexation of Naples to Italy his bank there was discontinued in 1860 and his sons went to Frankfort.

h) James (Jacob), born in 1792; married to his niece (the daughter of his brother, Salomon)—Betty of Vienna and died in 1868.

i) Julia, who married Mayer Levy Beyfuss.

j) Henriette, who married Abraham Montefiore.

Mayer Amschel's wife Gutta (Gudula) survived Mayer many years and died most quietly at the age of 96. Notwithstanding its filthy surroundings, the old house in the Judengasse was her home to the last. So Shnapper lived, until the thread of life was snapped.

"The movements of the Rothschilds are carefully watched, and are as important to the public as those of any Ministers. One enthusiastic inquirer was informed, that it was impossible to name all the members of the family, as a pedigree did not exist". (Reeves, 60)

When death approached, old Amschel called together his children, in Frankfort, and having read the satanic Talmud, he proclaimed:

"Remember my children, that all the Earth must belong to us, Jews, and that the Gentiles being mere excrements of animals, must possess nothing."

Explaining this, Amschel compelled them to swear most solemnly that they would always stick to one another and never undertake anything separately. This they did and it was repeated on Amschel's grave twenty-four years later, when Nathan for material reasons consented to become a "Christian" and "suddenly" died . . .

AMSCHEL DISTRIBUTES THE WORLD. HIS DEATH (1812)

Amschel allotted Germany, Austria, Great Britain, Italy and France to his five sons: Anselm, Salomon, Nathan, Karl, and James-Jacob. Later on a scion of Rothschild, known as Schoeneberg was accorded the United States and took the name of Belmont.

The Rothschilds did not wish to exhibit their name in America, because the Hessian soldiers, who so irritated the populaton there, were one of the herds which had been bought, equipped and sold by Mayer Amschel as "gun fodder."

This distribution of the world among the five sons of the old Jew of Frankfort is most striking and reminds one of how the world was also distributed just 1000 years earlier by the four grand sons of Charlemagne, Emperor of the Romans. Amschel hated nothing on earth more than the word "Roma," because there lived the leader of the Christians. **"Rome is the great foe of Bolshevism"** (A. Mond).

The Pope in Rome, the King of Rome (Napoleon II) and the Roma Nova (the Romanovs) in Russia, all of these made Amschel mad with satanic fury. He delegated agents to ruin all of them. Amschel created an Empire of Gold and Usury, more durable than the Empires of Charlemagne, of Napoleon I, and of the Romanovs.

Around a dirty table in the Judengasse, Amschel explained to his wife, the most greedy of all the Jewesses of Frankfort, Gutta Shnapper, and to his five sons and five daughters, the "lust of murder" and of making money out of plundering the Christians.

Having learned in the rabbinic school all the satanic program, known as the "Protocols of the Learned Elders of Zion," Amschel knew ahead of the assault on the royalty of race and its substitution by the royalty of gold. He preached to his children how to rob and not to be "pinched," and all the devilish tricks of the Kabbalah (see "The Kabbalah Unveiled," translated by S. L. MacGregor Mathers).

"The five sons started in business in five European capitals, but were acting in concert with the others.... The business of the Rothschilds since 1812 has been so immense, and the bonds linking the different members of the family together so interwoven, that to unravel them appears to be well nigh hopeless. The success achieved by the founder was due to the disturbed state of the world. Mayer Amschel was a child of fortune equally with Napoleon," (J. Reeves, p. 58)

But who started those wars and were they not the consequence of the criminal act of the Landgrave to confide his colossal fortune to a "satanist mankiller," forgetting CHRIST'S warning? Were not all the rulers right who tried to prevent the Jews from accumulating such tremendous fortunes in their hands?

95

Nathan was established in London, Salomon in Vienna, Karl at Naples and James in Paris.

Anselm, the first son, became the successor to the Bank at Frankfort, and remained the only real Mayer. He was an old-fashioned Jew. His father ordered him to marry the Jewess, Eva Hannan whom he disliked; he had no children. After his death he was succeeded by the sons of Karl, the chief of their bank in Naples, which was closed in 1860, when the Rothschilds found that the Pope was ruined, and that Italy could no more be plundered..

Salomon, the second son of Amschel, went to Vienna, then occupied by the five Jews Arnstein, Eskeles, Geymuller, Stein, and Sina. He promptly pushed out the first four and let the fifth live modestly in the shadow of the gigantic tree of Rothschild.

Karl, the fifth son, went to Naples, as the centre from which he could upset the Pope and plunder the Italian Kingdoms. He married a beautiful Jewess, Adelaide Hertz, who found favour with the King of Naples and thus helped her husband to . . . develop his affairs. Karl became the occult head of the "Alta Vendita." Karl's two oldest sons, Charles and William returned to Frankfort at the death of Anselm, and left the house of Naples to Karl's third son, Adolphe, who succeeded his father in 1855.

Adolphe had no Rothschild blood in his veins. In 1860 he liquidated his bank and preferred to live quietly. He was at the Coronation of the Tsar Alexander II. in Moscow, in 1856. He married a cousin Rothschild, but had no children by his own wife.

He was the image of the King of Naples... His title was-Marquis.

Salomon of Vienna had two children, one son, Anselm Salomon, and a daughter, Betty, who married her uncle James of Paris and the 3rd "Emperor of the World." All these satanists were happy after the exile of Napoleon to the island of Elba and it seemed that nothing could disturb their "beatitude." But he suddenly left Elba and re-entered France.

He was supposed by the people to be an Anti-Christ.

"Vox populi, vox Dei," says a wise, ancient proverb.

The people had a wonderful insight, and understood that he was "created" by the Satanic power.

When they said "Anti-Christ," they meant "anti-Christian."

Alexander refused to let Napoleon bleed Europe again.

A new Coalition was formed and war declared.

The Rothschilds financed all these powers.

THE "MYSTERY" OF WATERLOO

"'The battle of Waterloo is an enigma as obscure for those who gained it, as for him, who lost it. To Napoleon—it is a panic. Wellington does not understand it at all. All the historians suffer from a certain bedazzlement in which they grope about" (a genius Victor Hugo in his "Waterloo", p. 88).

Thousands of authors on Napoleon I. overlooked the "Tigers" of the "Political Zoo,"—the Rothschilds, and their agents, who, like rats were constantly engaged in undermining the foundations of his power. Historians have paid no attention to the numerous complaints of the great Conqueror, during his exile. In General Gourgaud's book "Talks of Napoleon at Helena," we read again and again, the disillusioned Emperor's bitter exclamations:

"Soult, my second in command at Waterloo, did not aid me much, as he might have done.... His staff, notwithstanding all my orders, was not organized... Soult was very easily discouraged... Soult was worth nothing... Why during the battle did he not keep order at Gemappe"! *

The Corsican genius did not know my "Theory of the Satanic Forces, which rule the world," and he, like Nicholas II. was too magnanimous: he did not arrest these mischievous Jews-Rothschild, when his Chief of Police, Prince of Eckmuhl, suggested it. Like Nicholas II., Charles I. of Austria, and Wilhelm II., Napoleon I. permitted Jews to occupy the most important posts in his empire and all four Emperors were betrayed, ruined and maligned by the Jews, whom they had imprudently honored. The same will happen to every country, ruler, or individual, who will place reliance in them!

All that puzzled Napoleon I. in the conduct of Soult, is explained by the fact that Soult was a Jew, i.e., he obeyed the orders of the Rothschilds. Though Napoleon promoted Soult Marshal, made him Duke of Dalmatia, and granted him an income of millions, this Jew did not hesitate to betray his generous Emperor. Some of my readers may remark, that the Jews rendered a yeoman service to Europe by putting down Napoleon. No! As soon as he attained a firm power, Napoleon became one of the most distinguished and meritorious Monarchs, who ever ruled. The Hidden Hand "created" him in order to make wars and ruin the Church, just as later it "created" Bismarck. But precisely when Napoleon abandoned this warfare, the Rothschilds found him too "Christian" and destroyed him. The difference between the Kaiser and Napoleon is that the Kaiser at last understood, that he was first lured on, deceived, and later betrayed by his Jews, as he confessed ("Chicago Tribune," July 3, 1922), but Napoleon never grasped the reason of his and Frances' disaster.

*) Napoleon was ill! Soult commanded and purposely lost the battle!

97

NATHAN ROTHSCHILD II. AT WATERLOO (1815)

Nathan became the legendary leader of the "coup de Waterloo."

Why did he leave the Exchange, go to Belgium and join the British army? It could not have been a voyage of pleasure because victory might have turned into disaster, had Marshal Grouchy not lost twenty-four hours on account "of the rain," as he himself justified his "mysterious" delay, although he heard the guns. Was he bribed by the Rothschilds; or deceived by his Jewish secretary, as his opponents affirmed?* Marquis Grouchy was honest.

The Rothschilds corrupted all the guides of the French army. Numberless Jews·spies were roaming in Belgium and all the plans of Napoleon were known. Just as in the World's war, the Jews spied in all Christian countries and did their best to incite both sides to exterminate each other.

Nathan did not rely even on Salomon, Karl and James, but found it necessary to go to Waterloo himself. He knew, that if Napoleon rose again the money which they had lent to many states might be lost, because of the eventual bankruptcy of Europe. He also feared that the Emperor would at last arrest the "Tigers".

Not a penny did they give to the warrior genius.

It was Ouvrard who lent him 50 million francs.

There were at that time only three banks in Europe, which acted as fiscal agents of Governments: Baring in London, Hope in Amsterdam and Ouvrard in Paris. Not until 1823 did the Rothschilds, thanks to Mr. Villele, put their hands on French finances.

Nathan came to the tremendous fifth act of the bloody twenty year drama of continuous murder by the Hidden Hand. In the last years it was not Napoleon, who was provoking the wars, but he was himself being provoked and compelled to unsheath the sword as "ultima ratio."

When the battle began Nathan's anxiety was such that he advanced to the very battle field in order to lose none of the incidents of the fighting. As soon as he saw the Prussians of Blucher arriving to help the British instead of the soldiers of Grouchy, expected by the Emperor, Nathan understood that Napoleon was crushed!

While the immortal Imperial Guard of the illustrious Corsican was falling under the rain of bullets, Rothschild, jumped on the fastest horse obtainable.

*) I was told by the well informed author of the "Democracy or Shylocracy," Capt. H. Sherwood Spencer, that he knew people, who had seen the box in which the gold has been carried from London to the camp of Grouchy.

He rode to Brussels, and without losing a second, proceeded to Ostende, but here he found the sea so rough that no fisherman would take him to England despite the bribes offered. Nathan began to tear his hair, as the Jews do in despair, when he discovered a sailor, bolder than the others, who consented to risk the crossing for two thousand francs. The devilish son of Amschel arrived at Dover, and the next morning the bankers found him leaning against a pillar of the Stock Exchange, with pale face and a very dismayed expression, as of a man who had just heard of a great disaster.

The Exchange people, who knew that Nathan has just landed from the Continent, plied him with questions.

Nathan, simulating not to grasp the meaning of what they asked, remained silent and sinister; but a rumor had been spread by his mouthpieces on the Exchange, that Blucher's army had been beaten at Ligny and that Wellington had been crushed. One can imagine the reaction on stock and bonds.

Nathan increased the consternation by ostensibly offering to sell all he could while prices were still good, but his agents re-bought all that was offered at the lowest panic price.

It was a gigantic plunder of the Britons.

Next morning came the genuine news of the victory of Wellington; and securities rose to a level unheard of before. "Honest" Nathan made by his brigandage $5,000,000 in one day. This fraud was forgotten in the joy which spread over England at the defeat of Napoleon, which Nathan's friends attributed to his tricks played through the Marshals Grouchy and Soult.

Before the death of Goldsmidt, Nathan had already in 1815, nearly all the English finance in his hands. Nathan's brothers, Salomon and Karl who founded banks in Vienna and Naples were Nathan's agents there as was his brother James in France. All these young hyenas were the usurers of the great aristocracy, whom they made pay 100% interest. It was always the money of the Landgrave which was used, but the Rothschilds reaped all the profits. The Landgrave had forgotten CHRIST'S warning.

Was it not a punishment of Providence, for the Landgrave's impardonable crime, when the descendants of Amschel ordered the execution of the descendant of the Landgrave—the Princess of Hesse, who, as the wife of Czar Nicholas II. perished tragically with all her five children, and husband—the Czar? And threePrinces of Hesse took part in Wilhelmsbad masonic convention.

The first English loan which Nathan Rothschild tried to appropriate, was $70,000,000 in 1819, but it was taken by the group of Francis Baring (a Jew) and Goldsmidt (a Jew). As Goldsmidt was esteemed in London, Nathan felt a terrific hatred for him: every Jew ought to bow to Amschel's son. The Goldsmidt brothers established themselves as "Bill Brokers" in London in 1777.

Thanks to the Rothschilds' gold Nathan started a campaign against the loan, using the most infamous methods. The loan began to go down, and Francis Baring died, Sept. 11, 1819, leaving everything on the shoulders of Abraham Goldsmidt. The Indian Company had large deposits with Goldsmidt. Nathan through intrigues succeeded in persuading them to withdraw these deposits. The loan went down still more, Goldsmidt lost his head and committed suicide, on Sep. 28th. "**The Morning Post**" stated on that date, that a declaration of war could not have produced a greater panic on the Exchange. Nathan exploited this also and earned a huge sum from the corpse of Goldsmidt. The Goldsmidt Bank was compelled to liquidate.

But the greatest coup of Nathan was the plundering of the London Stock Exchange on the day after the battle of Waterloo.

There was not a single sympathetic trace in Nathan: only moral and physical devilish impurity of a most repugnant character. His awful stinginess was proverbial. His clerks were literally starving though overwhelmed with work. They received the smallest salaries in the whole city.

When Nathan died in 1836 he did not give a single penny to his co-workers and servitors, not a penny to Charity.

"Nathan Mayer was a greater financier, a greater speculator and manipulator (than his elder brother—Amschel, who remained at Frankfort) of more solid and useful acquirements. The more weighty operations were planned and carried out by all the brothers in concert... We must seek the explanations of the problem, how they have been able to develop their business so amazingly. Circumstances, or, in other words, luck was on their side." (J. Reeves, p. 114).

No! Circumstances were created by them, because the fortune and the influence of the Landgrave was at the disposition of Amschel and this made all the Jews with their 3,000 year old Free-Masonic secret organizations recognise him as the AUTOCRATIC RULER of all the Jewish nation, and of all those deceived or attracted by them.

NATHAN R. SUBJUGATES THE BANK OF ENGLAND

As soon as Nathan Rothschild felt secure he laid his greedy hands upon the Bank of England. To the Rothschilds the Banks of Emission became banks of borrowing, where they took the cash needed.

Once when James wanted gold for the Bank of France and Villele, the bribed French Minister of Finance, Nathan sent to fetch the gold from the Bank of England. The Directors timidly begged Nathan to return the gold bars, when he would not need them any more. When the time came to return the gold, Nathan sent them some of his paper. They asked for the gold, but he answered:

"Send me back my paper, I shall exchange it into bank notes of the Bank of England and these I shall present to your cashiers to be exchanged into gold bars, to be returned to you. Since you have no confidence in my paper I have none in yours. You shall see me presenting at your counters all your banknotes owned by us."

The next day the Bank of England published an announcement, that the Rothschild paper would be accepted by it as if it were its own.

The Rothschild paper began to possess "**Legal Tender.**"

The same episode is described by the Rothschilds thus.

Once the Bank of England refused to discount a bill of exchange signed by the Rothschilds of Frankfort, under the pretext, that the Bank was not accepting private paper. Nathan screamed:

"I shall show what sort of private persons the Rothschilds are." He came to the bank and presented a banknote of $25 to be exchanged into gold, examined the gold coin and weighed it putting it slowly into a bag, then took from his portfolio a new banknote of $25, and continued such operations. His clerks proceeded to do the same with other cashiers, and in one day they drew $1,000,000 in gold. The Bank at first found this "very excentric indeed." But the next day Nathan and his nine clerks came again and he declared, that it would last for months, thus shutting the Bank to other clients. This meant also, that some $30 millions in gold would be taken away every month until the Bank would fail to pay its banknotes.

Then the Bank published, the above note that Rothschilds bills of exchange would be accepted as Bank notes. The truth is that the Bank of England, having received a blow in the face, and seeing bankruptcy, invented the story in order to turn the offence into a joke. Why was the bankruptcy imminent? Because all the Jews everywhere would have lent their banknotes to Nathan.

The defeat of Napoleon I, was a great triumph for the Rothschilds, but Alexander I. Romanov, the Habsburg and the Hohenzollern signed the **Holy Alliance**, a League of Nations, in 1815, recognizing CHRIST as the **Supreme Leader**. That is why the Rothschilds directed their activities especially against the above three Dynasties, which they upset in 1917 and 1918.

The murder of Alexander I. was accomplished in 1825.

The "Decabrist" revolution staged by the Free-Masons, headed by the Rothschilds, against Nicholas I. in 1825 **failed**, and a whole plan of murders and revolutions was elaborated by the "'Tigers.'"

They "created" for their purpose a series of able Jewish agents, such as Disraeli, 1805, Napoleon III., 1808, Bismarck, 1815, Gambetta-Gamberle 1838, not counting the Jews: Marshal Soult, Bombelles, Karl Marx, Ferd. Lassale, Hertz (Herzen), and others.

The next was the "death" of Napoleon II. in 1832.

This was accomplished through a Jew—Bombelles—the tutor of Nathan's son, Lionel, and described by Disraeli in his "Coningsby," as "Rebello," thus:

"A Jesuit before the revolution; since then an exiled Liberal leader; now a member of the Spanish Cortes: Rebello was always a Jew."

Disraeli's Rebello—a Jew—was ordered to be baptised and to feign the Jesuit Faith, in order to compromise it also.

Rebello—Bombelles—introduced to the **"Eaglet"** a pretty Jewish dancer, Fanny Elsner, who was ordered to make such violent love to Napoleon II., that he would die from exhaustion. And she succeeded in 1832. The same year the last son of Napoleon I. by Queen Hortense of Holland died from an "accident."

"Maria Louisa contracted an ignoble alliance, and passed the remainder of her life in comparative obscurity. She died in 1847" (Charles Macfarlane, "Life of Napoleon Bonaparte," p. 364)

This historian does not mention which alliance he named "ignoble." It was not the second with Count Neiperg, but the third with a criminal Jew Bombelles, introduced and "created" by Salomon Rothschild, who obtained him from Nathan.

"At Vienna Alexander I. had defended Marie Louise's rights with chivalrous ardor" ("An Imperial Victim. Marie Louise", p. 159, by Mrs Edith E. Cuthell).

THE ROTHSCHILDS SATANISE GERMANY

The upsetting of the Christian Church and of all monarchies, because they defend their nations, has been the program of the satanists-murderers — headed by the Rothschilds, since 1770. This was exposed in the "Protocols of the Learned Elders of Zion," as the Jews call the 300 members, composing the Hidden Hand. Every Christian ought to read the "Protocols," so much the more, since the Jews were characterized by CHRIST in only three words: "The Jews are satanists, murderers, liars." "The Protocols" confirm this to the last word.

Mgr. Jouin, the famous expert on Free-Masonry and Editor of the "Revue Internationale des Societes Secretes" (96, Boulevard Malesherbes, Paris) has written four enormous volumes, proving that every line of the "Protocols" is being brought about in life by the Jews. Why is not his brilliant work translated?

Also a complete plan was elaborated to ruin the Hohenzollerns, and Mr. Gilbert Stanhope in his "Frederick William II." quotes statements from Lord Malsmesbury's diary, that the Prussian King was in the hands of a fascinating Jewess—Miss Bethmann at Frankfort, daughter of a partner of the Rothschilds, an ancester of the German Chancellor, Bethman-Hollweg-Rothschild, the "hero" of the "scrap of paper" incident. The Hohenzollerns already had some Jewish blood in their veins through a Miss Eskeles—a Jewess, whose sister was also the beloved mistress of a Habsburg, Joseph II.

But it was not sufficient to overthrow two such ancient Dynasties as the Hohenzollerns and the Habsburgs, who practically created Germany and Austria. The Romanovs, who, having inherited a small piece of land around Moscow, (continuously invaded by foreigners) transformed it into one of the largest Empires, were also marked for destruction, as the most fervent Christians.

The Rothschilds decided to exploit the son of the Jewess Menken (married to Major Bismarck) and possibly of the Jew, Marshal Soult and to make of him a "Wallenrod" for Germany, a monstrous murderer of Christians, and a champion antagonist of the Mother Church of Rome.

Thus was created the "Iron Chancellor," Otto Bismarck.

The Jews, "who almost monopolised the professorial chairs in Germany," (according to Disraeli, "Coningsby," p. 250) made her hated and feared by all her neighbours, who were obliged to increase their armaments more and more.

Thus the "fever of armaments" began in Europe.

But, there is always a "but" even for Satan.

GOD inspired King George III. of England who proferred a remarkable political axiom:

"Every good Englishman ought to be a good Russian, just as every good Russian ought to be a good Englishman."

This alarmed the Spider-Emperor of Frankfort!

With England and Russia hand-in-hand, Christianity could look calmly to its future.

It was a titanic blow to the dreams of Amschel.

The satanist wanted to shout: "Indeed, CHRIST must be GOD." England with her best brains and high morals and Russia with her great heart and endless wealth, would together represent a moral and material strength unheard of before.

An Anglo-Russian Alliance would have saved the World. To prevent even a friendship between them no means was too costly. A Satanic plan was at once conceived to thwart it.

The English throne was surrounded by a veritable oak forest of ancient aristocracy, impenetrable to the Jews. Even his millions could not help Nathan and his son Lionel, to penetrate the British aristocracy and Court Society, or the Government.

A new "Horse of Troy" had to be invented, through which a score of Jews could slip into the Governmental machinery of the British Empire and into the House of Lords.

A "Konrad Wallenrod"* had to be educated who could be elevated to the highest power and then betray the country by doing the reverse of what its interests demanded, and create as many obstacles as possible to an alliance with Russia.

Such a Jewish "Wallenrod-traitor" was Disraeli!

Satanic ideas were infused into his young mind by Lionel Rothschild himself, as everybody can discern by reading Disraeli's own book "Coningsby," published in 1844.

*) Konrad Wallenrod was a Pole - Lithuanian, who entered the German Order of Knights of the Sword, and for years seemed to be their most devoted soldier, but when he became the Great Master of the Order, he abused his power to destroy it. This historical fact is in a masterly way pictured by the Polish poet Mitzkevich. The same "Wallenrodism" is constantly practiced by the Jews with the Jesuits and Freemasons and now with the Ku-Klux-Klan.

ROTHSCHILDS FOR THE DOMINATION OF THE WORLD

In 1812, Amschel Rothschild I., delegated his five sons い dominate the world. Their problem was to overthrow the French, English, Russian, German, Austrian and other dynasties, and especially the Church. The most capable of his sons was James, but he was yet too young. The most satanic was Nathan, and he became Rothschild II.

"The brothers, fully cognizant of his superior intellectual capacity, willingly acknowledged Nathan Mayer as the most rit to direct all their most important transactions" (J. Reeves, p. 64).

As the English aristocracy and people had a distrust of Jews, Isaac D'Israeli was ordered by Nathan to baptize his son Benjamin in 1817, and to make of him a ram and a "Wallenrod" in England. The task to depose at once all the Monarchs was too huge a task. The Rothschilds' interests demanded first of all the downfall of Napoleon I in order to save the Rothschilds' money invested with many other rulers.

Napoleon had one legitimate son and two illegitimate living. All of them were doomed ... As France had been very much "militarised" by Napoleon I., the Rothschilds decided it was necessary to have an Emperor for some time, but they created their own "mock" Jewish Napoleon III., and killed the two true Napoleonides.

The Occult Jewish dynasty had five chief branches—one of which the branch in Naples, was closed in 1860, while in the United States. Shoenberg,* a Rothschildian, was camouflaged as Belmont. But they all obeyed the one, chosen as the "Occult World Emperor." Insurrections within the dynasty were mercilessly crushed, as in the case with James-Edouard (died in 1881): Nathaniel, chief of the London branch, died in Oct. 1923) et al., who were said to be victims of "suicide".

* "August Belmont, the American representative of the Rothschilds. His father, August Shoenberg (the present form of the name represents its translation into French) came to America from the Rothschilds' Franfort banking house before the Civil War ("The World's Work", January, 1923.) Why this constant camouflage of names, just like the Jews-bolsheviks camouflaged into the Russians (Bronstein took the name of Trozky, a Governor General of West Russia). How wonderfully right was CHRIST (St. John, VIII, 44) when He said, that the Jews are the sons of the devil, the father of lies?... And what devilish part took this "Belmont" in helping the Jew, Judah P. Benjamin, the Secretary of State in the Southern Confederacy "the most adroit brain in the secession movement," according to Mr. Burton J. Hendrik in his non-adroit blandishing of the Jews in "The World's Work" of Dec. 1922 —to start the most senseless and meanest fratricide known as the Civil War? Then only Russia's help saved America.

105

DISRAELI THE "WALLENROD" OF ENGLAND (1817)

Benjamin D'Israeli settled in England in 1748.

His ancestors took this name "in order that their race might for ever be recognized." A Jew, he married in 1765 a Jewess, who, according to her grandson ,"lived until eighty without indulging in a tender expression."

Isaac D'Israeli father of B. Disraeli, was born in 1766 and in 1780 went abroad, where "he imbibed the 'liberal' sentiments," which were at that time so widely professed by the Free-Masonry of Amschel. .

With such a provoking name as D'Israeli, he was noticed by the "Illuminati" and like all Jews, Isaac could not fail to become an admirer of Amschel. At eighteen (1784) Isaac became a Bolshevik and wrote "Against Commerce." He returned to England, but the underground work of Amschel, attracted Isaac and he again ran to him.

"He lived with learned men," said Disraeli of his father, who again returned to England in 1788. These were the "Illuminati" and the "Learned Elders of Zion" or the "300 men."

"His son, Benjamin revealed deeper faith and stronger confidence than his father in the Asiatic Jewish type of character."

The future Lord Beaconsfield would never have abandoned his creed and become a Christian, if such an act had not been ordered by Nathan. Born a Jew in 1805, he was circumcised, and baptised in 1817, because the "coup de Waterloo" and the downfall of Napoleon opened new horizons for Nathan.

It became the chief desire of Benjamin to be Dictator of England, in order not only to conquer step by step all the barriers erected against the Jews, but to further their plan to dominate the world. He revealed to the Home Secretary Lord Melbourne his desire to become Prime Minister.

As in the case of Napoleon I., and of Bismarck the biographers of Disraeli were "amazed" by his "audacity of conception, his brilliant triumphs, though he has neither rank, nor wealth", nor friends * and had never been an able scholar. Benjamin had "that supreme confidence in himself, which amounts to virtual genius." He "has never shown discouragement."—Backed by the Rothschilds, he could be sure of his future and had any number of protectors, who were the retainers of the Rothschilds.

*) This statement repeated by many "historians" is absolutely false: Disraeli from his childhood was choosen, guided and supported by Lionel for the special Jewish plan of World Domination.

THE "MYSTERY" OF THE ALTA VENDITA (1814-48)

"The Supreme Government of all the secret societies of the wolrd was exercised by the 'Alta Vendita' (High Market) or highest lodge of the Italian Carbonari, which from 1814 to 1848 directed the activities of all the secret societies". (an expert, Mr. George F. Dillon).

Yes! But the "mystery" of this sudden role assumed by an Italian lodge over all the secret societies and Masonic Lodges, presided over by several crowned heads, can be explained only by the fact, that at precisely that time Karl Rothschild remained in Italy. Many historians and the best of these, Mrs. Nesta Webster, describe, that the Alta Vendita was led by a young "Italian" nobleman with the pseudonym of Nubius. His right hand, if not his "chieftain" was a "Piccolo Tigre," a Jew, who was always travelling all over Europe and was masquerading as an itinerant money lender, carrying instructions to the Carbonari and "returning laden with gold for the money chests of Nubius."

This "mystery" is partly revealed by the babbling Jew-traitor-Disraelli, who thus writes about Sidonia (Lionel Rothshild):

"When he was nineteen, Sidonia, who had then resided some time with his uncle (Karl) at Naples, made a long visit to another of his father's relative at Frankfort (uncle Amschel)."

"Between Paris and Naples Sidonia passed two years. It was impossible to penetrate him. His frankness was strictly limited to the surface. He observed everything, though overcautious, but avoided serious discussion. He was a man without affection," etc.

Is it not the description of these criminals of the Alta Vendita. like Nubius or "Piccolo Tigre," always moving like devils, seeking to devour some Christians?

"Sidonia at a great family congress held at Naples, made arrangements with the heads of the houses which bore his name, respecting the disposition and management of his vast fortune" . . .

"Sidonia was absent from his connections for five years"!!!
"They were aware of his existence only by the orders which he drew on them for payment" . . . "Sidonia resided some time in Germany and then settled in Naples. Of an interesting personality, he availed himself of the attentions of a court of which he was the principal creditor." Was not Sidonia the mysterious Nubius?

And Mr. J. Reeves in his "The House of Rothschild" confirms the above by saying, that Ferdinand I. of Naples was compelled to accept the condition named by Karl Rothschild viz. "the reinstatment in office as Minister of Finance of his friend the chevalier Medici, also a Jew" (p. 265). The Alta Vendita was not Christian.

BISMARCK'S SATANIC ORIGIN AND BEGINNINGS

The Rothschilds were the chief delegates of Satan—the "arch-murderer." Through their secret agents they were seeking for the most ambitious, unscrupulous and able men, whom they caused to be educated and promoted to become their agents. Tricky spies approached such youngsters and implied" all the kingdoms of the world and the GLORY will I give thee, if thou wilt fall down and worship me" (St. Matthew, iv, 8-9). Napoleon having been put down, the Rothschilds needed a new "mankiller." They created such a one of Otto Bismarck. His father, William, married Louisa Menken (the Menkens were **Jews**)—a little bourgeoise of "un-known" origin. He took her to his country place, which the French troops of Napoleon I. soon invaded, and in a nearby chateau Mar-schal Soult, a Jew, according to Disraeli ("Coningsby" p. 251), established his head-quarters.

"**Louise had been in imminent peril of violation**" . . . says history. The champagne of the Jew Marshal from Paris; his Asiatic persuasive power and the devotion of both to the idea of "Israel above all," appealed more to the heart of the Jewess, than the beer and heavy wits of her provincial German husband.

Soult has since always shown an extreme attention to Mrs. Bis-marck-Menken and to her son, the future "man of Blood and Iron." * A Jew and one of the "300" of the Hidden Hand, Soult occupied the highest posts in France until his death in 1851 and betrayed every Christian ruler. "The six years Bismarck passed in Plaman Institute in Berlin had left him but regrettable mem-cries". Pelman's Institute with a 6 weeks course would be better!

Like Disraeli, Bismarck was never an able pupil.

Bismarck was a "very pretty boy," as was Disraeli.

His life in Goettingen "obliged him to run into debts."

For years "their memory has pursued and saddened him."

He was found to be corrupting the youth of Jena. (This is pre-scribed by the "Protocols.")

"His reserved, disdainful, even haughty character, disconcerted his supe-riors, as it kept at a distance his inferiors and his equals". (p.21 J. Hoche).

As a Jew, he was sure of the "superiority of his race."

*) Carl Bonaparte (the father of Napoleon) took the field. His young wife (former Letitia Ramolini) who was pregnant with Napoleon, accompanied her husband, sharing in the hardships and dangers of a partisan warfare. This formed the military inclinations of Napoleon. The same love for "blood and iron" we see in Bismark. Does it not prove, that the battling Jew, Mar-shal Soult, was his real father and not the quiet Prussian small landowner the official father of Bismarck?

ROMANOVS, HOHENZOLLERNS AND HABSBURGS DOOMED BY SATAN

The three Christian Imperial Dynasties: Orthodox, Protestant and Catholic, were suddenly upset in 1917 and 1918, after centuries of useful reign. It was Satan's revenge for the Holy Alliance of 1815. In order to understand all the "mysteries" one must study the so-called Satanic Forces, which rule the world. And to graps the Cause of the Downfall of the three Monarchies we must return to the glorious year 1815.

The leading phrase of the Holy Alliance (Czar Alexander's League of Nations) was that Austria, Prussia, Russia and all the Christian nations have One true and Only Sovereign, to whom Alone all power by right belongs. namely, GOD Our Divine SAVIOUR, JESUS CHRIST.

"Divide et Impera" thus Satan commands the Jews to act. Those aims of Satan: to divide and to rule and to destroy the Christians, were counteracted by the proposition of the Czar Alexander I. of a Holy Alliance in 1815. Everybody knows, that the Tsar Alexander I. was its creator.

Let us return to the book, "The Curse of the Romanovs" by their worst foe, the Jew, A. Rappoport.

"The re-establishment of European peace has given the Czar Alexander I, great satisfaction. (p. 356)

But it was a nasty blow to the Rothschilds.

"Alexander directed his attention to the irreligiousness of the nations as the source of many evils. He conceived the idea of reviving religious fervour in the peoples and thus re-establish a patriarchal regime, purity of family life and obedience to law and authority. But the rulers must set an example and serve as models for their subjects. The sovereigns of Europe must carry out their mission as rulers of empires and kingdoms in the spirit of the FOUNDER of Christianity, which should be the link uniting the sovereigns to their peoples and among themselves" (p. 356).

Such plan was exactly the reverse of that desired by the satanists Rothschilds, whose chief aim was to annihilate it.

And all the following Czars imitated Alexander I.

Hence this boundless hatred of the Rothschilds against them.

"Alexander was the man of the best intentions. He showed himself persistantly favorable to views which, to say the least, were a hundred years ahead of his time. Alexander I came to the throne of Russia in 1801 anxious to carry out his liberal plans" (Mr. John Spencer Bassett in his "The Lost Fruit of Waterloo") .

The "fruit of Waterloo" was lost, because the treachery of the Jew Marshal Soult enthroned definitely the Jew Nathan

The Americans know about the Romanovs only what has been served to them by their "American" press, nearly all controlled by the Jews, and by servile authors, who know that their writings will be paid only when they obey the order of the Hidden Hand: "About the Romanovs—aut male aut nihil" (either bad or nothing).

This exact photograph of Alexander I. and of all the Romanovs is given by their violent enemy, the Jew, Rappoport, unconsciously, although he begins his book by cursing them, as a Jew would. And if this description be true, and it is true, how could Paul I., Alexander I., Nicholas I., Alexander II., Alexander III., Nicholas II, perhaps the most Christian rulers, who ever existed, have escaped the hatred of Satan, of his servants, the Rothschilds, and of all their numberless agents?

"Alexander I. felt sure, that if he had triumphed over the man (Napoleon) whose superior genius seemed invincible, it was because he had never glorified in his own success. 'Henceforward', said the Tsar and former pupil of Laharpe, 'the sovereigns of Europe must place their confidence not in the strength of their armies, but in the power of faith and religion.' Alexander, therefore, concluded a treaty by which the rulers solemnly vowed to govern their subjects in the spirit of Christianity, and to be guided solely by the principles of justice, love and peace. This treaty signed on Sept. 26th, 1815, by Alexander, the King of Prussia, Friedrich Wilhelm III. and Francis I., Emperor of Austria, is known as the **Holy Alliance**" (A. Rappoport p. 357).

That is why all the press and the writers, who depended on the Jews, were ordered by them to blacken the Holy Alliance, misrepresenting it, as if a "reactionary" organization, meanwhile the three rulers wished to make it purely Christian.

In 1818, speaking with the Bishop of Prussia (Dr. Eylert) Alexander I. explained its origin:

"After the defeats of Lutzen, Dresden and Bautzen, we (he and the King of Prussia) were obliged to retreat. We became convicted that, without the help and blessing of Providence, Germany was lost. The King said:

'We must pray, and with the help of God we shall conquer; and if, as I trust, God will bless our united efforts, then we will proclaim in the face of the whole world our conviction, that to Him alone the honour is due. Then came the victories. The emperor, Francis I, of Austria shared our Christian sentiments and willingly became a third in our Alliance. The Holy Alliance is not our work, but that of GOD. CHRIST HIMSELF has inspired us" (p. 358).

THE "FAIR ANGEL" OF EUROPE

A. Rappoport, a Jew, narrates about Alexander I:

"Alexander did not spare himself. Like Peter the Great, he rose at five o'clock in the morning. Every subject, no matter to what class he belonged, was admitted to his presence, and all petitions were received..." "He was extremely particuliar as to cleanliness, moral and physical."

In this he was the exact opposite to the Rothschilds, of whom Amschel never changed his clothes and underwear, until they fell to pieces. Nathan Rothschild II. began to change his clothes, but never took a bath or changed his underwear as long as it would hang together. Rappoport continues:

"Alexander—upright, generous, philanthropic and capable of most noble enthusiasm—well fitted for the work" (p. 316).

"Although intrepid in the midst of danger, Alexander had a horror of war, wrote Laharpe..." "The Tsar has shown himself extremely generous the campaign between Germany and France" (p. 362).

"Full of good intentions, kind of heart, possessed of unusual powers of mind, and, moreover, gifted with diplomatic clearness and fineness of judgment". (p. 318).

"I acknowledge no power as just, save that which is supported by the laws,' repeated Alexander. He lowered taxes by lessening the expenditures of the Court."

"Alexander with his charming manner and kindly smile, and his fascinating, almost feminine grace, produced a very favorable impression upon Napoleon" (p. 331). "Alexander's candour won for him the confidence of the French people as a whole" (349).

But the "too-Christian" and too peace-loving Alexander I. could not be allowed to live; all Satan's forces were concentrated against him and his followers. His "crimes" were too enormous. He proclaimed:

"The Sovereignity of CHRIST and of the Cross."

Alexander repeated the "crime" of his father, Paul I.

The reconciliation of the two Catholic Churches: Universal and Orthodox would be the severest defeat and retrogression for Satan ...

In my career I saw always, that the reunion of these Churches was most bitterly opposed by the most immoral men.

The Re-union of the Western (Roman) and Eastern (Orthodox) Catholic Churches was the main aim of the geniuses: Pope Leo XIII and of His State Secretary the Cardinal Rampolla del Tindaro.

But as soon as Czar Nicholas II. had agreed to have their Nuncio Mgr Tarnassi in St. Petersburgh, the latter was poisoned, by the Hidden Hand. The Pope and the Czar horrified, postponed the plan.

ROTHSCHILDS ATTEMPT TO "JUDAIZE" RUSSIA

"Czar Alexander I., one of the triumvirs of the Holy Alliance was cultivating in Russia the principles of paternal administration and Christian government" (a Jew, S. M. Dubnow, in his "History of the Jews in Russia and Poland," published by "The Jewish Judaic Publishing Society in America" p. 390).

But Rothschild hired a crowd of satanists "judaizers" with orders to transform Russia into a "New Judea." Imagine the grief of the devout Christian Czar, called "Fair Angel."

"The attention of the Russian authorities was diverted by the ominous spectacle of huge numbers of Christians embracing a doctrine closely akin to Judaism." (S. M. Dubnow, p. 401).

"The Judaizing sect came into existence through natural Jews" "The 'Judaizing heresy' spread rapidly to the villages and cities appealing alike to peasants and merchants. Whenever taken to task, the sectarians declared that they longed to return to the Old Testament and 'maintain the faith of their fathers, the Judeans." The central authorities were alarmed and resorted to extraordinary measures to check the spread of the schism. The Committee of Ministers approved the following project in 1823:

"The chiefs and the teachers of the Judaizing sets are to be impressed into military service, and those unfit for service deported to Siberia. All Jews are to be expelled from the districts, in which the sect of Sabbatarians or "Judeans" has made its appearance."

Thus the resolution of the Committee of Ministers proves, that the bloody money of the Rothschidls (i.e., of the criminal Landgrave, who disregarded CHRIST's warning) was corrupting Christianity in "Holy Russia" already one hundred years ago. And it is the same kind of money which is corrupting and "judaizing" America through all kind of "International Bible Students".

"Rationalism" and "modernism" are but new terms of "judaization," the first having been started by a Jew Spinoza.

But this decree was in reality announced to check their proselyting activities.

"As far as the Jews were concerned, the immediate results of the measures insignificant. The number of Jews involved in the decree of expulsion trom the affected Great Russian provinces was infinitesimal" (Dubnow, p. 403).

However. even this weak defense by the Czar of his Christian people seemed a real "persecution" to the Rothschilds. Their resolution was: "Revolution! Execution of the Czar."

The Czar's wife becoming ill, they went to the South.

"Alexander was unceasingly occupied in providing her comfort and devoted all his time to her." (Rappoport, p. 391).

Amschel Rothchild I. died on Sept. 12, 1812, on the eve of Napoleon's failure in Russia. His sons ordered the Jews of Poland and Lithuania to plunder and kill all the Christians, who wounded or ill, fell into their hands.

"The fall of Napoleon was the rise of Rothschild" (J. Reeves, p. 86).

When the Napoleonic Empire fell in 1815, the Emperor of Austria knighted all the Rothchilds. After that James called himself Chevalier de Rothschild. He did not forget the house with the Red Shield and the second-hand clothes sold by his mother—Gutta Schnapper.

On October 15th, 1822, the Emperor of Austria granted to all the Rothschild brothers the title of baron; and the four sons of old Amschel (except the Viennese) were nominated Consuls-General of Austria.

Such haste in promoting all the Rothschilds immediately after the battle of Waterloo and after the death of Napoleon I. by the most cautious and proud Austrian Government proved to what extent it understood the tremendous power of the Rothschild satanic clutches.

Since that moment the **Dynasty** of the Rothschilds was established in France on a basis more solid than that of the Bourbons, whose last representatives mounted the throne only soon to be exiled. The world since 1815 has practically been ruled by the Occult Jewish Dynasty of Rothschilds, who are as Rulers of Germany, Austria, England, France, Italy, the United States, and now they rule Russia through their pro-consuls, the Jews, Bronstein (alias Trotzky); Apfelbaum (Zinoviev); Rosenfeld (Kamenev); etc.

However, all these "Vice-Roys" obey one of the Rothschilds, who is the **World Emperor,** chosen not according to his age or heredity, but because of his personal qualifications according to Satanic standards; that is to say, the chosen World Emperor is the most demoniacal of those "tigers."

Since 1789 his Red (Roth) flag (schield) is the adopted worldly signal for all bloodshed. "The Jews have made this war," confirmed a Jew, Dr. Oscar Levy of London. All wars, bloodshed and troubles are being prepared and started through their Executives—the Free Masonic Lodges, governed by the Jewish Central Chancellery—The Universal Israelite Alliance in Paris.

I do not speak of the nice, but "pseudo" Free-Masons in America, many of whom are respectable gentlemen.

113

N. ROTHSCHILD II. VS. ALEXANDER I. ROMANOV

"Whilst on the one hand the Rothschilds provided supplies for the armies of Napoleon, on the ether, they raised loans for his foes. The Rothschilds belonged to no party, they were ready to grow rich at the expenses of friends and foes alike" (Reeves, p. 86).

No! The Rothschilds belong to the "party" of Satan and his lusts of murder (moral, mental and physical) they are eagerly doing.

In London, N. Rothschild, having won his $5,000,000 in one day, was strong enough to compel Lord Castlereagh, the Secretary for Foreign Affairs, to refuse to join the Holy Alliance under the blasphemous pretext, that CHRIST was not defined in the British Constitution. But the "thirty pieces of silver" received from Nathan were too heavy and Castlereagh, like Judas, committed suicide, by cutting his throat in 1822. He influenced the British Government to sent Napoleon to St. Helena and annoyed him by restrictions.

Gladstone called Castlereagh a most corrupt man.

The Czar's motto "CHRIST above all" had doomed him.

Rothschild revived his Masonic Lodges in Russia.

The political murders were organized through them.*

The Russians in Paris were attracted to these dens.

Colonel A. Pestel became a real pestilence in Russia.

The propaganda of "pseudo-liberalism" was spread.

"In 1815 Marshal Soult found papers which divulged horrible designs (of Russians attracted into Free Masonry in Paris). The Marshal hastened to make them known to the Emperor Alexander, who thanked him, saying that the danger was not so real as he thought. How the Emperor, with that rare sagacity and that clearness of judgement which distinguished him could not see the embers that smouldered in his own state." (Mrs. de Choiseul Gouffres in her "Emperor Alexander I.," p. 210).

The answer is: because this Czar ignored the Hidden Hand just as 115 millions Americans are today shutting their eyes to it. Just ten years later the Tsar was foully poisoned by the Hidden Hand.

It may take months for the Hidden Hand to destroy the United States, by staging a revolt, a Civil War and a circular foreign assault headed by Japan, whose attack is practically imminent.

"It is my firm decision to bring about the emancipation of the serfs," the Czar Alexander declared (Capefigue). Then his envoy Kotzebue, was promptly assassinated by Maurice Sand, a German Jew, and the Czar's favorite Semenovsky regiment was driven to mutiny, purposely provoked by its German colonel Schwartz, a freemason. Such interference from abroad made the Czar disappointed and suspicious, and after the early death of his five children, he found his only consolation in religion.

*"L'Assassinat Maçonique. Le Crime Rituel. La Trahison Juive" by "La Renaissance Francaise," 52, Passage des Panoramas, Paris.

ALEXANDER I. "MYSTERIOUSLY" POISONED

Let us continue the Rappoport's statements:

"Alexander showed the same respect toward Catholicism as toward Ortho doxy". "He held that their fundamental principles were one and the same".

Only through the efforts of Satan's agents has the Church remained disunited.

"He mingled with Christians, Moslems and Jews!" (p. 395). "He lunched at the Synagogue of the Jews and returned to Taganrog **mysteriously ill.**" "He now learned of the existence of a conspiracy to assassinate him" (p. 396).

He called out to his doctor, Sir James Wylies:

"Oh! my friend! What monsters, what ungrateful wretches! And I did so genuinely desire their welfare!"

He was poisoned by the famous Aqua Tofana, but the illness was declared to be typhoid fever, because of the fear that his people might organize wholesale pogroms against the Jews.

The poison worked slowly causing him great suffering. At one moment it seemed he could be saved, and the people receiving the news, "went wild with delight" (p. 399).

On Dec. 1, 1825, the Czar opened his eyes, unable to speak, and kissed the Empress' hand.

"A few minutes later, he breathed his last!" ... (p. 400).

His face became black as the result of Aqua Tofana!

The Hidden Hand which murdered him as usual spread various false reports, among others that the Czar went to Siberia and lived under the name of Feodor Kusmich.

The Jew, Rappoport, entitles the chapter about the last sufferings of the Czar, Alexander I. as **"Finita la Comedia"** showing his devilish joy and hatred against the Emperor, who dared to propose to the World the Leadership of CHRIST.

The daughter of a prominent German—Tisenhaus—wrote:

"The author shared her father's distrust of the Tzar (like the Americans do who are taught by their Jew-controlled press, that everything Monarchistic is 'rotten''); but after meeting him, in common with many others, was impressed with Alexander's frankness, energy, and nobility of character. This impression deepened into a loyal and devoted friendship" (Mrs. de Choiseul-Gouffres in her "Emperor Alexander I.", VI.).

The constant fear of the Satanists, that by a stroke of the pen the Romanovs might make the Orthodox Church re-enter the Universal, was one of the chief causes for the assassination of the last six Romanoff Czars.

Alexander I.'s death was exploited for a revolt. This was made to annihilate everything Christian.

JAMES ROTHSCHILD CONQUERS PARIS (1825-1830).

"Baron" James became a great personality. Kings and people were obliged to reckon with him and he justified this by financing a loan of 520 million francs to the Government of the Restoration, which needed money after the great wars of the Revolution and of the Empire.

In his "Juifs Rois de l'Epoque" ("The Jews-Monarchs of the Epoch") Toussenel wrote 50 years ago:

"One can take the fatal year 1815 as the era of the new power, though prior to this date the coalition of bankers who bought grain upset the campaign of Moscow.,. Moscow and Waterloo — these are the names to be remembered for the interference of the Jews in our (French) national affairs. Financial sovereignty reveals itself during the days of national disaster. It thrives on the misery of the people. In 1818,France, condemned to pay 1,500 million francs in war indemnity, became the prey of the international financiers, of Frankfort, Paris, London and Vienna who became as one to exploit her calamity."

Of course, Anselm, Salomon, Nathan and James Rothschild "made one." Did not Amschel on his death-bed order them all to "make but **One?**"

"Then began the work of High Financiers who became the councellors of statesmen, and grasped the monopoly, present and future, of national loans. France borrowed at ruinous terms because her funds were only at fifty percent and the Jews took mortgages on all her revenues". (Toussenel).

Yes! James Rothschild III. gave for each government bond of one hundred francs only fifty francs and received five francs as interest, which made ten percent on the money actually loaned and the following year the principal began to return twofold.

James became "**Lender to the Kings.**" This, added to his speculations on the Exchange, where he was able to influence the rise and fall of stocks and bonds, swelled the baron's earnings into millions.

The Rothschilds were not only financiers they later on became industrial magnates and merchants as well. Their immense capital like millions of leeches is attached to every human effort.

Between 1815 and 1830 the Rothschilds were simply plundering the five great powers: England, Russia, Austria, France and Prussia. Thus Prussia in 1818 contracted a 5% loan of 5,000,000 pounds sterling, but received for its government bonds only 3,500,000 or 70%, making the actual interest rate over 7%, but the chief point of it was, that the bonds has to be redeemed in a few years at 100%, i.e. redeemed by Prussia at par, or 5,000,000 pounds, thus paying a profit to the Rothschilds of 1,500,000 pounds, plus the interest.

In 1823 James took up the whole of the French loan.

In 1823 James received the order of the Legion of Honor.

LIONEL ("SIDONIA") SATANIZES DISRAELI

"The period of 1820 onwards became the age of the Rothschilds, so that by the middle of the century it was a common dictum, there is only one power in Europe, and that is Rothschild" (Prof. Werner Sombart, "The Jews And Modern Capitalism", p. 99).

What imbeciles or hypocrites then were all the Gentiles, who were constantly induced to make revolutions against all Mon-archs, but never (except a small revolt in 1848) against the "only power"—the Rothschilds.

While James Rothschild was organizing the revolution of 1830 and plundering France, young Lionel of London, the son of Nath-an, was satanizing Disraeli.

The grandeur of the Rothschilds was just beginning.

Even they believed the plan of the Jews—to dominate the World, was a dream. Hearing the confessions and boastings of Lionel, Disraeli, with Jewish acumen, thought it expedient to expose them in book form, and, sceptical as to the realization of these "mirages" —to make immediate profit from the exaltations of his patron. So in 1844 his political novel "Coningsby" was published in which a love story serves as a mere framework for the political statements of Lionel. Thus, the intense and traitorous greed of Disraeli to exploit his patron's confidence became a most convincing proof of the Jewish Peril.

During nearly 75 years the brave Britishers have read "Conings-by" and thought that "Sidonia" was a fiction. It was thanks to my articles in London, that England grasped, that "Sidonia" was a photo of Lionel.

"Many predictions made by the character Sidonia have been fulfilled. Perhaps this accounts for the interest re-awakened in Disraeli's novels, and especially in a study of Sidonia, who has been identified by a Russian author, Count Cherep-Spiridovich as portraying the first Lord Rothschild" (Plain English, Oct. 22, 1921).

"Between Sidonia (Lionel) and Coningsby (Disraeli) at once occurred companionship." p. 235. Of course! Two fiery Jewish conspirators!! There is no doubt that Sidonia, described by Dis-raeli in his "Coningsby" was Lionel, the son of Nathan Rothschild II. Mr. Lewis Apjohn in his "The Earl of Beaconsfield" states, p. 118:

"Beaconsfield has introduced living persons into his romances." Another such as Sidonia, as photographed by Disraeli, could not be found on the entire earth.

First of all, "Sidonia had unlimited wealth."

"His father (Nathan Rothschild II.) had established a brother in most of the principal capitals. He was lord and master of the money-markets of the world, and, of course, virtually lord nad master of everything else. He literally held the revenues of Southern Italy in pawn (through Karl Rothschild in Naples) and Monarchs and ministers of all countries courted his advice and were guided by his suggestions" ("Coningsby", pp. 213 and 214).

"Between Paris and Naples Sidonia (Lionel) passed two years". "Sidonia had no heart, he was a man without affections." (p. 217).

"What we call heart (said Sinodia-Lionel) is a nervous sensation like shyness, which gradually disappears in society" (p. 248).

Was not Lionel Sidonia a reincarnation of Satan?

"It was well-known that Sidonia (Rothschild) was not a marrying man" p. 235). Because their greed for gold and power their plan delegated by Satan, did not allow them to introduce strangers in their brigand den, the Rothschilds inter-married or occasionally took wives from other rich Jewish families.

"Sidonia, when he was nineteen resided for some time with his uncle (Karl) in Naples, and made a long visit to another of his father's relatives at Frankfort " (uncle Anselm).

Disraeli, through Rothschild (Sidonia) explains all the plans of their "superior race," and how "Jewish mind exercises a vast influence on the affairs of Europe." Alas! too vast! Sidonia Rothschild said:

"The first Jesuits were Jews; that mysterious Russian Diplomacy, which so alarms Western Europe, is organised and carried on by Jews; that mighty revolution (of 1848) which is at this moment preparing in Germany, is entirely developing under the auspices of Jews, who almost monopolise the professional chairs of Germany".

Yes! All the revolutions were staged by the Jews.

Thus, the Jew, Disraeli, himself confirmed that the Jew, Rothschild (Sidonia) knew several years ahead, what would happen in 1848. His book was published in 1844.

It is analogous to my book "L'Alliance Franco-Allemande et Les Forces Titaniques," (vide The British Museum), in which I met all the arguments of the French ex-Minister, M. Marcel Sembat, who suggested such an Alliance.

I foretold in it in May 1914 that in case of war, Rosa Luxembourg would upset the Kaiser.

Lionel-Nathan was educated in Germany at Goettingen, by Jew satanic professors. Elected to Parliament in 1847, he was seated only in 1858, and represented London until 1873.

SHORTEST SUMMARY OF THE YEARS 1800-1850

To make it easier for my readers to remember a mass of facts and actors in quite a new light, I feel it indispensable to disclose a short summary of events, which History fails to record.

Already in 1798, Nathan brought his gang of "Illuminati" from Frankfort, but failing to repeat the "French" Revolution in England, he began to plunder her.

In 1815, Nathan "knocked out" Napoleon I. But Alexander I. Romanov, proposed to the Hohenzollerns and the Habsburgs the Holy Alliance, with CHRIST as Leader.

Nathan doomed these three Christian Dynasties.

He tried to convert Russia to Judaism, but was thwarted.

For this Alexander I. was poisoned in 1825.

Nathan attempted a revolution in Russia in 1825.

Both sons of Napoleon I. were killed in 1832.

Nathan died and was succeeded by James in 1836.

Franz Joseph handed to a Jew to be satanized in 1838.

Lionel confessed to Disraeli in 1844, that revolutions were prepared by his Jews in Germany.

"I will fire on whoever shall fire first," the "anti-War" Emperor, Nicholas I. declared in 1850, and thus prevented a war!

Then the chief agents of James Rothschild III. Disraeli, Napoleon III. and Bismarck were mobilised in 1851-52 against Nicholas I.

They provoked that "war of crime" in Crimea in 1853.

Unable to win it, they poisoned Nicholas I. in 1855.

The World Assassins have created many "Apostles of Evil": Bombelles (Rebello), Disraeli, Bismarck, Gamberle (Gambetta), Aerenthal, Bethmann-Hollweg*, Adler (Kerensky), Bronstein (Trotzky), Cederbaum (Lenin), Masaryk, Venizelos (Beni Zelos), Millerand-Kahn, all Jews, and not counting such devils—Jews, educated by the Rothschilds, as Hertz (Hertzen), F. Lassale, Karl Marx, Ernesto Nathan, Lord Northcliffe, etc., etc.

The Assassination of the most noble Christian Tsar Nicholas I. marked the conclusion of the first half of the Satanic misrule of the World by the Rothschilds; as the murders of King Louis XIV, King Gustavus III and of Emperor Joseph II of Austria, all condemned to death at the Free-Masonic Congress at Wilhelmsbad in 1786, were the beginning.

The first Monarch was executed in 1793, the second in 1790 and the third in 1792, according te the Amschel's decisions.

*His mother was a Rothschild from Frankfort.

The revolts in South America in 1810 (Pedro became Emperor of Brazil); in Italy (after Karl Rothschild came to Naples), and in Petersburg on Dec. 14, 1825 (the "Decabrist") were, none of them organized by these nations, but always by the Free-Masons of the Grand Orient in Paris, led by the Rothschilds.

After Empress Elizabeth refused to take any profits from CHRIST'S enemies, and Catherine II., obeyed HIS warning, (St. John, viii, 44)—Amschel Rothschild I., started in Russia many branches of the Grand Orient like the "Union of Salvation," the "Union of Benevolence," etc.

Young Russian officers, who accompanied Alexander I., to Paris, were attracted into the Lodges and duped by empty, grand, eloquent phrases and the "secrecy" of the rituals. The enrollment of imbeciles and crooks, and exciting them to revolutionary actions, grew to such proportions that the Czar, on July 25, 1822, was compelled to forbid Free-Masonry in Russia. The Satanists poisoned this true "Fair Angel," this Republican-Emperor, the most liberal of Monarchs that ever existed. His good reforms were paralyzed by the plots of the Free-Masons, who were ordered by Rothschild to organize at any cost a revolution, which was so much more easy, because the brother of Alexander, the eldest Romanov, Constantine, repeatedly refused to accept the sceptre and remained far away in Warsaw, and that Nicholas the next brother did not wish to become Czar. **All the Romanovs disliked to be Czars...**

The sons of the "father of lies" persuaded the mob and the young soldiers, that the real Czar was Constantine and his wife was Constituzia ("constituzia" is Russian for constitution). And so the people shouted: "Constantine, Constituzia," believing that thus they were loyal to the throne and that Nicholas I. was an usurper.

This despicable trick to provoke "murder" failed because of the marvelous courage of Nicholas I.—the "Demi-God," as he was called by the foreign writers, for his extraordinarily beautiful and majestic appearance. He rushed to the rebels and thundered:

"Children, on your knees." And the masses obeyed . . .

When investigation proved, that the Free-Masons were deliberately executing the orders of the Hidden Hand their lodges were closed in Russia in 1826. Thanks to this, Russia had a glorious period of thirty years of prosperity. The four power alliance of 1853-55, started and cemented by the satanist Rothschilds, could do nothing against her, though Prussia and Austria betrayed her.

THE "MYSTERY" OF BOMBELLES-REBELLO

Who was the mysterious Bombelles-the Jew-Jesuit?

Very little is known about this great criminal.

The Hidden Hand carefully hides him from daylight.

Bombelles entered the Jesuit Order only to become for the Jesuits, a "Konrad Wallenrod," who would degrade this Order and thus scandalize the whole Christian World, or to exploit the Order for his own advancement.

It is perfectly obvious that this devil, Bombelles, Jew and Jesuit, is the same scoundrel, described by Disraeli in his "Coningsby,"

"The young Sidonia (Lionel) was fortunate (from the Jewish, i. e., Satanic point of view) in the tutor whom his father (Nathan, a brigand satanist and plunderer) had procured for him, and who devoted to his charge all the resources of his trained intellect and vast erudition. A Jesuit before the Revolution; since then an exiled Liberal leader; now a member of the Spanish Cortes: Rebello was always a Jew".

The superlative satanism of Bombelles inspired Salomon Rothschild of Vienna, whose mere clerk became the notorious Prince Metternich, to warmly recommend Bombelles, as tutor of Napoleon II., and thus to put him as a Satan-tempter of the ex-Empress Marie-Louise, widow of Napoleon I.

The genius Emperor accustomed his wife to spend money lavishely and the Rothschilds knew it. Before tempting her by the love alone of the handsome Jew Bombelles, they carefully put the "Imperial Victim" into a golden web.

"In December 1827 Marie Louise raised a loan of ten million francs from Rothschild. On February 22, 1829 she lost her husband Count Neipperg (or Neuberg).. ("An Imperial Victim", by Mrs Edith E. Cuthell).

The death of Neiperg remained "mysterious for the historians."

Metternich, told Bombelles, that he "wished a man who could guide the weak character of Marie Louise". Thus the bargain was settled, and the "Nouveau Larousse" says, that Bombelles was already in 1830 secretly married to Marie Louise...

Thus Bombelles — "Rebello", a Jewish Macchiavelli, who "educated" Lionel, was recommended to be the slow annihilator of Napoleon II; became the confident of the widow of Napoleon I, Empress Marie-Louise and married her.

Thus was accomplished one of the most satanic murders by the Rothschilds of an innocent person—the scion of the Corsican Eagle.

Finally the Jew, Bombelles, using all the satanic tricks practically compelled the widow of Napoleon I. and this Archduchess of Habsburg to marry this dark snake of a ghetto....

121

Bombelles appears in the "L'Aiglon," the fine tragedy of Rostand, who went to Schoenbrunn in order to study the details, of how Bombelles did Napoleon II. to death through the "love" of the Jewess-Fanny Elsner, who was introduced through Bombelles to the young "King of Rome" with the special mission to conveniently murder this Napoleonid.

Fanny Elsner through her charms purposely brought the young Prince to exhaustion and death in 1832. She executed the orders of the Hidden Hand.

Edmond Rostand, author of "L'Aiglon," shows Bombelles very friendly with the Empress Maria-Louise who then was yet Countess Neiperg. The greatest actress, who played "L'Aiglon," the Princess Bariatinska-Yavorska, who was superior in this role to the Jewess, Sarah Bernhardt, and who learned all the details from M. Rostand himself, says that Bombelles in 1832, must have been forty years old and extremely handsome, according to the information procured by Rostand, from the Schoenbrunn archives.

Charles R. Bombelles is thus described by Mrs. E. E. Cuthell:

"He has even more ambition. With his soft voice he whispered in the ears of women"... "Bombelles wished to marry a M-lle Cavanagh, who had money He gained his object. His wife died, bequeathing him her heart in a leaden case. He buried it. A year later he had a desperate passion for another rich heiress, who declined it" (p. 321).

After the death of Marie Louise, Charles R. Bombelles was appointed the Comptroller to the Emperor of Austria, while Philippe Bombelles had become his "satanizer" since 1838.

"Rumours that she had died of poison floated about Parma and spread farther" ("An Imperial Victim" p. 373).

Bombelles's satanic work consisted in demoralizing the heir to the throne, the future Emperor Franz - Joseph II to such an extent, that the last failed to prevent nine murders within his own family, which caused his discredit and the downfall in 1918 of the Habsburg dynasty, whose "prime offense" was to sign the Holy Alliance with the motto "Christ above all".

Disraeli himself narrated, that a Jew "Rebello" (Bombelles) "educated", or rather, "satanized" Lionel Rothschild.

Having murdered all the direct Napoleonides and two Czars of Russia, the Rothschilds were anxious to get rid of, or, at least, to undermine the Habsburgs and to become "Above All" in the beautiful capital of Austria.

ROTHSCHILDS BEGIN TO DESTROY HABSBURGS.

But how to ruin the Habsburgs: this most ancient dynasty, strong ly supported by the Mother Church at Rome? Rudolphus of Habsburg was chosen Emperor in the year 1273. This dynasty had im mense merits, because it cemented thirteen different peoples, who otherwise would be cutting each others throats. The Habsburgs were the bulwark of Europe against the invasion of the fanatical Asiatic Turks; they were also the Pillars of Catholicism.

The best way to annihilate the Habsburgs and thus to weaken the Church, was to "bore the family from within", this favorite Jewish satanic trick, i.e. to educate the heir to the throne into a real monster. To this end a true satanist, a Jew Bombelles, (Rebello) a mock Jesuit, was introduced by the Viennese Salomon Rothschild as the best "educator"; first to the King of Rome, son of Napoleon I and grand son of the Emperor of Austria, and later to the heir of Franz-Joseph himself. I repeat this insistently.

Bombelles supported by Salomon and his clerk Metternich, was uplifted in 1838 as "educator" or "satanizer" of the future Emperor of Austria, Franz Jozeph. Thus the Habsburgs forgot the warning of CHRIST, as ninety-nine percent of the Americans are doing, who assure us: "There are good Jews. Therefore, let the bad Jews do what they like." What was the consequence of the "spitting" on CHRIST?

Bombelles was the responsible author of the most awful disloyalty, baseness and cruelty of Austria, which began to amaze the whole world since 1848, when Franz Joseph, only eighteen years, old became the Emperor de jure, and Bombelles was the "power behind the throne," receiving and executing the orders of Rothschild. Their first act was to betray their word to Nicholas I., who put as "condition sine qua non" mercy for the Hungarian generals Sheczeny and others. Franz-Joseph-Bombelles strangled them, as soon as the Russian troops left Hungary.

As was promised to the victorious Russian field marshal Paskevich, "not a hair had fallen from the heads of the most gallant patriotic Hungarian prisoners."

Yes! A Jew of Portugal, Bombelles, similar to Disraeli, was helped by the Rothschilds to become the husband of an Empress and thus the member of the House of Habsburgs'!

Out of 115.000.000 Americans, 15 heard Bombelles' name!

Billions and honors did not satisfy Satan's delegate, James. He aimed at murder, as CHRIST stated, and the ruination of HIS work. If the rulers resented his exactions, he provoked rows, bloodshed and, as Disraeli revealed, all the mischief makers were salaried by L. Rothschild. Thus no danger for the Rothschilds, but only for the imbecile and cowardly Christians, who "spit" at **CHRIST**.

Nathan wished to penetrate into the high British society in order to rule England and tried to prove himself more "English," than the Britishers themselves. He spread Pan-Britanism and inflamed England against France. James and Nathan searched for pretext to cause a war.

James knew the Christian convictions of King Charles X. of France, and demanded that his (James') wife should be received at Court, where she could step on the toes of the Queen. But the Duchess of Angouleme answered:

"You must not forget that the King of France is the **most Christian King**," i. e., since OUR LORD designated the Jews as satanists-mankillers, we ought to avoid them."

James ordered his press to wage a venomous campaign against the Bourbons. In order to defend himself, the King accepted the advice of his Minister, Polignac, to restrain the obscenity of the newspapers. This was exploited by James, who ordered his freemasons to unite the Bonapartists, Orleanists, republicans and the slums against the King. After 1770 Amschel established his Jews as agents in many places. Thus a Busnach was at Algiers, where he, thanks to the Rothschild's credit, became the Jew "King of Algeria," bribing the stupid Turkish janissaries, who elected the Dey, i. e., the Viceroy of the Sultan of Turkey. To humiliate King Charles, to compel France to act and to anger Great Britain, Busnach was ordered to excite the Dey. At a reception in 1827 the Dey slapped the face of the Consul of France, M. Deval, with a fly fan. It was an unheard of offense. France demanded a reparation. Meantime Nathan succeeded in having the Duke of Wellington, a foe of France, made Prime Minister.

The attack of France on Algeria helped Nathan to irritate England and on July 27-29 she supported the above groups to overthrow King Charles X. and to enthrone the son of Phillipe Egalite, Duke d'Orleans, who was for twenty years the Grand Master of the Grand Orient and who criminally voted the death of King Louis XVI.

J. ROTHSCHILD III. GRABS THE RAILROADS

"With the French July Revolution the firm entered upon a period during which its influence and position attained a height which would have surprised Amschel Mayer. History does not record another instance of any one private firm holding so prominent a position, or exercising such a powerful control over the destinies of nations, as is furnished by the Rothschild family" (J. Reeves, p. 87).

The greatest endeavour of the XIX Century, was the construction of railroads. The Rothschilds grabbed most of them. Read the conditions which James Rothschild III. compelled France to accept for financing its North Railroad.

The Government took upon itself the obligation to spend 100 million francs in order to build the roadbed. James consented to spend some 60 millions in providing the rails cars, etc. He received during 40 years 17 millions yearly by way of income, i.e. 620 millions in interest, plus the principal of 60 millions. In this undertaking the Rothschilds used 60 millions of their depositors' money for which they paid them 4% interest or 2,400,000 yearly, thus getting 14,600,000 francs per annum for their signature.

The "Journal des Debats" in order to deceive the nation stated in July, 1843, that Rothschild is **"begging for the privilege to ruin himself."** The French press acted the role of agent provocateur as early as fifty years before the scandal of Panama.

The Jews have coveted this rich prey—the railroads—at any cost. At one time the Government passed through an interval of honesty and had the temerity to stem their aggression. In 1838 M. Martin, from the North, suggested to Parliament a net of railroads to be built by the State. If Mr. Martin's plan, based on two pillars: monopoly of banking and of transportation had been approved by Parliament the financial feodality would have been killed in its inception. But the Rothschilds, through the press controlled by them, found the way to acquire the railroads. In 1840, the West and South lines were conceded to the Rothschilds and the Foulds. By 1845 all the great lines belonged to these two companies.

They ruled the Exchange and by regularly plundering the public, made 150 millions yearly. Through their press the Rothschilds excited the appetites of the public and sold all they could at the highest point, and in 1823 began to withdraw their capital and did not reinvest it. Of course, many banks failed and millions of individuals were ruined.* In 1825 the Rothschilds rebought their stocks at the lowest possible prices.

*Just as the Federal Reserve Bank acted with the farmers in 1921 22.

ROTHSCHILDS DEMORALIZE BRITISH NOBILITY

In all European countries the aristocracy earnestly served their nations but did it gratuitously, and by so doing spent its ancient wealth, acquired in wars by rewarded courage, while the middle class would not move one finger without being paid, and thereby enriched itself.

As I have said, the British aristocracy gave all its best to save the future of England in her struggle against Napoleon's supremacy and was pauperised. The plunder by Nathan Rothschild II. of $5,000,000 in one day after Waterloo, made most of England nobles and statesmen's mouths water. However, Nathan was physically too unclean to be received in London society. This was understood by his son, Lionel, one of the trickiest satanists.

"Ten times since 1833 had the Bill for the admission of Jews to Parliament been carried in the House of Commons and rejected by the House of Lords, who now at last gave way, and Baron Rothschild took his seat on July, 26, 1858," wrote Sir Algernon West in his "Recollections", p. 157.

To defeat the noble Lords, who remembered the warning of CHRIST, that the Jews are "satanists-menkillers," Rothschild compelled Lord Derby to unite his forces with Disraeli. Lord Derby again became Prime Minister with Disraeli as his Chancellor of the Exchequer, thus making many Lords dependent for their economic needs on L. Rothschild whom they knew to be Disraeli's "boss." How the Rothschilds captured the British nobility in their nets can be understood from the following two statements of Sir Algernon West:

a) "Many a time when he (Whyte Melville) met me with Baron Rothschild's hounds, he would say a kind word, which gave infinite satisfaction" (though, perhaps these words were given to please the Roehschild's dogs) p. 233.

b) "Dining one night at Baron Rothschild's, Lord Granville was asked to take in Lady. — Certainly not; I hardly know, if I can take myself in, answered Lord Granville, Secretary for Colonies" (p. 425).

Whether Baron Rothschild thought that the best company for Sir Algernon West would be his dogs; or that Sir A. West would rather be with the dogs than with their master—could not be traced in his "Recollections."

Many hundred years ago a prophet, Mahomet, stated:

"Who ever is a friend of a Jew, belongs to them, becomes one of them. GOD cannot tolerate this mean people. The Jews have wandered away from divine religion (given by Moses). They are usurpers. You must not relent in your work which must show up Jewish deceit." (Koran).

NATHAN BETRAYS JUDAISM. DIES "MYSTERIOUSLY"

Nathan Mayer Rothschild married in 1806 the richest Jewess in London Johanna Levi Barnet (Barnato?) Cohen. Their son, Lionel, was born on Nov. 22nd, 1808, later than Disraeli (born on Dec. 21st, 1805) whom he entirely captivated.

Bombelles (Rebello) a Jewish Machiavelli, was made the tutor of Lionel and taught Nathan such satanic contempt of all moral and religious traditions "which should be a man's only guide," that the totally unscrupulous Nathan, seing that the Londoners distrusted his Jewish creed, condemned by CHRIST, became ready to commit apostasy, the easier to accumulate wealth and attain titles and power in England.

But his intentions became known to his eldest brother, Anselm, who immediately summoned his four brothers to Frankfort, and there and then, on the tomb of Amschel Rothschild I. Nathan was tried, convicted and doomed . . . Nathan "suddenly" died . . . All the other brothers had sworn to be faithful to their creed and to the testament of the "great Exterminator of Christians," Amschel.

To be sure that Lionel would not embrace Christianity for his own ambitious ends the brothers Rothschilds, his uncles, ordered him to marry Charlotte, the daughter of Karl Rothschild of Naples, whose wife was Adelaide Hertz.

"Nathan went to Frankfort to be present at the marriage festivities. He was suffering from a carbuncle. On the day of the wedding he was taken seriously ill and died on the 28-th July, 1836. (Reeves, p. 201).

"The superiority of Nathan's intelligence was proved on several occasions. He was the first to inform Lord Aberdeen (a Minister) of the Paris July revolution, as he had been to announce the defeat of Napoleon at Waterloo." (p. 169).

Of course, Nathan could announce it, once the Rothschilds were at the head of the Hidden Hand, which organized all the bloodshed, as I stated in my "Science of Political Foresight."

Of course, the arrival of the Landgrave's $4,000,000 to London in cash, when England was on the eve of bankruptcy, did not demand a genius to make tremendous profit, especially if the owner of this capital was a real satanist -mankiller, as was Nathan Mayer, future Rothschild II.

"The amount of fortune he left always remained a secret. The Business was to be conducted by the four sons in co-operation with their uncles abroad. To each of his daughters he left $500.000, which was to be forfeited if they married without the consent of their mother and their brothers. There were no legacies to his employes and no charitable bequests" (p. 203).

127

NATHAN R. II. WAS A FILTHY CRUEL BEAST

I take the following notes about Nathan from the book " The Rothschilds: The Financial Rulers of Nations":

"The first occasion on which Nathan assisted the English Government was in 1819, when he undertook the loan of $60,000,000" (p. 177).

From 1818 until 1832 Nathan issued eight other loans for a sum of $105,400,000.

"With Spain, or the South American states, which had formerly acknowledged the Spanish flag, he would never have anything to do" (p. 179).

Explanation: The Spanish Inquisition.

"In 1831 Nathan Mayer took control of the quicksilver mines at Idria in Austria and, simultaneously similar mines in Almadena, in Spain. Thus all the mercury, indispensable as medicine, was in his hands, and he doubled and trebled its price. It had a terrific consequence upon the sick and suffering of all nations." This is not all that this "good" Jew did. Now the mercurial preparations, because of the price of pure mercury, are no longer manufactured from the metal as obtained from the mines, but from the refuse of other articles containing quicksilver, such as the foil of old mirrors and looking glasses" (p. 181).

"Nathan never paid his employee a cent more than was necessary for their bare subsistence, or at least not a farthing more that they could compel him to pay," (Mr. Martin in his "Stories of Banks and Bankers".

Did he not merit the censure of the World?

"One cause of his success was the torturous policy with which he misled those who watched him" (Reeves, p. 189).

Nathan constantly created false panics and plundered like a highwayman, all who came within his power.

"A general suspicion and mistrust followed him in all his action" (p. 190).

"They who preached loudest against mammon, bent lowest before the mammon worshipper" (p. 194).

"Nathan had ruined many a man of business" (p. 197).

"The direction of old Mayer Amschel of Frankfort, that his sons should always remain united, were carried out to their fullest possible extent, by the practice of intermarriage" (p. 201).

"The control of the London branch was confided exclusively to Lionel".

This was because he was the most satanic of the family.

"Lionel concentrated his thoughts exclusively on the consolidation of the immense fortune. Great prudence marked his enterprises. In the negotiation of foreign loans Lionel was particularly active, as this business, at once lucrative and comparatively free from risk, was one which he preferred before all others. During his lifetime his firm was interested in the issue of no less than eighteen Government loans, amounting in the aggregate to seven hundred million dollars. To enter into the details of these transactions would be to give the financial history of Europe i . the last fifty years" (Reeves, pp. 205—207).

128

THE FAMILY OF NATHAN ROTHSCHILD II.

Nathan had four sons and three daughters:

(1) Lionel-Nathan, born Nov. 22, 1808. He was the "satanizer of Disraeli, who described him as "Sidonia." As GOD made the rattlesnakes produce noise in order to warn us, so He made the Jews boastful, that they should betray themselves and their deadly danger. The "educator" of Lionel was a Jew, whom Disraeli pictured as Rebello and who in turn became Jesuit, Liberal, courtier; who "educated" to death the King of Rome, and finally became the third husband of the second wife of Napoleon, as Count Bombelles. Lionel married his cousin Charlotte, daughter of his uncle Karl of Naples and Adelaide Hertz, in 1836 and died in 1879, having compelled Europe to keep the Christians of Macedonia under the Turkish knife in order to exterminate them, and also to create new pretexts for wars. Lionel became a British Baronet in 1846; but being the personification of a real satanist he was unable to overcome the British nobility's distrust of the Jews the "satanists-man-killers"—as CHRIST called them.

I shall return to him later.

At the death of his father Nathan Rothschild II., Lionel could not maintain his power because his uncles suspected him óf being "de-satanized" and because of the extraordinary satanic capacities of his uncle James, who thereupon became the World Autocrat, and World Assassin-Rothschild, III.

(2) Anthony, born May, 26, 1810; died July, 4, 1876. He married his cousin Louise Montefiore, whose father Abraham was married to Henriette a daughter of Amschel and sister of Nathan. Anthony had only two daughters, one of whom, Constance, married Lord Seymour, and Anna, who died early.

(3) Nathaniel, born April, 2, 1812; died in February, 1870. He married his cousin Charlotte, daughter of James Rothschild III., and of Betty, daughter of Salomon Rothschild of Vienna. He lived in Paris until his death. He left two sons: James-Nathan or James-Edouard and Arthur. The first, born on Oct. 29, 1844, married his cousin. Louise-Therese, daughter of Charles of Naples, the son of Karl Rothschild, (the leader of the "Alta Vendita"). James-Nathan revolted against the tyranny of Alphonse Rothschild IV., and was compelled to commit "suicide." His throat was cut . . .

The same happened with the grandson of Lionel, Nathaniel Rothschild in London in 1923, who was also found with his throat cut... Beloved execution of the Rothschilds.

THE THIRD GENERATION OF ROTHSCHILDS.

James-Nathan left a son, Henri (who married a Jewess, Weis-weller) and a daughter, Jane, who married a Jew, baron Leonino.

(4) Mayer, born June, 26, 1818; died February, 6, 1874. He married in 1850 his cousin, Juliana Cohen, daughter of the brother of his mother, who was Johanna Levi Barnet Cohen, the wife of Nathan Rothschild II.

The only daughter of Mayer, Anna, who died in 1910, married Lord Roseberry, and thus infused the Jewish blood into another noble British family. According to Jewish law the children of a Jewess are Jews (M. Joseph Santo).

The three daughters of Nathan Rothschild II. were:

(a) Charlotte, born in 1807, who married her cousin Anselm Salomon, son of Salomon (the second son of Amschel Rothschild I.) and of Caroline Stern. The Sterns of Frankfort were the ancestors of the Harmsworths in England, one of whom became camuflaged as Lord Northcliffe and another as Lord Rothermere. Both chose their names "North" and "Roth" as much similar to Rothschild as possible. Roth-er-mere or "mere-Roth" (schild).

(b) Louise, born in 1820, married her cousin Charles, son of Karl Rothschild of Naples.

(c) Anna married an Englishman, Henry Fitz-Roy.

The daughters received as dowry only $2,500,000 each.

THE ROTHSCHILDS "ABOVE ALL"

One of the two publications which tell the whole Truth*) "The British Guardian," (40, Great Ormond street, London) published by the brilliant British homeopath and patriot, Dr. John H. Clarke, says in its issue of December, 1922:

"And how this potent firm (the Rothschilds) governs the Government of France and England alike may be gathered from two recent incidents. The French Secretary of Legation M. Thierry at the Embassy of London, some months ago married a Jewess of the Rothschild clan. And now the hidden mentors of Mr. Bonar Law's (who promised to follow the policy of Disraeli, i. e., of his patrons, the Rothschilds) new "Conservative" Government induced him to send as Ambassador in Paris a non-diplomatic "Liberal", Marquis of Crewe whose wife is the daughter of Hannah Rothschild, Countess of Roseberry. Here we have the actual basis of the Franco-British Entente. "R. F." (R. F. means Republic French and also "Rothschilds Freres" i. e., Rothschilds Brothers) covers the British Empire, the French Republic, and most of other republics and kingdoms between Moscow. Angora and Washington.

*) The other being the Patriot — 2, White friars, London.

130

DISRAELI BETRAYS HIS RACE AND ROTHSCHILD.

Disraeli, boastful, like all Jews betrayed himself. In his novel "Coningsby", Disraeli acknowledged the protection of Lionel Rothschild (Sidonia).

This is clearly evident also from the official "Letters of Lord Beaconsfield to his sister." He does not hide how Lionel advised him to go to the Bar; and that after having envenomed Disraeli with his satanic ideas, offered him financial and political support.

Disraeli was to Lionel what Weisshaupt was to Amschel; Gamberle to James Rothschild III..; what Poincare was to Alphonse Rothschild IV. and is to Edouard Rothschild V. or as was and is Kerensky-Kirbis, a Jew, to E. Rothschild V.

The English aristocracy had not been exterminated by the Revolution as had been the French; and with all their money, Nathan and his son, Lionel, could not triumph over the quite justifiable distrust of the Jews in England; these "sellers of CHRIST," as they are called in Europe, and whom CHRIST Himself designated as "the sons of the devil, and the executors of his lusts."

A handsome, ambitious young Jew was needed, to build a path across the united aristocracy, in order that this road could be used by the Rothschilds for their vast scheme of World domination. When one takes into consideration the influence of the Hidden Hand upon Beaconsfield, then all that seemed so extraordinary, so "mysterious" and so "secret" to all his biographers becomes perfectly clear.

In "Coningsby," he writes of Lionel's tutor "Rebello" (allusion to his Jewish rebellious nature and the consonance with "Bombelles", which is pronounced in French, like "Bombelle"):

"Jesuit before the revolution, since then an exiled Liberal leader; now a member of the Spanish Cortes; Rebello was always a Jew."

Like him, Disraeli became a Christian, then a Conservative, but always remained a Jew and a rebel.

This is proved by his poem, Lyridon:
"Shall cool those chariot — wheels now hot with blood;
And blessed be the hand that dares to bare
The regicidal steel that shall redeem
A nation's sorrow with tyrant's blood"!
("The Earl of Beaconsfield" by Mr. L. Apjohn, p. 66).

Disraeli was the Horse of Troy slipped into the upper classes of Great Britain, carrying inside a score of Jews, as future Lords and Ministers. Now they entirely rule her, as I exposed it in my pamphlet — "**Let Us Prevent The Second World War, Already** Prepared", which was my report to Pres. Harding in 1921.

131

"MYSTERY" OF DISRAELI REVEALED.

Those who write about Disraeli and other "great" Jews, who in reality were only great mankillers, uplifted by the Hidden Hand such as Gambetta, Venizelos,*) Millerand-Kahn, Kerensky, Trozky, etc., have failed to disclose the "secret" of their "success", and have made the most absurd hypotheses.

And Mr. H. W. W., who reviewed in "The Daily News" of June 7, 1920, the fifth and sixth volumes of Mr. Buckle's "Life of Disraeli", exclaims:

"No career in English history is more marvellous than that of Disraeli, and none has hitherto been enshrouded in greater mystery".

The "marvel" and "mystery" is simply that Disraeli was a servant of the Rothschilds, like all the above named "great men".

Mr. H. W. W., afraid to give his name, reminds us that Disraeli was quite rightly called "adventurer" and "superlative Hebrew conjurer" by Carlyle. In an outburst of vile flattery, Mr. Buckle attributes most high qualities to this Jew. Mr. H. W. W. entertains a feeling of shame in behalf of Mr. Buckle and hides himself.

Mr. Buckle's statement, that Disraeli „triumphed over all patrician prejudices by sheer capacity" is most preposterous, because all the wealth of the Rothschilds and all the Satanic Forces were at the back of Disraeli — their "Wallenrod" for England. (vide "Coningsby", p. 452, or "Lord Beaconsfield's Letters" of June 1839, 2 December 1842; May 1844; March 1848; etc.)

The statement that Disraeli "raised England to the highest position" is absurd also, because he was a mere tool of the Hidden Hand, which at that moment was preparing a whole series of wars, including this last great war, always in order to "exterminate the Christians" to overthrow the Church and to grasp "all the Kingdoms." The brilliant English nation does not need Disraelis.

Disraeli imbued whole generations of British statesmen with the lie, that "a great Russia is a danger" for Great Britain.

"Suppress a truth of which we have good evidence, and, like the stone of stumbling and rock of offense, it may fall upon us by and by and grind us to powder" (H. W. Rankin).

*) It was through his complicity that the German cruisers Goeben and Breslau could reach Constantinople and menacing to bombard the Sultan's palace and to destroy the town, they compelled Turkey to join the Central powers, which caused the prolongation of the World War for many months. It was the Venizelos' "lust of murder" and his desire to upset the excellent Christian Monarch, which started the absurd Greco Turkish war. The poor King Constantin was compelled to follow Venizelos and accept the war and atone this crime of Venizelos with throne and very life. The late King was one of the most refined persons of the Nordic Aryans. King Alexander I. of Greece was also 'mysteriously" killed by the same Hidden Hand.

132

ROTHSCHILD EXPOSES JEWRY UEBER ALLIES.

«The Minister cannot pay the interest on the national debt; not an unprecedented circumstance, and has applied to us (Rothschilds). I never permit any business of State to be transacted without my personal interposition; and so I must go up to town immediately» confessed "Sidonia" ("Coningsby," p. 248).

After these last phrases of »Sidonia» could there yet be any doubt, that he is the life like photograph of Lionel, whose father Nathan smashed nearly all the other bankers in London, and who, "devoted all his attention to Governmental loans. "Sidonia" added:

"Can anything be more absurd than that a nation should apply to an individual to maintain its credit, and, with its credit, its existance as an empire!"

Rothschild thus revealed the Jewish Peril, if the existence of the British Empire depended on his caprice.

Is it better with America? Not the least. Has not Senator Edwin Ladd rightly warned her that she is facing an imminent bankruptcy, as I proved in my »Gentiles Review« No-8? Out of 550 members of the American Congress there is none, who understands the catastrophic situation, or has the courage to tell the truth Why?

Because when Abraham Lincoln wished to prevent the bankruptcy and forthcoming moral, mental, political and financial slavery of his beloved country, a Jew * John Wilkes Booth, obviously an agent of the Hidden Hand, murdered the patriotic President. And no American seems to know this or dares to reveal it....

When another honest President, Garfield said:

"Whoever controls the money of a nation, controls that nation".

This truth and courage cost him his life! He was shot, as was Lincoln, for the same reason, by the same Hidden Hand!

"I was the most powerful man in 1918", said a Jew, B. M. Baruch.

"The President will do exactly what I tell him to do", bluntly told me the secretary of President Roosevelt, a Jew Loeb, in February 1907.

"Justice Lubitz Brandeis, a Jew, ruled the White House by secret telephone" ("Chicago Daily Tribune", July 22, 1922).

A brilliant Captain Harold Sherwood Spencer in his book "Democracy Or Shylocracy" describes, how he got hold in 1917, of a telegram, saying that »Brandeis cabled Rothschild yesterday«. Was Brandeis asking E. Rothschild's orders to the White House? Or was Justice Brandeis communicating to Rothschild what he had found out about the White House?..

But the people find it all-right that the Jews murder the American Presidents, or rule the more servile ones and imagine that America is a free country! Yes! Free for the 135.000 slayers, who are over-running the country, according to Justice Marcus Cavanaugh.

*) Read the "Truth About The Jews", p. 58, by Walter Hurt, Chicago.

133

LIONEL NATHAN DE ROTHSCHILD.

Educated by the Jew-Machiavelli — Bombelles — ''Rebello,'' Lionel continued to increase his fortune. His brothers married cousins: Anthony, Louise Montefiore, and Mayer Juliana Cohen. Both went into society to prepare their entrance into the nobility.

The ancient Amschel, the grandfather, never changed his underwear, or his clothes, until they fell to pieces.

His five sons were as dirty as he in underwear, but sometimes changed their outer garments. His grandsons, i.e. the third generation began to change both.

When Nathan bought or sold consols, people in London asked what dirty speculation he was then engaged in.

When Lionel sold, the people foresaw some diplomatic trouble. **He started eighteen Governmental loans and even became financial agent for the Russian Empire.**

He also financed the 'Government of England, when it bought the shares of the Suez Canal from the Khedive for $20.000.000. For his mere endorsement of the obligation of the British Government for a very short time Lionel pocketed 500,000 pounds.

The Russian loan was offered to Lionel, but he hesitated. The reason was that at that very moment he was endeavouring to enter the House of Commons. That is why, in order to create a favorable impression, Lionel preached the freedom of nations, and shouted against the autocrats.

We must not forget that according to Disraeli (''Coningsby,'' p. 218-219). Sidonia Lionel was supporting all the outcasts and revolutionaries of the world. Thus Lionel found it somewhat embarassing to help them in their destructive work against the Monarchs, in order to create the mankilling demanded by the Talmud and to finance the Monarchs **simultaneously!**

When, after a long struggle between his greed and his profession of liberalism, he decided to take the loan, this had been given to a competitor. Lionel could never console himself, and swore revenge on Russian Czars.

In 1847 Lionel presented his candidature in the City of London and was elected with his colleague, John Russel, thanks to bribes.

A law had to be enacted to permit a Jew to become a Commoner.

It was supported by Mr. Gladstone, and opposed by Mr. R. Inglis, a British patriot. After a discussion, it was adopted.

This decision cost the Rothschilds dearly but it was rejected by the more honest and independent Upper House.

DISRAELI MERE CLERK OF THE ROTHSCHILDS

The politics of Disraeli consisted chiefly in his satanic Jewish, (not English) hatred of Russia. Disraeli had to neutralize the sane advice of King George III, whe most wisely said:

"Every good Englishman ought to be a good Russian, just as every good Russian ought to be a good Englishman".

This wise Christian motto ruined the reputation of this monarch ιn the Jewish press of the world, which did everything possible to defame him, making him responsible for the outbreak of the American Revolution, though in reality it was Amschel Rothschild I, who through his Jews: Haim Solomon, four Franks and others staged **all the bloodshed,** which could have been averted·

Taken by Lionel under his guidance, Disraeli henceforth assumed a sort of triumphant scorn, that would be worthy of a Mephistopheles. As he was luridly pale with flashing eyes and black hair, he adopted a dress coat of black velvet lined with white satin, white gloves, hanging fringes of black silk, white ivory stick with black tassels. All this together was devilishly combined in order to make a stronger impression on influential old ladies.

And through them, Benjamin learned in London all the secrets, needed for his patron-Lionel, with whose money Disraeli stepped into the highest spheres.

Lionel made most persistent efforts te procure the abolition of the civil and political "disabilities" of the Jews, which were practically suggested by the warning of CHRIST HIMSELF, who pointed out the Jews as "satanists-murderers." To remove these "disabilities" was to disobey CHRIST. But there were any number of the breed of Judas, who for 30 or more silver or gold coins were ready to betray their country and even CHRIST.

"Mr. Disraeli, then the Tory member for Buckingham (and who wrote poems praising the regicide steel) also supported the resolution, making an earnest appeal to the House to perform a great act of national justiee, and to discard the "superstition" of the Dark Ages, which influenced them in their opposition" (J. Reeves, p. 216).

It is understandable that for the satanist Disraeli the warning of OUR SAVIOUR seemed "superstition," but the Lords grabbed the 30 silver coin in cash or "in dogs," as Sir Algernon West implied in his "Recollections" (p. 233) when he stated: "Many a time he {White Melville) met me with Baron Rothschild's hounds."

Since then British politics became satanized; and the United States should beware. Even the Tsar an Ally and a cousin of the King of England was basely betrayed by an Ambassador of Sassoon-Rothschild, Sir George Buchanan.

LIONEL MAKES HIS WAY INTO PARLIAMENT.

Nothwithstanding the Rothschild's dogs and other bribes the honest Lords long resisted. In 1850 Lionel, reelected, walked up impudently to the table of the House of Commons, and demanded to be sworn on the Old Testament, but was forthwith requested to withdraw. In 1852 Lionel was again reelected. Once more the Lords showed their opposition (i.e., their honesty). On July 26, 1858, Lionel was again requested to withdraw. Lord Russell then moved a resolution, that the words: **"on the true faith of a Christian"** should be **omitted** from the oath, and, this being carried, Lionel was re-admitted." (p. 222). Of course, CHRIST was so far distant and the Jew with his 30 silver pieces and gold coin, and his hounds and all kinds of good things, was knocking at the doors. The House decided to scorn the warnings of CHRIST . . .

"Claiming to be fully as good citizens as the Roman Catholics, the Jews saw no reason why they likewise should not enjoy the same political and civil privileges as Protestants and Catholics now possess in common" (p. 213).

The Roman Catholics and the Protestants can be good Englishmen, or Americans, but, as the trial of Capt. H. H. Beamish and Sir Alfred Mond proved, a Jew cannot be a good Englishman (or American): a Jew is always a Jew, i. e., a satanist and a mankiller, as long as he does not drop Talmud, which preaches hatred of the gentiles, which Catholic or Protestant creeds do NOT teach. A million times it has been proved that the Jews do not care about the country, in which they live. Every great man from Diodor to Ernest Renan, confirmed this.

Was Mr. J. Reeves to receive some "30 silver coins" from the Rothschilds? He is criminally wrong.

"The Christians were influenced by "prejudice" by the stigma which has always been connected with the Jewish race" (p. 213).

declared Mr. J. Reeves, thus implying, that the warning of CHRIST was a "prejudice" or contempt.

"Although all impediments in the way to municipal offices were removed, the Jews found themselves still barred from entering upon parliamentary career, owing to the Oath of Abjuration which every member was bound to take before being allowed to sit and vote in the House. This oath concluded with the words 'on the true faith of a Christian', which no Jew could conscientiously repeat. No move was made to procure the abolition of the Jewish 'disabilities', as any agitation for that purpose would have been vain, owing to the great repugnance which the Tories displayed to all such measures. Lionel was elected in 1847 a member for the City of London with Lord John Russel as his colleague. Accordingly his Lordship, who was then the Premier, took an early opportunity of moving a resolution favorable to the Jews." (p. 214).

ROTHSCHILDS "ABOVE ALL" IN LONDON.

"For great as had been the services rendered by them to the nation in time of need, the Jews were still regarded as an outcast race, not worthy to be ranked on the same level as their Christian fellow citizens" (Reeves, p. 212).

Never have the Jews rendered service without compensation! They helped England to dispose of Napoleon I. but only after he, their own creation, had exhausted England, and became peaceful.

Without the support of the Amschel's millions and Free Masonry, there would have been no Napoleon; and there would have been fewer wars, less bloodshed and not so many useless revolts.

Mr. Reeves ventures to imply, that as the Roman Catholics in England had acquired the same rights as the Protestants, the Jews ought also be accorded the same rights. It is blasphemy to compare Catholics with Jews, who alone were branded by CHRIST as liars." Does Mr. J. Reeves, like many Gentiles, imply that CHRIST made a mistake, and he, Reeves and the Gentiles, KNOW BETTER?

In 1830 Robert Grant endeavored to extend all rights to the Jews. They were "unable" to take the oath of allegiance which was required to be sworn upon the Gospel. Neither could they take the oath of abjuration which contained the words, "on the true faith of a Christian," (p. 383) wrote Thomas Erskine in his "The Constitutional History of England."

The Jews were "unable" to take the oath of allegiance or of abjuration, not because the Christians were unjust to the Jews, but because an oath made by Jews to Christians remained "void" or a "scrap of paper," according to the satanic teachings of the Talmud. And the Christians acted wisely, when finding the Jews "unable" to take the oath, they regarded them as "unreliable," as characterized by CHRIST HIMSELF.

But Nathan and Lionel-Nathan hired all kinds of valets, like Robert Grant and others, and in 1847 Lionel N. Rothschild was returned to Parliament from London. The Lords proved to be honest and clever Christians. Then Lionel, through Disraeli, offered as reward his support to Lord Derby, whom he uplifted to the Premiership.

"The Lords, yielding to the persuasion of the Conservative Premier, Lord Derby, agreed to a concession. The Commons would thus be able to admit a Jew member, the Lords to exclude a Jewish peer" (Th. Erskine).

And W. E. Gladstone "suddenly" changed his ideas about the Jews, as Judas changed his of CHRIST.

And four Jews were returned to Parliament in 1859.

J. ROTHSCHILD "ABOVE ALL" IN PARIS.

James Rothschild, born in 1792, misruled from 1836 until 1868. He married ugly Betty, the daughter of his brother, Salomon of Vienna. Because of the "crime" of Nathan the latter's son Lionel was deprived of the World's Throne. James became Rothschild III.

Thus decided Amschel (Anselm), Salomon, and Karl Rothschilds, who all gathered in July 1836 at Frankfort in order to judge and presumably to execute Nathan, possibly the only Rothschild, who through a total lack of principle, wished to become a Christian, only that he could the easier deceive and enslave the English people

Lionel, the eldest son of Nathan was then only twenty eight years old and "who knows, if this Jew - Jesuit Bombelles had not shattered his Jewish creed?", thought his tiger uncles. Lionel was ordered to marry the daughter of his uncle Karl, a most orthodox Jew, so as to be under the supervision of a fanatical Jewess.

Could the old Amschel Mayer have foreseen that his son James would be knighted in 1815, when he was only twenty two years old; become a baron at thirty or that in 1842 he would come in a halo of gold into the salons of Marshal Soult, also a Jew, bearing on his breast the Star of Grand Officer of the Legion of Honor!

The political events during the fifteen years of James mother's life created a great difference between Nathan and James. The former was satisfied to be the king of the Exchange, to ruin the bankers and to use the brokers as his valets, while the latter aspired to make use of Governments and chose his valets among the Ministers of Cabinet rank, beginning by Marquis de Villele, the French Minister of Finances.

The Britishers showed greater resistance against the Rothschilds of London, than the Frenchmen against those of Paris.

"During the reign of Louis Philippe (1830 - 48) the influence of James was all - powerful. The reign was called the reign of stockjobbing and speculation. The splendour and luxury of the entertainments given by James, were never equaled by any given by the Court. To procure an invitation from James was more highly sought for than a presentation at Court. James took delight in humiliating those who cringed to him. His roughness of manner and his blunt, if not coarse, mode of speaking were well known, as was his utter disregard of politeness. The Prince of Wurtemberg once accepted James's invitation for dinner, during which James persis ted in addressing the Prince in a most annoyingly familiar tone. The Prince left the table." (Reeves, p. 344).

138

ROTHSCHILDS RECOGNIZED AS KINGS.

Already in July 27th, 1844, Guiseppe Mazzini, the renowned Italian patriot, wrote from London, that "the Golden Calf is all powerful in France, and that Rothschild (James I) could be **King** if he conspired". ("The Birth of Modern Italy", p. 62, by Mr. Jessie White Mario).

And the Russian revolutionary, Hertzen (the Jew—Hertz—born in 1812), called the Rothschilds — kings.

"The notorious author, Alexander (?) Hertzen (Hertz), one of the pioneers of the Russian revolutionary movement, was compelled to leave the country (Russia). He fled to England, where he started a Russian paper called "The Bell" Hertzen, however, was a rich man, who before going into exile had converted his property into Government bonds. The Russian Government knew the numbers of Herzen's bonds and when they were presented for payment upon the exile's arrival in London, Nicholas I, hoping thereby to crush his enemy, ordered the Government Bank of St. Petersburg to refuse payment. The Bank naturally obeyed. But 'fortunately' for Hertzen he found a champion in the elder Rothschild (James). The latter informed the Czar that as Herzen's bonds were as good as any other Russian bonds, he was reluctantly compelled to conclude the insolvency of the Russian Government. Should the bonds not be paid immediately, he would declare the Czar bankrupt in all the European money merkets, Nicholas I was beaten. He put his pride in his pocket and paid. Herzen himself relates this story in 'The Bell' under the title "**King Rothschild and Emperor Nicholas I,**" (The "Fortnightly Review" April, 1911. by Dr. A. S. Rappoport, p. 655)

Both "patriots" (Mazzini, educated by the Jew, Nathan, father of the recent mayor of Rome, and Herzen, illegitimate son of the Jew Herz, a Rothschildian) fought violently their Christian Monarch, but would rather die than write one word against the Rothschilds, whom they themselves called "Kings."

Just as the Jew, Karl Marx, attacking capital, never dared to whisper one word about the personification of Capital—James!

And in "The Fortnightly Review" of November 1920, after a remarkable article by the talented and well informed Mr. John Pollack (son of Frederick Pollock, Bart.) about the murder of the Czar by the Jews, a "defender" of the Jews, Dr. Hagberg Wright, confirms, that James Rothschild III has been financing a Jew, Herz*), who assumed the name of. Al. Hertzen, and was the same to Russian Bolshevism, that John the Baptist was to Christianity.

With Rothschild's money, Hertzen had opened a sort of "manufactury of bolsheviks," to which he had invited young Christian students and transformed them into atheistic assassins!

It was a kind of moral "canape" of Alphonse I.

*) Karl Mayer Rothschild married a Jewess, Adelaide Hertz.

139

"THE MYSTERY" OF THE DUKE OF ORLEANS'
DEATH (1842)

Some patriots openly called the Rothschilds "The Thieves of France". In many pamphlets were revealed some of their most amazing brigandages The pamphlets had as titles:

"Story of Rothschild 1, King of the Jews"; "Rothschild 1,—his Valets and his People"; "War to the Scoundrel"; "The Contest between Rothschild I and Satan"; "Universal Conspiracy of the Jews"; etc., etc.

Then there were yet men, who were not afraid to tell the truth. The people hated these aliens. The upper classes were not then as servile to the kings of gold, and the illustrious families had not then dishonored their name by selling themselves to the satanists.

The heir presumptive to the throne, the Duke of Orleans, was an avowed anti-semite. This Prince, so charming and so kind, treated writers and artists as equals, yet would never entertain a Jew.

In 1842, when Baron A. Rothschild (son of Nathan) wished to be present at the Chantilly races, the Duke refused to see him in his tribune. Everybody knew the feelings of the Duke regarding the Jews. The Royal Prince was troubled over their increasing evil influence and their desire for still more! He said:

"Those Jews violate power, crush the people and may turn against the innocent throne all the maledictions of an outraged nation"...

The noble Prince, like the Duchess d'Angouleme, believed in CHRIST's warning... But "accidentally," of course, the Duke,of Orleans perished in an "inexplicable" carriage accident in Neuilly....

And the nation, outraged by the artificial famine staged purposely by James Rothschild, "turned against the innocent throne all its maledictions!" Just as it happened in Russia in 1917.

Disraeli is proved to have been a cynical valet of Lionel.

Though having written so much about the insignificant details of Paris life, Disraeli does not dare to say a single word about the "mysterious" and tragic "accident" to the duke d'Orleans, who met with death by falling from an ordinary carriage (as P. Deschanel, the President of France did from a train) after his refusal to admit Anthony Rothschild to his box at the races at Chantilly.

But the Jewish instinct of revenge in Disraeli did not permit him to abstain from dancing on the grave of this enemy of his patrons: In a letter of October, 1842, Disraeli mentioned that "Anthony de Rothschild succeeded the Duke in his patronage of the turf."

A decade earlier the Hidden Hand murdered the Duc de Berry.

JAMES R. III, PLANS REVOLUTION OF 1848.

Honors and billions of money could not satisfy James, the satanist murderer. Satan urged bloodshed and James wished to break the Monarchy in France. He had had enough of being "Second" in Paris, when he "ought" to be the first. He read the "Protocols of the Learned Elders of Zion" and revived in his memory its prescription: "**Create want**", i.e. **famine!***)

This was so much easier as the harvest of 1846 was very poor and it suited the plan of James. He ordered one of his subaltern Jews, Ephrusi, to "corner" all the grain available; and being a true son of the father of lies, Ephrasi bought all the rotten grain and damaged flour as well. Becoming the sole master of the food market, James doubled and trebled prices, happy as a satanist, to see people starving to death and ready for a new bloody revolt.

James ordered his Jews Goudchaud, Cremieux and others who controlled the French Free-Masonry to prepare all their "Milukovs, Goudchkovs, Lvovs" and other bought valets free-masons to start a revolution and promised them instead of "30 silver coins", they would receive ministerial posts, which would yield that gold!

"A great Masonic Congress was held in 1847" (Deschamps, p. 281)

"Beyond the Masons and unknown to them, though formed generally from them, lay the deadly secret conclave, which nevertheless used and directed them for the ruin of the world, and their own selves" (a scientist G. F. Dillon, "The War of Anti-Crist with the Christian Civilization', p. 72).

The best British historian, Mrs. Nesta Webster in her "World Revolution" masterly describes all the insects and reptiles of the then Political Zoo, which produced the Revolution of 1848. But like other writers, she forgot the "Tigers" Rothschilds and wrote:

"Organized by the Secret Societies, directed by the Socialists, executed by the working men and aggravated by the intractable attitude of the King, the second great outbreak of World Revolution took place" (p. 129) Yes!

But why not mention, who headed these Secret Societies and, that the King was inspired by the same James, who led these societies and who was the chief promoter of the Revolution of 1848, as of all other bloodsheds, according to Disraeli!!! Mrs. Webster says:

"But the working classes were not admitted to the inner councils of the leaders: the place of the vanguard was on the barricades when the shooting began, not in the meetings , where the plan of campaign was drawn up"

If admitted in the meetings, the workmen might have exclaimed with Robespierre:

What are all these aliens (i. e. Jews) doing here.''

*) Just as in February 1917, the free masons, Bublikoff and others: all valets of Rothschild went over Russia and purposely stopped the food trains which were going to Petrograd, in order to provoke its population to revolt.

141

The workmen were only the "gun - fodder" of J. Rothschild.

The artificial starvation, contrived by James in order to provoke bloodshed, revolution and the downfall of the last French dynasty, enraged the people and might have cost the "lenders to Kings" very dearly. The people at last became very angry.

The palace of the Rothschilds in Suresnes (a suburb of Paris) was plundered and burned. Becoming frightened, the son of Am-schel was ready to flee from France, when the Perfect of Police, Caussidiere, put at his disposal a company of the Republic Guards, who day and night protected the baron's precious life against the rage of the poor. Caussidiere was appointed by the Hidden Hand.*)

As a reward to Caussidiere, when he was no more Prefect of Po-lice, James lent him $1000. But some people say, that he only began to buy wine from Caussidiere, who had started a wine shop. In any case, James's generosity was very meager. As soon as the danger was over, he pretended to forget the service rendered.

Naive people thought that the Revolution of 1848 would be fatal to Rothschild, especially immediately after the famine and "cor-nering" of grain, which had embittered the people, against the starvation practices of Laffitte street (where the Bank of Roths-child is).

But always "accidentally" some "Johnny on the spot", some Jews - Cremieux and Goudchaux climbed "accidentally" into the provisional Government of 1848, like Kerenski, a Jew into that of 1917. When Cremieux's name was proposed as a Member of the Goverument, the Assembly protested unanimously. But he went intc the room, where the Government was sitting and refused to withdraw, saying, that it was he and his friends (Rothschilds) who organized all the revolt.*)

Goudchaux, who snatched the portfolio of Finances was a broker for a small bank. He pitilessly exploited Parisian merchants in need, with the secret aid of Rothschild, who was a villainous usurer.

The "Archieves Israelites" assures us that Goudchaux "conce-ded" to the solicitations of the Provisional Government to accept the Ministry of Finance. But the truth is, that Rothschild imposed him on them. Meanwhile Lamartine seeing the Fatherland in dan-ger was crying :Let us save France!", Goudchaux had no other occupation, except to save Rothschild - his master.

*) In times of revolution authority remains with the greatest scoundrels'' (Danton).

THE "MYSTERIOUS" EXCLAMATION OF PROUDHON.

If James contemplated to flee from Paris, it was not only because of the revolt, provoked by his shameless speculation on the shortage of grain. In 1847 he endorsed a loan of 250 million francs. After November 1847 until February 1848 he was able to place this loan with a trivial profit of 18 millions.

But James did not consider that sufficient.

He kept the funds in his Bank, awaiting better times and when the Revolution broke out, he cynically refused the 170 millions.

J. Rothschild **simply declared himself bankrupt.**

The Government should have put him in the prison of Mazas, which had just been built.

But Goudchaux, a Jew, considered as did Rothschild, that a word given to a goy (Christian) was not obligatory upon a Jew because, according to the Talmud, it was only a "scrap of paper!" Not only did he secretly allow James, who had betrayed his engagements to the State, to participate in a new loan, but he himself even furnished him with funds to start a loan to Greece.

However, the anger of the people and this false "bankruptcy" compelled James to seek some oblivion and his "enthronement" in France had to be postponed for twenty years at least. Rothschilds, the leaders—rulers of the German Jews—Ashkenazim, found it wise to keep in the shadow and give the place to the Portugese Jews— the Sephardim, known as the "Jews of Saint-Simon".

This is why the famous Proudhon said after 1848:

"France has only changed her Jews"....

Just as in March 1917, the Jews Simonovitch (who guided Rasputin) and Manuiloff (who guided the Prime Minister of Russia— Stuermer) were "exchanged" for the Jew Kerensky, who became the Dictator of Russia until November, when he was "exchanged" for the Jews "Trotsky" (Bronstein) and Co.

Note well that Proudhon unlike Al. Lamartine was almost an anarchist and was the first to post a placard demanding the deposition of the King. The chief of Police Caussidiere, placed by Rothschild, was the first to proffer the word "Republic". In some book I read that **Caussidiere was a Jew!**..

From all these numerous proofs that the Jews are the organizers of all the bloodshed, as CHRIST pointed it out (St. John, VIII,44) could we not deduce **without the smallest doubt,** that it will be Jews, who will plunge the United States into an ocean of blood in the nearest future, unless the Americans open their eyes and drop their blind groundless optimism....

L. Rothschild continues his revelations:

"There has been no friendship between the Court of St. Petersburgh and my family." (p. 251). No! It was a perpetual assault against the Romanovs; these "Fair Angels" as the people of Europe called them.

And that is why the Czars have all been exterminated.

"The world is governed by very diffrent personages from what is imagined by those who are not behind the scenes" ("Coningsby", p. 252).

explains Sidonia-Rothschild—and develops his main idea, that "a superior race" (Jewish) ought to govern the world and that "the Jewish mind exercises a vast influence on the affairs of Europe."

That is why Europe is going to destruction.

Indeed, too vast, and not only in Europe, if one can believe the words of Bernard M. Baruch, a Jew, who "spat" in the face of the American Senate, that he (and not the American President) was "the most powerful man" in 1918.

And the Senators seemed to find it quite normal ...

The declarations of "Sidonia" were published by Disraeli in 1844 and no Britisher had understood, that it was L. Rothschild's confessions, betrayed by the Jew Disraeli, until in the fall of 1920 my 16 large articles. appeared in the "Plain English" of London.*)

Since the American Revolution the Jews have also been the real rulers of America and their power is constantly growing and becomes deadly in every sense, as the Jews themselves confirm it.

Nobody knows where this sinister band of Rothschilds, through Disraeli, Bismarck, Gamberle-Gambetta and similar Jews, would have brought the world, but for the most Christian, patriotic and energetic resistance of the Romanovs, and partly of the great Britisher Mr. H. Gladstone.

Sir Henry Lucy (the "Westminster Gazette" of Sept. 22, 1920) describes that Disraeli on Jan. 20, 1835, met "Gladstone, who had not until then even noticed the Jew."

"They met again at a dinner in 1850, Gladstone being particularly agreeable."

He did not then realize what a hyena he had met; but he knew well, who was behind Disraeli.

"If we ignore the existence of this concerted (Judeo-Mongol) attack and neglect to examine the nature and history of the forces by which Christian civilisation is now threatened, we deserve ALL , that the International Revolutionists are working to bring about." (Lord Sydenham, House of Lords).

*) Note that the French Revolution of 1789 was all prepared at the great Masonic Congress in 1782 at Wilhelmsbad (then a palace of the Langrave of Hesse, managed by Amschel Rothschild). This Congress decided the death of the three best Christian Monarchs, who later on were foully murdered...

"MYSTERY" OF BISMARCK'S SUCCESS· HE WAS TRAPPED.

Lionel satanized Disraeli and took him often to Paris, where he introduced him to James Rothschild III. They were visited by a Jew, Count Arnim, the Prussian Minister ("Lord Beaconsfield Letters", Dec. 2, 1842). Through Lionel, Disraeli became his friend. The Jew, Soult, was a Cabinet Minister of France and spoke much, perhaps, of his son, or the son of his Jewess-mistress, ex-Menken* — Mrs. Bismarck. Thus this gang of Jews decided to capture young Bismarck, who was in great need and was, at least, a half Jew, who already in 1839 was "compelled to struggle against disaster, which threatened his property". In 1840 "there followed a series of infernal raids and orgies, which were the terror of the country".

But the Rothschilds, Disraeli, Soult, Arnim were already watching him and all sought to use him. Even in 1839 at Aachen Bismarck had shown himself as rebellious, as had Disraeli, who in his poem wrote "blessings to the regicide dagger." But James required that Bismarck and Disraeli display "arch-Conservatism" (which then was winning) in order to slip into the high society and to acquire power.

Therefore, Disraeli and Bismarck dropped the hymns to "regicide daggers" and became ultra conservatists· Both were ordered to become very "mundane". Oscar Arnim married Bismarck's beloved sister Malvina in 1844. He was a member of the Reichstag and a Jew, according to Disraeli ("Coningsby," p. 252).

Bismarck was entirely under their influence.

Some readers might find a contradiction between the warning of CHRIST, that "the Jews are doing the devil's lust of murder" and the facts, which prove that the two chief "reactionaries" Disraeli and Bismarck were Jews.** I must remind that in the same time there were the Jews: Karl Marx, Ferdinand Lasalle (an agent of Bismarck), Engels and others, who were the leaders of the then "bolsheviks". And both Jews: Bismarck and Disraeli did their best to put their two countries into wars.

*) "The Jewish Tribune" of New York confirms on January 9, 1925, that the Menkens are Jews and descendents from the Jew Haim Solomon, who practically "gave all his fortune" to start a revolution in America and at the same time "remained the richest man in America," which proves that he must have given Rothschild's money, and not his own — to start a war!

**) Lionel Rothschild ("Sidonia") assured Disraeli, that the Jews are religious and "essentially monarchical," and, however he said, the Jews are giving funds to undermine every Church and every Government" ("Coningsby," p. 249).

145

"TO STAGE A REVOLT — INFLAME PASSIONS·"

Lionel confessed that the revolutions are not caused by the discontent of a people, but are purposely staged. By?....

Rothschild remarks, that England was very rich and comfortable in 1640:

"Yet she was on the eve of the greatest and most violent changes that she had yet experienced. The imagination of England rose against the government. When that faculty is astir in a nation, it will sacrifice even physical comfort to follow its IMPULSES."

"Accidentally," of course, the Jews (expelled in 1290 from England by King Edward I. because according to Mr. John Speed in his "History of Great Britain," they ate the English nation to the bones") wished by any means to re enter into England, and "accidentally" of course, the revolution in 1640 returned them to England or better to say returned England to them.

Lionel said also, that the religious question does not play a role in the form of government.

"That would be recurring to the old error of supposing that you can find national content in political institutions". Because reason does not influence a nation.

"We are not indebted to the reason of man for any of great achievements which are the landmarks of human action and human progress. Man is only truly great when he acts from the passions; never irresistible but when he appeals to the imagination. England is governed by Downing Street, once it was governed by the Kings".

Rothschild is sure that each "Slaughter" and "bleeding white" of Christians is "human progress," i. e., Jewish progress, because the Jews assert, that the Christians are a lower order of creatures.

Later Lionel offered "Coningsby"-Disraeli his help to reach the highest pinacle, i. e. to assume command of Downing Street and thus of England; but, of course, on condition that he obey the orders of the Rothschilds, as Disraeli and all his followers have done down to Mr. Lloyd George, who according even to a socialist Mr. John Spargo, is following Disraeli's, i. e. Rothschild's politics. ("Independent", April, 9, 1921).

Even when recently Mr. Bonar Low wished to become Prime Minister, according to The Christian Monitor, of Nov. 11, 1922, he declared, that he would follow the policy of Disraeli (read of Rothschild). And Bonar Law became the British Prime Minister· Lionel openly bribed Disraeli ("Coningsby," p. 452).

In 1878 'at Berlin Disraeli "controlled many Cabinets."

DISRAELI EXPLOITING OLD WOMEN.

Mr. Buckle, in the "**Life of Disraeli**," implies that "the secret of this great career" was the gift of this Jew to love simultaneously **four** ladies, whose combined ages approached 300 years.

Thus his pathologic capacities surpassed those of Rasputin.... **Mr.** Buckle's description of Mr. Disraeli portrays the latter as being very similar to Rasputin. He says about Queen Victoria:

"None of the Monarch's Ministers has ever shown her more consideration and kindness than he." "Words are too weak to say what the Monarch feels (after Disraeli's death); how overhelmed she is with the terrible, irreparable loss, which is a national one. His kindness and devotion to the Monarch on all and every occasion; his anxiety to lighten her cares and difficulties, she never, never can forget, and feels her loss cruelly. Four days after his funeral she visited and wept over his grave, and laid on his coffin a wreath; and from her privy purse, she erected a personal memorial to him with the noble text, etc."

Disraeli flattered Her Majesty by saying: "**We** authors, Madam", and then he boasted, that "the Queen paid me a visit in my bedchamber."

"Disraeli was never in the least shy; he did not insinuate; he spoke in terms most unconventional; and the Queen thought she had never in her life seen so amusing a person."

Just as Rasputin spoke with the Empress of Russia:

Just as the Jew Balsamo with Marie Antoinette:

And as the Jew Bauer with the Empress Eugenie. Disraeli, on the one hand played the role of clown, on the other he tried to reach the Queen's heart by writing her most sentimentally.

Nothing proves "his devotion to the Queen was sincere."

Mr. Lewis Apjohn in his "The Lord Beaconsfield" (p. 66) states, that Disraeli was a liar, and this is proved by Mr. O'Connor, M. P. and by Mr. Bright.

Mr. W. Gladstone declared, that there were only two things Lord Beaconsfield cared for, and about which he was thoroughly in earnest — his wife and his race. (p. 19).

Disraeli obsequiously flattered the Queen's poor book. On receiving it he at once wrote to her, that only the Bible, Dante and Shakespeare could compare with it.

THE RITUAL MURDER OF DAMASCUS (1840)

"Every foreigner, who glorifies Sunday (i. e. a Christian) must be killed without asking him" (the Talmud, Sahanderin, p. 58).

Since immemorial times Jews have committed "Ritual Murders," i. e. bleeding white Christians, whose blood was collected for ritual purposes. There is a satanic meaning in this. Satan asked Faust to sign his obligation not with ink, but with blood. (The Jews took every precaution, that such crimes should remain hidden*). But there are too many proofs, that the "ritual murder" is practiced even to-day.

"Why do we not discover it?", an American may ask. It is because the American press is so enslaved by the Jews, that everything disagreable to them can be at once suppressed. Well, I am convinced that the crime of Anvers street in Chicago in 1921 by a Jewess Pinhes was a failed "ritual murder".... But the father of the victim, a policeman McLauglin, entered the house of the Jewess and she killed the child by suffocating it.

On February 5, 1840 in Damascus (Asia Minor) a monk, Father Thomas, and his servant both disappeared. Count de Ratti-Menton, Consul of France, informed the Governor General, Cherif-Pasha, who ordered a public investigation. A barber Suleiman, a Jew, denounced 7 other Jews and said, that he was ordered to cut the throat of Rev. Thomas, who was tied with ropes. After all the blood was collected, the body was cut into pieces and thrown into the sewer, where it was found.

"What is done with the blood?" the Consul asked.

The blood is used for Fath' ir (holiday of the Azymes)—, was the answer of the Jews. After long inquiries the Jews confessed that they killed the monk to obtain his blood, which they put in a large bottle and gave to the chief rabbi.

The accused said, that the use of Christian blood is the secret of the grand rabbis. Ten Jews were condemned to death. But the Rothschilds were alarmed and sent their most tricky agents: Moses Montefiore (cousin of Lionel) A. Cremieux and Munck with unlimited credits to save and exonerate the condemned Jews· They went to Mahomet Ali (Vice Roy). All their gold could not induce even him (who sorely needed money) to exonerate the criminals, but only to free them.

*) There is a series of books exposing the "Ritual Murders:" "Le Crime Rituel Chez Les Juifs", by Albert Monniot; "Le Crime Rituel. La Trahison Juive," etc., "La Renaissance Francaise," Passage des Panoramas, Paris.

148

BISMARCK CREATED BY THE ROTHSCHILDS.

The late Dictator of Germany Rathenau, a Jew, wrote:

"Only 300 men, each of whom knows all the others, govern the fate of Europe. They elect their successors from their entourage. These German Jews have the means in their hands of putting an end to the form of Government of any State which proves unreasonable" ("Plain English" June, 11, 1921).

Everything Christian is utterly "unreasonable" for a Jew.

As the Czar of Russia did not know any of the Rothschilds, it means, that speaking about those "who govern the fate of Europe," Rathenau did not include the Czar. So much the more as the Czars did not "elect their successors," the latter being indicated by the priority of birth.

Thus Rathenau only repeated the declaration of Disraeli, that "the world is governed by very different personages from what is imagined by those who are not behind the scenes," i. e. not by the Czars, Emperors, Presidents, but by "the 300 German Jews," who compose the World Government, known as the "Hidden Hand."

Forty years after the declaration of Disraeli and forty years before the statement of Rathenau, Bismarck said the same:

"To those who insisted upon treating Bismarck as a great political genius, a man of fate, marked, like Napoleon, with the seal of a tragic predestination, Bismarck would repeat, that he did not believe in great providential men; that according to his belief, political celebrities owed their reputations, if not to chance, at least to circumstances which they themselves could not have foreseen."

Is it not the Rathenau idea, that the "successors in governing the fate of Europe (and of America, of course) are being elected by the 300 German Jews"?

Soult, a Jew, of the "300" was perhaps the real father of Bismarck. However, Mrs. Bismarck was Soult's mistress. And Soult might "elect Bismarck as his successor," as one of the "300" in governing the fate of Europe. The same with Disraeli and a series of Jews, who played a great role in the World affairs. Soult died in 1851.

What Bismarck practically says is nearly this:

"Not my talents and capacities made me great. But the fact that my mother was the mistress of Soult, one of the '300', who all helped me".

"There is no error so vulgar as to believe, that revolutions are occasioned by economical causes. They come in, doubtless, to precipitate a catastrophe; very rarely do they occasion one" ("Coningsby", p. 238).

NAPOLEON III. WAS NOT A NAPOLEONIDE.

I have told how Amschel Rothschild I, little by little became disappointed in his champion "exterminator of Christians," Napoleon I, who ceased to be agnostic and anti-Catholic: and began to increase his girth and had no more enthusiasm for shedding blood.

Amschel decided to de-throne the Corsican genius.

However, so much money and effort had been spent on making Napoleon that Amschel looked on him as his pawn.

Disraeli and Bismarck became agents of Rothschild. Now I shall throw light on the third agent of the Jewish World Emperors, the strange personality of the supposed nephew of the great Napoleon.

The next Napoleonide ought to be entirely Amschel's!

The historians often falsified the facts·

His mother was Hortense, step daughter of Napoleon I.

But who was the real father of Napoleon III.?

Cardinal Fesch (a half-brother of Napoleon I.'s mother (Letitia Ramolini) states in his narratives:

"When it comes to fixing the father of her children, Hortense is always confused about her datas."

The famous physician of Napoleon I., Corvisart des Marets, declared openly in 1808:

"The King of Holland is an invalid, a scrofulous subject, impotent.... I would swear to it."

"He was the **putative** father of Napoleon III.," the "Universal Encyclopaedia" says of Louis Bonaparte, Hortense's husband.

The King Louis of Holland, brother of Napoleon I., disliked his wife — Hortense — and he admits it many times in his "Documents Historiques." From 1802 to 1807 they only lived together four months, at three different periods separated by long intervals. But the fact is: Louis and Hortense never actually cohabited together, because they were repulsive to each other.

It is also a notorious fact, that Hortense distributed her affections somewhat promiscuously....

Josephine, her mother, was repeatedly unfaithful.

Well, like mother, like daughter, they had the same passionate temperament. Most of the people who surrounded Napoleon I., have denied a liaison between him and his step daughter.

Let us suppose that Napoleon I., was the father of Hortense's first two sons born in 1801 — but, who was the father of the third son, who later became Napoleon III.?

NAPOLEON III "MYSTERY". WAS HE A ROTHSCHILD ?

A **Danish** lexicographer says he was "probably the fruit of her (Hortense's) liaison with the Dutch admiral Verhuel."

The first son of Hortense, Charles, died in 1807.

He could possibly have been the son of Napoleon I.

Napoleon I was much abroad in the summer of 1807 - in Tilsit and elsewhere. When he returned to Paris, Hortense was at Cauterets in the South of France. Thus the attempts of the partisans of Napoleon III to prove that he was the son of the greatest warrior, fall flat.

It was not Napoleon I. It was not King Louis!

Who was the real father of Napoleon III?

"All is darkness and mystery", say the historians.

As always they overlook the "Tigers" in the Zoo!

There was a conspiracy of silence about them.

King Louis of Holland preserved in his apartments all the portraits of his relatives and children, except that of the future Napoleon III.

If Napoleon III had been the child of Napoleon I, then Louis would have liked him, as he did the other sons of the Corsican.

And in the Vatican's archives is to be found a letter of Louis in which he calls Hortense a **Messalina.**

Napoleon III was not a **Napoleonide** at all!

On April 20th, 1808, the future Napoleon III was born in the very **den of the Rothschilds** in their hotel in the rue Cerutti, now rue Lafitte, at No. 17 (Baron d'Ambes, p, 47)

Why did the Queen of Holland go to a private House?

Thus he began his career in the Rothschild Bank.

His father "de jure" was the invalid King of Holland.

The Empress Josephine was this child's grandmother.

But who was the real father of Napoleon III?

Surely it was not the decrepit King of Holland.

Was it one of the young Rothschilds, the youngest of whom Jacob (James) was then 16 years old, his brother Karl, 20 years, or the 31 years old Nathan, who constantly rushed from Frankfurt to London through Paris - Dunkerk. Nathan personified the type of an "itinerant jeweller and moneylender", described by Mrs. Nesta Webster in her "World Revolution" (p. 87).

HOW THE ROTHSCHILDS CREATED AN EMPEROR

The Rothschilds have been the greatest smugglers of sensual "love," as well as of goods. They have with satanic design poisoned the French and English aristocracy by infusing into their veins as much Jewish blood as possible.

Since 1798 Nathan was constantly travelling between Frankfort and Paris. How could this re-incarnation of Satan, watching day and night what was going on in France (which Amschel granted to his beloved Benjamin-James) neglect such a chance to "create" his own "Napoleonide"?

The Imperial Police in Paris, faithfully registered the movements there of the young Rothschilds, owners of an unheard-of fortune, then one billion of francs. Those young devils had been ordered by Amschel to have their own French Emperor, and above all to humiliate the very "anti-semitic" **Napoleon I.**

Hortense was the easiest woman to conquer.

Her revenues were never sufficient to pay her debts and expenses. And she sought to seek the aid of the Jewish usurers.

And she constantly appealed to the Rothschilds.

The Jewish blood of Napoleon III. soon revealed itself.

Thus, he hated all studies, except German (Yiddish).[*]

This is confirmed by the Abbe Bertrand, his teacher.

The story about admiral Verhuel is a mere screen.

This middle-aged, torpid and penniless admiral could not pose as a rival to the fiery young asiatics, with their fabulous fortune and desperate desire at any cost to have their own French Emperor. In their house remained the famous "sofa" on which the Rothschilds received ladies, who needed their financial support. ....

The truth was too compromising for Napoleon III. and that is why the most polite and reserved Nicholas I. called him a "parvenu." And in his features Napoleon III. had nothing "Napoleonic." **He looked as if a Rothschildian!.**

Since his birth Verhuel became a fiery "anti-semite."

It is a clear case of atavism, that although he knew that Napoleon I. was ruined, and Napoleon II. even murdered by the Rothschilds, he always appealed to them for guidance.

One of the true Bonapartes, a nephew of Napoleon I. nicknamed "Plon Plon" never wished to recognize Napoleon III.

"Napoleon III. had not one honest streak in his character" (Mr. **Cyrus** Hamlin, D. D., in his "The Armenian Massacres," p. 356)

*) For every orthodox Jew — Frankfort — remains his "Mecca."

THE ROTHSCHILDS OF VIENNA.

"The Jews for centuries played a very distinguished part in the affairs of Austria, and in Vienna especially, were to be found in the highest circles of society, wielding not only a large influence, but also holding prominent positions among the leading public men. The great authority they commanded was due simply to their money. They know how to amass fortunes by evil means, for in the Frankfort "Relationen" of 1667 it was stated that 'Hirshel Mayer had been arrested for having defrauded the Emperor of no less than two million gulden, contributions of coreligionists.''

"Joseph II., in 1783, created the first Jewish baron — the banker Joseph M. Arnstein, whose wife, Fanny Itzig of Berlin, was a special favorite of the Emperor, (just as the wife of Karl Rothschild was the mistress of the King of Naples). During the Congress of Vienna the families of the sovereign money kings, Arnstein and Eskeles were conspicuous. Their wives were daughters of the rich Jew, Itzig of Berlin, well known during the reign of Frederick II.'' (J. Reeves, p. p. 274-275)

"Under the rule of Maria-Theresa and Joseph II. Austria s finances assumed a flourishing aspect. Its loans were arranged through the Dutch bankers Hope and Goll. Austrian bonds were in great favor and saleable at par.'' (p. 276)

But the Jews Arnstein, Eskeles, etc., offered not only money, but their wives as premiums, and Austrian financial affairs entered a decline.

Salomon Rothschild eclipsed all the Viennese Jews. He negotiated the Government loans at 60 and forced them up in the market until they were redeemed at 109. Soon after Salomon ruined all the bankers of Vienna, even the Jewish, just as Nathan did in London. Many were arrested or ran away. He also established a Fire Insurance Company. In 1836, Salomon began to plunder Austria through the building of railroads. He robbed everybody on the Stock Exchange. The Jews Brentano, and later Morpurgo, were his agents in Trieste.

After the death of Salomon the bank passed to his son Anselm (Amschel), until he died in 1879, when his 3 sons Ferdinand. Nathan and Salomon Albert succeeded him. The youngest was the most satanic and he ruled the bank. Ferdinand became an English citizen, and married Evelyn, daughter of Lionel.

The Rothschilds begun by making Metternich their tool. Then they imposed a Jew Ch. Bombelles as a member of the Habsburgs' House by marrying him to Marie-Louise, and making his cousin, Ph. Bombelles, the "satanizer" of Franz Joseph. **Thus the Habsburgs were destroyed "from within!...**

"ONLY BLOOD AND IRON," BISMARCK'S MOTTO.

"**Only blood and iron** could improve the condition of Germany," Bismarck said in 1849.

When the list of a suggested new Cabinet was presented to Frederick William IV. in the same year 1849, he drew a thick line through Bismarck's name and wrote:

"Red-hot reactionary. Likes the smell of blood."

As a Jew,* according to CHRIST, he was a "mankiller."

"Every foreigner, who glorifies Sunday (i. e. a Christian) must be killed without asking him," states the Talmud, chapter Sanhedrin, p. 58 ("La Vieille France N-276).

In 1847, Bismarck conciliated Conservatives by his simulated violence against the Liberals (as Disraeli) and won the favor of the King of Prussia. Thanks to the efforts of the above Jews, Bismarck married Johanna Puttkamer in 1847, a remarkable woman, who moderated his Asiatic Jewish outbursts of fury, which otherwise would have ruined his career.** He knew in advance from Disraeli all about the revolt of 1848, exploited it and placed himself at the head of he Prussian reactionaries. In 1849 he founded in Berlin the "Gazette of the Cross," which was to defend the "divine right of Kings."

"He had himself elected to the 2-d Prussian Chamber" ("The Real Bismarck"). In 1851 he attended the Diet of Frankfort as deputy. Count Arnim ably assisted Bismarck and recommended him to the presiding Minister of Prussia, Manteufel, and to the future Emperor Wilhelm I. Many flattering German authors have written that Bismarck "triumphed by sheer capacity." We know how. All the "300" supported him. He repeated:

"I sold myself to Satan (Rothschild) but he is German" (Jew).

"When Bismarck was old, his eyes never lost their amazing power"...
"He had by nature a contempt for anything weak, sentimental, and among his the objects of his disdain he included several of the Christian virtues" (Prof. F. M. Bowicke, "Bismarck and the German Empire," p. 5)

"The Jews were the only people who could exploit Bismarck in such a way, that all the liberal reforms in Germany after the Sadowa (a battle, where the Prussians defeated the Austrians in 1866) — introduced by Bismarck — served all to the benefit of the Jews." (Valbert in the "La Revue des Deux Mondes" in 1880. vol. 28, p. 203).

*) Was Bismarck the son of the Jew Marshall Soult, nobody can tell. But doubtless he was the son of the Jewess Menken, and according to the Jewish laws, a son of a Jewess is a Jew.

) It was not easy, because the intuition of the father in law — Herr Puttkamer made him think persistently that Bismarck was a "devil.**"

THE JEWS OF ST. SIMON

When Napoleon III, became President in 1848 and Emperor in 1851, James Rothschild III., because of the people's anger caused by the artificial famine, thought better to "go into the shadow," giving place to the Portuguese Jewry, represented by the Pereires, Millauds, Solars, Mires and others.

For the method of usury Rothschild substituted State loans. The Pereires created a new financial system: under high sounding shibboleths such as: "the Beneficence of credit," "Circulation of capital," etc. They enveloped it all in a sort of philosophy and created a special literature: "the rapproachement of nations," "end of pauperism," and so on. They showed to their intimate friends the skull of Saint-Simon, whose ideas the Pereires had simply appropriated, and which enriched Israel in the XIX Century.

Napoleon III. was himself a dreamer,—a kind of Saint·Simon— and had fatally preferred the method of those Jews, who touched socialism and literature, to the rude barbarian German-Jew, who could only offend his "humanitarianism." He knew, that the Rothschilds upset Napoleon I. and they were anxious, lest he might take revenge.

The Pereires with the gang of Jews from the South in their train cleverly took advantage of this monarch's frame of mind to plunder France. The Pereire, Mires & Co. became the "benefactors" of the people by emptying their pockets through all kind of public subscriptions.

Baron James was watching the new chief of State and taking time to digest the billions which were "burdening the Rothschilds. So James permitted his southern coreligionists to "operate·" He continued, however, to deal in funds, whenever occasion offered.

Count de Morny the right hand and brother of Napoleon III., happening to want some information, went to the office of Rothschild to get it. Rothschild received him without deference, merely saying:

"Will you take a chair?" and continued to write. At last Napoleon III's foster brother was tired of waiting and exclaimed:

"You are addressing the Comte de Morny."

"Will you then have the kindness to take two chairs," said Rothschild with irony; and returned to his letters.

"De-Christianize, and all the kingdoms are thine." (Satan).

155

THE YOUTH OF CZAR NICHOLAS I.

Nicholas I., born in 1796, was the son of Paul I.

The historian Schilder says in truth:

"Nicholas indeed lived and died as a true knight."

"Nicholas was passionately devoted to his 'lioness nurse,' as he called Miss Lyon, daughter of a Scottish sculptor" ("The Court of Russia" by an excellent historian, Mr. E. A. Brayley Hodgets)

"Her attachment to her august charge amounted to a passion, a fanaticism. Nicholas was ardently devoted to his nurse — indeed he was ardent in all his attachments, and cherished his respect for her and the memory of his former feelings up to the day of her death in 1842... The heroic, chivalrous, bold and frank nature of this 'lioness-foster-mother' exercised a very strong and happy influence on the formation of the character of the Russian eagle and hero."

In his travel diary in 1816, Nicholas wrote:

"The wealthy Poles had never exhibited any loyalty to Russia, had all sworn allegiance to Napoleon I. The general ruination of the peasantry is attributed to the Jews. They exploit to the utmost the unfortunate population. They are everything; and they are so tricky in squeezing and cheating the people. They are regular LEECHES, who suck up everything and completely exhaust this province (Poland)." (p. 161).

That is why Lionel Rothschild said to Disraeli:

"There has been no friendship between the Court of St. Petersburg and my family; and our representations in favour of Polish Hebrews, have not been very agreeable to the Czar." (Coningsby, p. 251).

He would like to make of each Jew—"leech"—a banker!

"Nicholas went to England in 1816 and earned universal praise and respect by his personality and courteous manners. He has pleased everybody by his amiable ways and his noble nature and frankness. Everybody has been struck by his distinguished and modest bearing and his easy conversation and sound sense." ("The Court of Russia" p. 167).

The Princess Royal was married to Prince Leopold, who describes Nicholas "as an exceptionally handsome and charming young man, as straight as a pine. He was very abstemious in his food and drank only water."

The lady-in-waiting, Mrs. Campbell, noted for her severity in judging men, said:

"Oh! what a charming creature. He will become the most handsome man in Europe."

Nicholas—all his life was greatly devoted to his family.

Such was Nicholas I. His accursed enemy and real murderer, Rothschild, was described by Disraeli as "a man without affections," whom the individual never touched. Woman was to him a toy, man a machine." ("Coningsby," p. 217).

"Nicholas was married to Princess Charlotte of Prussia, whose tender and affectionate husband, he ever after remained." (p. 169).

NICHOLAS I. DESCRIBED BY ENGLISHMEN AS "DEMI-GOD"

He made his wife very happy because of "his frank cheerfulness and love of fun."

The first trouble of Nicholas occurred when Alexander I. died, making him heir to the throne, instead of Constantine, who was the elder. Nicholas was then only 28 years old...

Nicholas as all the Romanovs, and with the highest principles of a Romanov, did not wish to accept the throne and only the great insistence of his mother, and of Constantine himself, and the conspiracy of the Free-Masons, known as Decabrist revolution, forced him to assume power.

An officer, Rostovzev, warned him of the plot to make the transfer of the oath of allegiance the excuse for revolt. Nicholas told him not to name anybody, if he considered that by so doing he would be acting dishonourably.

The French Ambassador, Count La Ferronnaye, wrote:

"The Emperor combines in his person all the best qualities of a truly chivalrous and most noble-minded Monarch, with those of deep feeling, and besides those he is endowed with extraordinary energy. This Prince is in the full acceptation of the word, one of the most estimable men ever known"!

Yes! But he was "too-Christian" and so he perished.

A. de Custine, who travelled much in Russia states in his clever book "La Russie En 1839," that in the Czar's estates the poor peasants were so exceptionally kindly treated that in 1839 a deputation of the peasants came to the Czar to beg him that their districts would be added to the royal domains.

Nicholas I. received them most kindly and all his sympathies were with the people. It was he who visited Robert Owen at New Lanark to study his schemes of social reforms. He answered to the peasants with great gentleness, that he regretted he could not buy all Russia, but he added:

"I hope that the time will come when every peasant of this Empire will be free; if it only depended on me Russians would enjoy from to-day the independence that I wish for them and that I am working with all my might to procure for them in the future."

James's satanic hatred of the most Christian and most peace loving Romanovs was well known. This made him hesitant about grabbing the construction of the railroads in Russia. But a group of Jewish bankers headed by Pereire and Stieglitz in St. Petersburg succeeded in obtaining a concession for the construction of a network of railways in Russia. James' hatred against the Tsars was thus furthermore increased and his press was ordered to attack the Romanovs.

ROMANOVS DISTATESFUL TO ROTHSCHILDS

Lord Loftus, the British Ambassador in Russia, wrote:

"Nicholas I. was the most majestic and most handsome figure of a man, who ever occupied a throne. There was something eminently grand about him. He was a fine character, noble hearted, generous and much beloved by those in his intimacy. His severity, was rather obligatory than voluntary. The Tsar talks with vivacity and with perfect simplicity and good breeding. Everything he says betrays a brilliant intellect, but he is never guilty of common-place jokes. He is said to be an excellent engineer and a good mathematician. He reads a good deal. He possesses in a supreme degree that power of attention, which is nothing else but Genius."

Another eminent Britisher, Mr. Edward Tracy Turnerelli stated: ("What I know of the late Emperor Nicholas"):

"It is a positive truth, that during my long sojourn in Russia all that I witnessed, and, all that I heard, was favourable to the Czar. I heard of no bad action. Wherever I went the tone in which Nicholas was spoken of was one of unwearied admiration and respect. With the lower classes this was even carried to a degree amounting to worship."

"No one can deny that in European events, Emperor Nicholas I. influence has been a moral and religious one, opposed to everything immoral and impious" (Blaze de Bury in "Germany as It Is", p. 321).

And this man was described by the valets of the Rothschilds, as a "narrow minded monster" . . .

To the Imperial Council, the Czar Nicholas I. repeated:

"I love truth, and, relying upon your experience and loyalty, I invite you to express your opinions with absolute frankness and without any regard to my own convictions."

"The Czar was animated in all he did by a devout spirit of Christian humility and a profound desire to act justly and wisely." (Korff).

Disraeli describes the dispositions of James and Nathan and their devilish underground organization. Now all the power of the Rothschilds was directed to destroy Nicholas I.

One of the main objects of the World Jewish conspiracy of the Rothschilds was to prevent the operation of the wise axiom of H. M. King George III. Everything was done in order to compel England and Russia to fight. It was a delight to the Rothschilds, with their countless agents, to organize awful massacres of the Christians by the Turks, and thus to awaken Russia from her lazy dreaming, and provoke her Christian sentiments and indignation.

After the Empress Elisabeth refused to accept incomes from the foes of CHRIST and because her heirs continued the same distrust of the Jews, the Rothschilds invented and spread their motto:

"A great Russia is a danger to England."

THE "ANTI-WAR" CZAR NICHOLAS I.

"While Emperor Nicholas distinguished Joukovsky (a poet) and even confided to him the education of the heir-apparent, he could treat other poets with considerable severity. For example Polejayeff, a student, who wrote a most scurrilous poem against the Tsarina and spread it, felt the Tsar's severity. The Tsar called Polejayeff, and ordered him to read aloud his insulting poem. The Emperor then said: "I will give you a chance to purify and redeem yourself". He kissed him on the forehead and dismissed him. Soon the young poet was appointed as a non-commissioned officer to an infantry regiment." ("The Court of Russia", p. 266).

A few months later he was promoted officer...

Such was the "barbarian cruelty" of Czar Nicholas I.

This recognition by Alexander I. of CHRIST as "**Supreme Leader**" of his Holy Alliance, brought the death sentence to this most chivalrous man.

And the bold declaration of "Anti-War" Nicholas I.:

"**I shall fire on the first who fires,**" paralyzed at once the efforts of the Rothschilds to murder the Christians, by starting a new war. These words, uttered in 1850, "**saved Europe from a War,**" when the Prussians had invaded Hesse, according to Charles Lowe in his "**Prince Bismarck,**" (p. 108).

The Rothschilds at once mobilized their champions.

Bismarck was elected as Deputy to Frankfort in 1851.

Napoleon III. was made Emperor, December 2nd, 1851.

Lord Russell's Government resigned Feb. 23rd, 1852.

Disraeli became Chancellor of the Exchequer in 1852.

As soon as Disraeli became influential thanks to Lionel and several old women of high standing, his first satanic work was to exploit his friendship with Louis Napoleon, prepared by Lionel.

"Napoleon was the companion of Mr. Disraeli's youth" (Mr. L. Apjohn, p. 167, in his "Earl of Beaconsfield").

"French affairs were the subject of frequent discussion in England, in which Mr. Disraeli took part. Napoleon gradually obtained the goodwill of the English public beginning with the Court and Society." (p. 168).

They were associated in the same free-masonic Lodge.

"Napoleon III. had a personal grudge against Emperor Nicholas, who addressed him 'Sire and Good Friend' instead of 'Brother,' as is customary among monarchs. Though Napoleon answered him, acknowledging the compliment implied from the fact, that one may choose one's friends, but not one's brothers, yet he never forgot the slight." ("Secret Diplomacy," p. 56, by Dr. P. S. Reinsch).

This was exposed by the Jews as one of the reasons, why Napoleon allowed himself to be persuaded by the Hidden Hand to declare war on Russia. The second reason, according to the liars, was the desire of Napoleon III. to show himself a hero·

ROTHSCHILDS START THE WAR IN CRIMEA—"WAR OF CRIME"

Endless calumnies were rumored against the Romanovs. Every author knowing this, has kept silent about the good side of the Romanovs, and blackened all their deeds.

Disraeli with typical Jewish boastfulness explains in his book the vast underground organization of the Rothschilds. It was a trifle, a joke, for them to induce the Turks, to organise massacres of the Christians, and thus provoke Russia. This done, it was easy to persuade Napoleon III., that his new throne needed military glory and that "he ought to defend the Holy Places." Thus "the Greatest Murderers of Christians" through Disraeli, induced also England to foully attack Russia.

Napoleon III. was a member of the Carbonari Lodges, and according to Disraeli, these were supported by the Rothschilds. Thus the war in Crimea was organised and started—a true war of **Jewish Crime**, which was the tragic mother of all the wars that followed, not excluding the last Great War, which alone cost the Christians 40,000,000 in casualties and $350 billions in monetary losses.

All this has been done by the Rothschilds!

"Nicholas I. had done ALL he could to prevent the war," stated even an Englishman, Mr. Brayley Hodgets, in his most interesting book "The Court of Russia," (p. 50).

Since the "Distribution of the World" by Amschel Mayer R. I. and the overthrow of Napoleon I. by Amschel's five sons, these World Emperors have been disobeyed and hindred only by Russia and the United States.

And James resolved to destroy these two great powers.

As Napoleon III. was probably a Rothschildian (illegitimate **son** of Nathan) and as he pretended to be a good free-mason, i.e., a servant of the Hidden Hand, he was not opposed by James in seizing power in 1848, when James was in panic, and because he knew, that Napoleon could be inspired to make new wars.

And the Rothchilds through Disraeli induced England to basely shed blood, ostensibly to prevent Russia putting an end to the "mankilling" of the Christians in Turkey, but chiefly to prevent an Anglo-Russian Union! Disraeli was saying, that a "great Russia was a danger," a lie, repeated by the Hidden Hand, in order to ruin Russia, which the Rothschilds achieved in 1917.

The Jews also organized pogroms in order to irritate all the other nations against Russia.

160

NICHOLAS I. BETRAYED BY HIS JEW MINISTER.

Even the worst foes of Nicholas I. admit:

"He did not want the Crimean War; he had an honest and sincere respect and admiration for the English people, and earnestly desired to cement these personal feelings by a political alliance." ("The Court of Russia," p. 272)

Lord Loftus in his "Diplomatic Reminiscences," wrote:

"Had the four Powers declared to the Emperor, that the passage of the Pruth would be regarded by them as a casus belli, it is very certain that the Emperor would not have crossed the Pruth, and war would have been averted. But he was misled by the reports of his Ambassadors in London and Paris, who both expressed the opinion, that an alliance between England and France would not be brought about."

These two asses, like true diplomats, paid attention only to official diplomats and overlooked the "Tigers" of the Political Zoo: James R. III. and his Jew puppet, Napoleon III. in Paris and Lionel and his Jew puppet—Disraeli in London.

Also the English Quakers from Manchester, received by the Czar, affirmed that, because of the Czar's very friendly feelings towards England no war was possible.

The British Ambassador to Petersburg, Sir Hamilton Seymour, reports the Emperor's words to him:

"Our two countries should be upon terms of close amity; our interests are upon all questions the same. It is essential for the two Governments to be on the best terms. Turkey itself seems to be falling to pieces. England and Russia should come to a perfectly good understanding and neither should take any step of which the other is not apprised."

The Czar's plan was to give autonomy to Servia and Bulgaria, and to let England have Egypt and Candia.

All this was splendid for England and Russia, but where would the Assassins of the Peoples be, with their aims, bequeathed by Satan, to exterminate all Christians and rule "all the kingdoms of the world"?

The Tsar was poisoned by his doctor Mandt, bribed by the Hidden Hand·

"He lay on his camp-bed, covered by a soldier's cloak'"*...

"He made the sign of the cross, stretched out his feeble hand to his wife, and grasping her's turned his dying eyes on the angel of his life".

On March 2nd, 1855, the "Anti-War" Tsar was no more!

The Jews "leeches" and "tigers" were revenged.

This awful murder was the end of the first half of the Rothschilds' misrule and murder (1770-1925).

*) Nicholas I. had as Minister of Finances, a Jew, Kankrin, who knowing that James was staging a war on Russia, persuaded the Czar, that the railroads were mere toys, and delayed their building. This caused the failure of the war. Disraeli confirms: Kankrin was a Jew. ("Coningsby," p. 257)

NICHOLAS I. POISONED. ROTHSCHILDS' TRIUMPH

The death of Nicholas I. gave an opportunity to James R. III., who until his death in 1868, was practically the Autocrat of the World and the Greatest Murderer of Christians. James commanded his chief executioners, the Jews: Disraeli, Napoleon III., Bismarck, Gamberle-Gambetta, and a whole band of "revolutionists," like the Jews: Karl Marx, Lassalle, Hertzen, all falsely called "great men," because mis-educated by the Jewish press and authors, we are all duped by the "immoral doctrine of success," i.e., when a man is successful, we think: "He is a great man" while he is only a great criminal, uplifted by the Hidden Hand.

After 1855 James R. III. remained the "Dark Angel."

The "Fair Angel" became Alexander II., the Liberator of the peasants and the Saviour of the United States.

In England Lionel was demoralising Disraeli and inducing him to start some new war.

In France James was satanizing Gambetta for the war of 1870.

We know how the 5 great powers had been distributed to the heirs of Amschel Mayer and these united under one of them as their head have been working to upset all the rulers of their respective countries and the Church, and to establish as Presidents, their own servants.

The murder of A. Lincoln, of Garfield, and of McKinley, Presidents, proves that the Hidden Hand wishes the Presidents to obey it. When Pres. Wilson ceased to do it, he was surely drugged with "kurare," as was Pres. Th. Stein of the Orange Republic by the same Hidden Hand. When Pres. Harding wished to free Alaska from Guggenheim, a Jew (possibly of the "300") this most gentle of the Gentiles "suddenly" died...

America finds it quite "normal" and pets the Jews!...

The purely Rothschildian "War of Revenge" in Crimea was absolutely useless to the nations, which shed their blood and spent their money in it only for the glory of the Rothschilds, who profited immensely. The war weakened the powers, giving a great temptation to Prussia to try Pan-Germanism, inspired by the Jews, who according to Disraeli, "monopolized the professorial chairs of Germany," and led Pan-Germanism, according to Prof. R. G. Usher.

The Crimean war proved to the Germans, that Russia after all was not "invincible," that she was a "giant with clay feet." This discovery greatly encouraged militarism in Germany and helped the Rothschilds to produce a series of wars, including that of 1914

THE ROTHSCHILDS OF THE FRANKFORT BRANCH

"Amschel Mayer (son of Amschel Rothschild I. and brother of Nathan and James) could at his pleasure raise or depress prices to the discomfiture of all who might happen to oppose him." (J. Reeves, p. 129)

"At entertainments Amschel Mayer sits, but never touches any dishes that have not been prepared in the Jewish fashion" (p. 117). "Strict Jew, opposed as he was to every innovation in the doctrine and ritual of the synagogue, and exact as he was in his observance of the Sabbath, he nevertheless did not hesitate to trade and make money on feast days."

Amschel Mayer understood the necessity of keeping the nobility in constant dependence, to further the program of "Israel Above ALL " Thus, we find, that he gave Henkel v. Donersmark 1,125,000 gulden (p. 127) with which to display a "rich German" in Paris and there prepare the overthrow of the Christian Dynasty of Napoleon III. in order to establish the Jewish Autocracy of the Rothschilds. A Jewess, Paiva, was supervising Henkel.

After the death of Anselm-Amschel Mayer Rothschild, head of the Frankfort branch (Dec. 6, 1855), the business of the Frankfort bank was managed by his nephews, Baron William and Baron Charles, sons of Karl of Naples, who died on March, 10, 1855. The Naples' branch was closed in 1860, when the Holy See was practically deprived of its temporal power, and the materialistic Rothschilds believed the Catholic Church doomed . . .

Karl Rothschild, the soul of the "mysterious" anti-Christian "Alta Vendita," before leaving Italy established there a cousin Nathan — to continue his satanic work of making anarchists and atheist out of the Italian patriots. His son was Ernesto Nathan.

This pig bought there a palace with a chapel and made of its altar a latrine for his free-masons.

The making a latrine of a Sacred Altar enthused the true free-masons. Thus Nathan's father a Rothschildian, a satanist, found Mazzini and "instructed" him to "spit" on CHRIST and Nathan's son did himself likewise. Mazzini was poor and having consented to become an Italian Kerensky, Nathan presumably was sent from London with the funds of the same Lionel, who according to Disraeli, supported all the anarchists, bolsheviks etc. Nathan was born in 1845. The "judaization" is proved by Nathan's letter to Mazzini from "Le Diable au XIX. Siecle."

"Ernesto Nathan was a Jew, coming from England. His very beautiful mother united in her drawing room many Italian revolutionists: Mazzini, Crispi, etc." (Roger Lambelin, "L'Imperialisme D'Israel." p. 152, Paris).

The "judaized" Crispi surrendered Italy to Bismarck.

This caused the Russo - French entente and the World War.

THE "MYSTERY" OF MAZZINI REVEALED.

The Jews themselves are the worst "anti-Semites," because, fond of boasting, they reveal their own rascalities. "The New York Times" owned by a Jew, Adolph Ochs, and edited by a Jew, Miller (now dead), narrates on April 11, 1921, of the late Jewish scoundrel, Ernesto Nathan, ex-Mayor of Rome. The paper says:

"The father of Nathan of Jewish parents was a banker of the Frankfort branch of the Rothschilds. Among the inmates of the shabby(!) lodging house in which Ernesto was born, was the Italian patriot Giuseppe Mazzini, whose works Ernesto published. In 1859 his father died and his mother's house became a refuge for patriots. Ernesto became the business manager(!) of 'La Roma del Popolo,' a paper started by Mazzini... In 1907 Nathan was chosen Mayor of ROME(!) by the Anti-Clericals, who upset the tradition of appointing as Mayor a member of one of the old Roman families. Never was a Mayor received with such vituperative attacks, passing all plausible bounds. Nathan, who was a mason, rose in that body to be Grand Master, and later Honorable Grand Master."

Thus the Jewish newspaper states that a Rothschildian—Nathan—went to Italy to "satanize" Mazzini and other patriots.

In Nathan's following letter (see "Le Diable au XIX Siecle") is confirmed "The Plan Of Hell," mentioned by Lemann, a Jew.

"The multitude disillusioned of Christianity, whose deist soul will up to that moment be without compass, thirsting for an ideal, but not knowing where to bestow their worship, will receive the True Light by the universal manifestation of the pure Luciferian doctrine, made public, a manifestation which will arise from the general movement of 'reaction,' following the destruction of Atheism and Christianity, both at the same time vanquished and exterminated."[*]

"Mazzini, professing Christian and patriot though he was, had joined the ranks of Carbonari, where his activities merely excited the derision of the Alta Vendita, which held that the mind rather than the body should be the point of attack." (Mrs. Nesta Webster, "World Revolution," p. 122)

"Mazzini on his part suspected that the secrets were being kept from him by the chiefs of the Alta Vendita, and Maligari, assailed by the same fears, wrote from London to Dr. Breidenstein these significant words: 'We form an association of brothers in all points of the globe, we have desires and interests in common, we aim at the emancipation of humanity, we wish to break every kind of yoke, yet there is one that is unseen, that can hardly be felt, yet that weighs on us. Whence comes it? Where is it? No one knows, or at least no one tells. The association is secret, even for us, the veterans of secret societies." ("World Revolution," p. 123).

The secret association is the "Hidden Hand." It disliked Mazzini and Maligari, because they were Christians and patriots. And it does not want to "emancipate humanity" from the Jewish yoke. It wants to enslave humanity under its Jewish heel...

* The Luciferian doctrine is now preached in Russia, Japan, etc.

The Second Rule of my Science of Political Foresight always demands the question: "Where is or will be the Hidden Hand."

The historians overlook the "Tigers" of the political Zoo."

The "War of (Rothschilds) Crime" in Crimea nearly ruined England and France. The former had 4.000 million dollars of debts. Europe was impoverished.

Whom to plunder next? Whom to embroil in new conflicts? The Rothschilds were looking for fresh victims.

In 1857, at the marriage of Lionel's daughter, Leonora, to her cousin Alfonse, son of James of Paris, all the Rothschilds were assembled in London. The sinister Jew, Disraeli, said:

"Under this roof are the heads of the family of Rothschild — a name famous in every capital in Europe and every division of the globe" (Reeves, p. 228).

Yes! But what could not fail to happen! The following. After dinner James Rothschild III, Lionel and Disraeli sat together and "conspired". James, always harsh, could not fail to grumble:

"How about the globe? The New World is not yet ours."

Disraeli could not resist jumping to his feet and boast:

"If you like, we shall divide the United States in two parts, one for you (James) and one for you (Lionel). Napoleon will do exactly, and all, that I shall advise him, and to Bismarck will be suggested such an intoxicating program, as to make of him our abject slave."

The three Jews decided then and there to destroy and plunder the United States, as we shall see.

Even a hundred years ago the issues between the Northern and Southern States produced greater dissensions and outbreaks. But the Hidden Hand was not interested then in the disturbances. Now the Hidden Hand decided to smash America and a tricky Jew, Judah P. Benjamin, was selected. According to Mr. Burton Hendrick he "was the brain of the revolt".

War is the "harvest of the Jews", according to Professor Werner Sombart of Berlin. The Jews Franks and other agents of the Hidden Hand tried to increase the discord between the South and the North, which was carefully inspired for "freedom of the slaves". Once the North began to insist, the South was encouraged by the Jews to resist. Mr. Burton Hendrick gives a proof of it, saying in his interesting book, "Jews in America":

"At the time of the Civil War Jews were found in every city, every village, every plantation, every mining camp" (p. 107).

"The Emperor Nicholas I. had done all he could to prevent the wars."

The "sudden" death of the "Demi-God"- Nicholas I. gave the throne to his son Alexander II.

The future Tsar-Liberator, born April 29th, 1817 (when Disraeli was "converted") was "the most delicious baby with plump body, large dark blue eyes, and already smiling at six weeks." ("The Court of Russia," p. 2, by Mr. E. A. Brayley Hodgets).

"At the age of eight he was already a Cornet in his Regiment of Hussars and at a review he attracted the attention of the French Marshall Marmont, Duc of Raguse, who was struck by his pluck and agility. Marmont in his Memoirs says: "The education which Nicholas has given his son is admirable. He is a charming Prince of rare beauty, whose good qualities have no doubt developed with time." (p. 5)

The priest Pavsky, Doctor of Divinity, became his instructor in the tenets of the Christian religion.

"The light of a beautiful soul radiated from him   (p. 14). Alexander astonished his instructors by his intelligence and quickness."

The famous poet Jukovsky wrote a recommendation to the Czar on how to educate his son Alexander:

"Respect the law. Live and promote culture. Respect public opinion. Love liberty and justice. Rule by order, not by might. Be true to thy word. Respect thy people. Love thy people. Have faith in virtue. That faith is the faith in God." (p. 12)

This so pleased the Czar, that Jukovsky was appointed tutor of the Grand Duke. Alexander studied various trades and crafts, visited factories and workshops. He built a cottage with bricks which he laid himself, and made all the furniture for it. He was taught the use of pencil and brush and studied music·

"The Czar became interested in the fate of the Jews. He opened schools for them and opened for them the doors of the universities and exempted them from paying the taxes, encouraged them to occupy themselves with the agriculture, manual working, art and sciences. He appointed to the very honorific posts those of them, who knew the Russian, Polish or German languages" (P. Mignot, "Le Probleme Juif," p. 50).

"Alexander II. tried to grant to the Jews all the concessions. Every Jew, who was working on the agriculture, or served in the army or achieved some school received all the rights of the best citizens of the Empire. But the Jews joined all the conspiracies and tried joining the anarchists to undermine the bases of the State. Their plot — the assassination of the Czar liberator has produced a violent wave of anti-semitism·" (P. Mignot, "Le Probleme Juif," p. 51)

The two members of the Holy Alliance, Austria and Prussia, having betrayed Russia, the Jew Nesselrode, the Minister for Foreign Affairs of Russia, ought to resign.

ALEXANDER II. THE LIBERATOR AND SAVIOUR

"I was convinced that the Emperor desired peace, and would not en. gage in any ambitious designs on India, nor have I attached importance to the refuted will of Peter the Great. The Czar in referring to it declared it to be apocryphal and to have been forged in Paris." (Lord Loftus, Ambassador).

The Marquis de Custine thus describes him:

"The habitual temper is gentle and benevolent. His expression is one of kindliness; his gait is graceful, easy and distinguished. He is truly a Prince. He is modest without timidity. His appearance gives the impression of perfect breeding. If he should ever reign he will exact obedience by charm of his natural grace and manner. He is both imposing and agreeable. He appears to me to be one of the finest models of a Prince."

Princess Metternich in her diary says that Alexander was handsome amiable, and amusing, and that everybody was astonished at his tact, cleverness and modesty.

Lord Palmerston spoke of him, when he was in London, as humane and conscientious to a most remarkable degree.

In 1840 he was admitted to the Council of Ministers.

"The somewhat philosophic, but extremely good-natured Emperor." (p. 41). "He was remarkably handsome, though less of a demigod than his father, Nicholas I." (p. 42). "He was perfectly urbane, courteous, tactful and indulgent." (p. 46). "A modest, well-educated, tactful gentleman, who was at no time of his life very much convinced of his own attainments, who would have been quite as content to lead the life of a simple private gentleman. Such was Alexander II. Add to that a certain religious fatalism and a refinement of mind. He was every inch a soldier and a grand seigneur." ("The Court of Russia," p. 47).

Count de Morny wrote to Napoleon about Alexander II:

"All that I learn about him, his conduct of his family, his relations with his friends, bears the stamp of fair-mindedness and of a spirit of chivalry. He does not bear malice. He never hurts anybody's feelings, he is true to his word and extraordinarily generous. It is impossible not to love him. He is worshipped by his people and Russia breathes freely."

Napoleon and Alexander met at Stuttgart in 1857.

"When Austria, Prussia, Sweden and even Spain were ready to join England, France and Sardinia in their Satanic desire to save Turkey and thus continue the extermination of the Christians, Alexander II. was determined to collect all the material and moral forces of Russia and lead them to repel and scatter the enemies." (p. 49).

This fact and presenting of Alaska for really nothing* prove once more, how absurd was the "Russian Danger," invented by the Rothschilds in their antagonism towards the Romanovs.

But nearly all the statements of the Jew, Disraeli, about Russia, were lies invented to precipitate her downfall, as the Pillar of Orthodoxy and to increase the "mankilling," desired by Satan.

* The $7,200,000 was the money spent by Russia to organize Alaska.

J. ROTHSCHILD'S APPEAL TO THE JEWS (1860).

The successful murder of the "Anti-War" Czar Nicholas I. and the uplifting of the H. H.'s agents: Disraeli in England; Napoleon III. in France; Bismarck in Germany; Mazzini in Italy, so encouraged James R. III. that he decided to try the "American coup," suggested by Disraeli.

This required the mobilization of the entire Jewry . . .

James decided to make public the Chief Chancellery of the Supreme Jewish World Government and called it "The Universal Jewish Alliance," in French "L'Alliance Israelite Universelle."

He made one of his Jewish valets, Adolphe Cremieux Grand Master of the Grand Orient of France, the Chief of his "Ministry for Foreign Affairs." "The Morning Post" of London, on Sept. 6, 1920, reproduced his Manifesto to all the Jews of the Universe:

"The union which we desire to found will not be a French, English, Irish or German union, but a Jewish one, a Universal one! Other peoples and races are divided into nationalities; we alone have no co-citizens, but exclusively co-religionaries."

"A Jew will under no circumstances become the friend of a Christian or a Moslem before the moment arrives, when the light of the Jewish faith, the only religion of reason, will shine all over the world! Scattered amongst other nations, we desire primarily to be and remain immutably Jews. Our nationality is the religion of our fathers and to recognize no other nationality. We are living in foreign lands and we cannot trouble about the ambitions of countries entirely alien to us.

"The Jewish teaching must cover the whole earth! No matter, where fate should lead—though scattered all over the earth, you must always consider yourselves members of a chosen race. If you realize that the faith of your forefathers is your only patriotism, — if you recognize that, notwithstanding the nationalities you have embraced, you always remain and everywhere form one and only nation, — if you believe that Jewry only is one and only religious and political truth, — if you are convinced of this, you Jews of the Universe, then come and give ear to our appeal and prove your consent."

"Our cause is great and holy, and its success is guaranteed."

"Catholicism, our immemorial enemy, is lying in the dust, mortally wounded in the head. The net which Jewry is throwing over the globe of the earth is widening and spreading daily."

"The time is near, when Jerusalem will become the house of prayer for all nations and peoples, and the banner of Jewish mono-deity will be unfurled and hoisted on the most distant shores."

"Let us avail ourselves of all circumstances. Our might is immense — learn to adopt this might for our cause."

"What have you to be afraid of?"

"The day is not distant when all the riches and treasures of the earth will become the property of the Children of Israel."

CIVIL WAR STARTED BY THE HIDDEN HAND

The Manifesto of A. Cremieux was understood by Jewry, as an appeal to some grand act and the Jews and their free - masons promised their support.

Orders were sent to the U. S. to create pretexts for war and on Jan. 3-d, 1861, the Governor of Alabama seized the arsenal of Mount Vernon. Everybody knows the rest of the Civil War. On May 26, 1865 the last armed force of the South having been vanquished, the hope of succor by France and England, as was promised in 1861, vanished with the surrender of General Kirby E. Smith.

David A. Wells says the total cost of the war was $8,165 millions. If this sum had been used to compensate the Southerners for the liberation of their slaves, there would have been no war. But the Rothschilds wished the enslavement of the New World. Therefore the Union army had 385,245 killed and wounded and at least 100,000 were killed in the Confederate Army.

As I said, crowds of the Jews, agents of the Hidden Hand, could be found in every place. The chief agent was a Jew, Judah P. Benjamin, who later became the State Secretary of the South. Their fiery speeches started the Civil War. The Hidden Hand in Europe persuaded Napoleon III, that he would glorify his sceptre by restoring Louisiana to France and by creating a new Empire of Mexico and the Southern States. The Rothschilds persuaded public opinion of England and France, that the most propitious moment had arrived to recover the losses, caused by the Crimean War.

Lionel's "straw men" revived the doctrine of Pan-Britanism (led by Pan - Judaism) and persuaded some of the statesmen most domesticated by Lionel, that the North could be returned to its former state of a British colony, or be annexed to Canada.

In May 1861, England and other powers recognized the Confederates as belligerents.

"Lincoln found his foreign relations unsatisfactory! England and France were in the main ill-disposed toward the North. Southern privateering received their assent. In October news came, that a combined English, French and Spanish fleet was preparing to move against Mexico 'for the purpose of collecting defaulted debts ' The Russian Czar, however, declined Napoleon's invitation to join the league." (Mr. Edwin Emerson in his "The 19-th Century And After," p. 867).

Emerson knew nothing about the "Tigers", who ruled Paris (James) and London (Lionel) and their Hidden Hand.

ENGLAND, FRANCE AND SPAIN LAND TROOPS IN MEXICO.

The Envoys accredited by the Confederates to England and France having been seized by Captain Wilkes of the U. S. Navy, Lord Russell (personal "friend" of Lionel) drafted a peremptory ultimatum, and the Secretary of State Seward released them. This policy drew England into a quasi-partnership with the South. The war against the North was a question of months. But it was preferable first to let the Americans themselves do the fighting.

"A poor excuse of so flagrant a breach of the law of nations was found in England's persistent violation of neutrality. The worst instance was the famous Alabama case." (Emerson, "The 19-th Century And After," p. 867).

English, French and Spanish warships landed their forces at Vera Cruz in 1862. Since June 5, 1863, the French Gen. Bazaine had occupied the capital of Mexico. On May, 28, 1864, Napoleon's nominee, Maximilian, landed in Mexico. The Rothschilds, having huge plans as to the United States, made a preliminary loan to Maximilian of 201.500.000 francs through a subordinate London banker. Meanwhile the Confederate army understood that its situation was desperate:

"Hood saw his men breaking at all points."

The Confederate States were eleven in number; Texas and Louisiana were two of them. The Confederacy was governed by a written constitution with limited powers. It was established in 1861 for the principal purpose of defending the asserted right of the 11 constituent States to secede from the Union of the 34 States, or from the 23 States of the North. The power to bargain away two of their number was not among the powers granted to the Confederate States, either with or without the consent of the two. But the alternative was to lose all or to save the other nine States by perhaps the temporary sacrifice of two of the original eleven. The hatred of the Southerners was so inflamed by the Hidden Hand's agents, that it was decided to appeal to Napoleon. He accepted the bargain and the author of the plot, Disraeli, assured the support of England, overexcited by the "Alabama" incident, exaggerated by the Rothschilds' agents.

Numerous "historians" have written the History of the Civil War, but none dared to reveal the Truth, which seems to be practically ignored by the historians of the United States.

CZAR THREATENS THE FOES OF THE U. S. (1863)

In 1863 the Confederate States offered Louisiana and Texas to Napoleon III. in exchange for his intervention with French troops against the North. The French troops at that moment occupied the capital of Mexico.

"Napoleon's object was to assure the predomination of France over the Latin races, and to augment the influence of these races in America. Napoleon ardently desired to recognize the independence of the rebellious American States, and repeatedly urged the British government to join him in so doing" (Mr. Mackenzie in his "The 19-th Century," p. p. 297-298).

The danger was indeed great. It taxed even the genius of Lincoln; and the skill and patriotism of General Grant's heroes could not have withstood such a combination. But the United States had its most faithful admirers in the Czars of Russia. For a long time they had contemplated the liberation of the serfs, but were checked by the then rampant "Prussianism" and by the landowners.

As early as 1842 Czar Nicholas I. in his decree of April 14, appealed to the great land-holders to liberate their serfs ("The 19-th Century and After," by E. Emerson, p. 619).

It was Czar Alexander II.'s magnanimous act of emancipating the Russian serfs by his Imperial decree of February 19, 1861, which greatly influenced the similar movement in the United States. Some 47.000.000 souls in Russia were freed. Many peasants were discontented by such freedom and in several places the troops had to interfere (Rambaud's "History of Russia"). The same object which by the Czar was obtained by a stroke of his pen, required in a Republic an ocean of blood and billions of treasure. Why? Because the Hidden Hand so desired it. On the same Febr. 19, 1861, the newly inaugurated Provisional President Jefferson Davis, named his Cabinet.

Thus the Czar followed every step of the drama with keenest attention, and when the above plan of the Hidden Hand became known to him, he, through his Ambassadors in Paris and London informed France and England, that their interference against the North would be regarded as a declaration of war against Russia.

Is it possible, that no one has ever cared to dwell upon these facts, concerning Russia's services to America during the Civil War. Did not Washington Irving insist on re-writing the World's History in America?

ALEXANDER II. SENDS HIS FLEETS TO AMERICA.

Simultaneously, the Czar dispatched his Atlantic fleet to New York harbor and his Pacific squadron to San Francisco with orders to fight every fleet, or force, which would attack the Northern States. **He put his ships at the disposal of Lincoln!**

The South was ready to sacrifice 2 States to secure the help of Napoleon's victorious army already in Mexico rather than face complete disaster alone. It was also assured by the agents of the Hidden Hand, that the French yoke would not continue for long. Thus the Confederates had some idea of recovering the bait after it had served its purpose. As the **Polish revolt of 1863 embittered** the Franco-Prussian and the Franco-Russian relations, France's yoke was not feared as being of long duration by the Southerners. They were ready to face any sacrifices to avenge themselves upon the supporters of Lincoln. Both sides ignored entirely that they were dupes of the Hidden Hand, and inflamed by its agents: like the Jews, Judah P. Benjamin, the Secretary of State of the South, also John Wilkes Booth, etc., etc.

A friend of mine, General James Grant Wilson of the Northern Army related these facts to me; and I heard in my youth from Admiral Lessovsky himself the details of the Russian naval demonstration. He was the commander of the Russian Pacific squadron which watched the safety of San Francisco.

At the first annual dinner of the Lincoln Fellowship, held at Delmonico in New York, February 12, 1908, I made a speech in the presence of nearly a hundred of Lincoln's co-workers, citing all the above. Everything I said was confirmed by them.

In Russia this story was kept secret, because the victories of Prussia over Denmark in 1864 and over Austria in 1866 revealed to Alexander II. the Pan-German peril, staged by the Hidden Hand, as implied by Disraeli himself. The Czar even went to Paris in 1867, in order to become reconciled with Napoleon III.

Russia did not wish to remind Frenchmen and Englishmen, that she ruined their golden dreams; inspired by the Rothschilds, of reconquering and dividing the opulent United States, which once belonged to them. So these facts ever remained secret.

In 1908, when many more survivors of the Civil War lived than today, everyone of them knew it. The oldest people never failed to say to me:

"We, Americans, must never forget, how much we are indebted to Russia for our salvation in 1863-64."

ALEXANDER II. SAVED THE UNITED STATES (1864)

France and England remembered the heavy losses and the colossal expenses of the Crimean war imposed upon them by the Rothschilds and their tools. After the hard struggle the allies captured only what was practically a village-Sebastopol.

Only the signature by Austria, guided by Salomon Rothschild, of a treaty with the four allies, who fought against Russia;, the hostility of Prussia and the poisoning of the "Fair Angel"-Nicholas I. by the Hidden Hand, saved the allies from a failure...

That is why France and England felt it would be madness to renew their fight against Russia only to please the Rothschilds, and accepted the warning of the Czar. None could doubt, that the attack of the five powers, which landed their troops in Mexico in 1863, would have given the decisive victory to the Confederates, the United States would have been disrupted and soon the South would have been annexed to Mexico and the North to Canada!

The History of the United States was written for the Americans by the Hidden Hand's hirelings. This explains, why this "incident" is carefully omitted from American History. But not all Americans ignore it. ...

"Russia was astonished when American public opinion supported the cause of Japan during the war between those empires in 1904-5. It was a rude awakening from the dream of American gratitude, based upon her action in making a naval demonstration at New York and San Francisco in a critical period of the Civil War," stated the former Assistant Secretary of State, (Mr. J. Callan O'Laughlin in his interesting book "The Imperial America").

The above stupid and base betrayal of Russia by the United States must be laid entirely at the doors of the Jews in America led by Jacob Schiff, who deceived public opinion to such a extent, that the Americans committed the most shameful act in their short History!

By helping Japan, which traitorously attacked unprepared Russia, who saved the United States in 1863-64 from a mortal danger and who proved her lack of desire to come into the New World, when she absolutely made a gift of the richest Alaska, the Americans created a veritable Japanese peril, which may prove fatal in 1925-26, unless this book opens the eyes of America to this terrific Jewish World Conspiracy, of which the United States is now again the target...

The above incident of vital importance to the United States is purposely withheld from the knowledge of the American nation by its publishers, writers and press, all controlled by the Jews.

THE HIDDEN HAND MADE THE CIVIL WAR.

Though since 1812 disputes had existed between the South and the North, the Civil War would have been postponed for 50 years or might never have happened, if the Hidden Hand had not decided to divide the United States at the Rothschilds' wedding in 1857. Here is one more proof of it, Mr. George P. Messervy, who surely took his materials from the Rothschilds themselves, says in his book "The Quick Step of an Emperor":

"Lord Rothschild (Lord Lionel-Nathan was also an Austrian baron) greeted Mr. Davidson, whom he introduced to Baron James de Rothschild (who came from Paris for this meeting) — as the representative of the English house of the Rothschilds in Mexico. Baron James said: 'The Emperor Napoleon is much interested in this Mexican undertaking; and our intimacy with him and his government is so close, that I deemed it desirable to be present, for IT IS CERTAIN they (the affairs of Mexico) WILL PLAY NO SMALL PART in the EVENTS of the next years, which will see the making and unmaking of national credits'' (p. 17)!

James Rothschild, was the most cunning of men.

He thrust four powers against Russia in the "War of Crime" (senseless as it was) and poisoned Nicholas I.

In 1857, James decided to disrupt the other great power (with which government he was not "in so close intimacy") by throwing against it five powers: Belgium, England, France, Spain, and Austria. But as the failure of the attack on Russia had discouraged England and France, James started the Civil War in the United States and thus weakened his eventual New World victim through fratricide.

And when half a million men were killed in America, James found, that the above five powers could land their troops in Mexico and proceed to occupy the Southern States with their partial consent.

Had not James forseen the DISAPPEARANCE of the United States as a separate power, never would he have solemnly stated that the affairs of Mexico would produce the "making or unmaking of national credits."

In order to take for himself Mexico, Louisiana and Texas and to grant to Lionel (his nephew, whose daughter — Leonora was the wife of James's son — Alphonse) the Northern States, James was ready to grant a loan. But, of course, this loan had to be largely guaranteed by some property.

James Rothschild III. was the vicar of Satan.

THE VATICAN WAS TO PAY THE ROTHSCHILDS' RISKS.

A Jew, Sir Alfred Mond, the former Minister of Health of England, revealed in his "English Review:"

"**Rome is the greatest enemy of Bolshevism.**"

As the brilliant President of the Society "The Britons," Mr. H. H. Beamish and many other of the best informed men have confirmed, Bolshevism used Communism only as a mask, but Bolshevism is in reality an agency of Pan-Judaism (the Hidden Hand).

Did not Mr. Madison Grant warn us also:

"Now Asia, in the guise of Bolshevism with Semitic leadership and Chinese executioners is organizing an assault upon the western Europe" (the introduction to the most interesting book of Mr. Lothrop Stoddard — "The Rising Tide of Color").

By saying that Rome is the greatest enemy of Bolshvism, i. e. of Pan-Judaism, Mond wished to point out the Vatican to the Jews as a foe and as target.

The same James conceived a demoniacal plan.

"At least one foe must be weakened." If for some reason, the conquest of the United States by the two Rothschilds, united still closer by the wedding of 1857 should fail there was still in Europe another hated foe the Vatican, which must be made to pay the bill.

The problem now was how to ruin the Holy Father?

The Hidden Hand has always had Jews in the Catholic hierarchy for such emergencies. So a new "Rebello-Bombelles" (pronounced Bombelle), a Jew Jesuit, Father Fisher was discovered and introduced to the Archduke Maximilian to create the Mexican Empire and promised the Pope, that it would be Catholic.

The unfortunate Archduke was finally induced to accept the throne of Mexico, which according to Fisher would greatly help the Christian cause.

Napoleon III., possibly a Rothschildian himself, permitted the Hidden Hand to introduce to his wife, the Empress Eugenie, a Jew "Catholic" priest, a notorious Bauer.

Thus the Rothschilds of Paris, Vienna and London, through the Jew "Catholic" priests Fisher and Bauer secured complete control over Napoleon III. and Maximilian, and through their Jew agents Davidson in Mexico and Judah P. Benjamin in the United States, they started the Civil War, which was calculated to bring about the entire disruption of the United States.

Judah P. Benjamin and Davidson did not fail to have a crowd of "Franks," grand-sons of the Franks who offered to Benedict Arnold the "30 silver coins."

Let us return to the declaration of James R. III.:

"Davidson has come to us from Mexico with a proposition from the clerical party there for borrowing 125.000.000 francs, giving as security therefore a portion of the most valuable property of the Roman Church in Mexico" ("The Quick Step of an Emperor")

"Father" Fisher is thus described by G. P. Messervy:

"A slight German Hebrew cast of countenance and of dark, almost swarthy complexion with large penetrating eyes. His garb was that of the Order of Jesus" (p. 20).

Fisher's entire attitude indicated, that he was a man of the Rothschilds. He certified, that the property was 15 times the value of the desired loan.

The French Ambassador was present at this meeting of the two Rothschilds and said in a positive and assertive manner:

"The world is soon to see the great Republic of the West (U. S.) BROKEN in twain — its Southern member allied to monarchy (France — behind the Mexican Empire) and its Northern member arising out of anarchy into a military despotism, ruled by a dictator." (p. 26).

Of course, this "dictator" of the Northern States would be selected by Lionel Rothschild, as Trotzky was selected for Russia by Lionel's grandson, Edouard Rothschild V.

The poor Emperor Maximilian was the victim of the satanic desire of the Rothschilds: to destroy the Habsburgs, as the Pillars of Catholicism, and to divide the United States between England and France, which the two Rothschilds regarded as their own domains.

Before his tragic death there must have appeared before the eyes of Emperor Maximilian, as in a vision, "a huge figure with Hebrew jowl, in the garb of a priest of the Society of Jesus, then the cry of the Cross "My God, My God, why hast Thou forsaken Me"? (p. 275). This Jesuit, a Jew, betrayed Maximilian, when he realized that the satanic plan of the Rothschilds to conquer and crush the United States was paralyzed by the Czar's threat to "fire on the first, who fires on America."

"The Pope had never heard of Fischer" (G. P. Messervy, p. 73).

We must not forget, however, that besides the Rothschilds, who deceived the Habsburgs, there was also the brother of the arch-beast Bombelles, who married the ex-Empress Marie-Louise, aunt of the Emperor of Austria. Bombelles became the "educator" (i. e., the "satanizer") of Franz-Joseph.

ROTHSCHILDS' ORDER TO AMERICAN BANKERS.

To pay the soldiers the Government issued its Treasury notes, authorized by act of Congress, July 17, 1861, for $50.000.000, bearing no interest. These notes circulated at par with gold. The Rothschilds' agents inspired the American banks to offer to Lincoln a loan of $150 million. But before they had taken much of the loan, the banks broke down and suspended specie payments in Dec. 1861. They wished to blackmail Lincoln and demanded the "shaving" of government paper to the extent of 33%, an extortion which was refused. A bill drafted for the Government issue of $150 million, which should be full legal tender for every debt in the United States, passed the House of Representatives Feb. 25, 1862, and was hailed with delight by the entire country. But the Wall Street bankers were furious.

Sen. Pettigrew reprints the so called "Hazzard Circular" sent in 1862 by the Bank of England (ruled by the Rothschilds):

"Slavery is likely to be abolished by the war power and chattel slavery destroyed. This I (Rothschild) and my European friends (the 300 men) are glad of, for slavery is but the owning of labor and carries with it the care of the laborer, while the European (read 'Rothschildian') plan led on by England (i. e. the Rothschilds) is for capital to control labor by controlling wages. THIS CAN BE DONE BY CONTROLLING THE MONEY. THE GREAT DEBT THAT CAPITALISTS WILL SEE TO IS MADE OUT OF THE WAR must be used as a means to control the volume of money. To accomplish this the BONDS must be used as a banking basis. We are now waiting for the Secretary of the Treasury to make his recommendation to Congress. It will not do to ALLOW the GREENBACK, as it is called, to circulate as money any length of time, as we cannot control that."

Thus the order of the Rothschilds was clear: "Capitalists WILL SEE TO IT that a DEBT is MADE out of the war."

The result was that by "hook and crook" the Rothschilds enslaved this country. And Schiffs, Baruchs & Co. are the rulers.

The Chairman of the Committee on Ways and Means of the House of Representatives, Mr. Thaddeus Stevens explains how the United States was captured by the Rothschilds:

"The agents of the banks fell upon the bill in haste and disfigured it."

In the Senate this amendment was tacked upon the bill:

"Good for all debts and dues of the U. S. EXCEPT DUTIES ON IMPORTS AND INTEREST on the PUBLIC DEBT," ($150 million above mentioned, plus $70 million, a pre-war debt).

"Thus equipped this bill went forth to rob every American and turn the ownership of this nation into the hands of capitalists." (Mrs. Hobart).

When the bill came back to the House, Mr. Stevens said: "We are about to consummate a cunningly devised scheme which will bring GREAT LOSS to all classes of people, except one" (the Rothschilds' branch of the Wall Street). The bill was passed.

ROTHSCHILDS OVERPOWERED CONGRESS (1862).

The Rothschilds were in possession of 80% of the gold in the country. They had a "corner" on gold. By securing this discrimination against the "greenback" by means of the "Exception clause," they made a market for their gold.

"Importers were obliged to go to Wall Street to buy gold to pay duties on their goods, and the Wall Street gamblers held the power to fix the price. Gold went to a premium. Had the greenbacks been permitted to retain their full legal tender quality, there would have been no need for gold to pay import duties. The price of gold rapidly rose and before the war closed had reached the price of $2.85, measured in greenbacks. The gold bought in Wall Street to pay import duties became the revenues of the government and was by it paid back to Wall Street as interest on the public debt. As fast as the bankers sold the gold it was returned for interest on the public debt to be sold again. Thus during the entire war these gold gamblers speculated in gold, making fortunes from the blood and tears of the American people," (Mrs M. E. Hobart in her "The Secret of Rothschilds," p. 54).

Two more issues of $150 million each, with the "Exception clause" were authorized in July, 1862 and in March, 1863, making in all $450,000,000. They bore no interest. When these issues were exhausted and necessity arose for additional money the bankers demanded that Treasury Notes should no longer be made in the form of DOLLARS, but in the form of BONDS: the bond draws interest, the dollar does not.

A gigantic war costing seven billions was carried through without gold. Why? Because everything was supplied at home, and American money, the "greenbacks" were gladly accepted.

"How then was it that this government, several years after the war was over, found itself owing in London and Wall Street several hundred million dollars to men who never fought a battle, who never made a uniform, never furnished a pound of bread, men, who never did an honest day's work in all their lives... The fact is, that billions owned by the sweat, tears and blood of American laborers have been poured into the coffers of these men for absolutely nothing. This 'sacred war debt' was only a gigantic scheme of fraud, concocted by European capitalists and enacted into American law by the aid of American congressmen, who were their paid hirelings or their ignorant dupes. That this crime has remained uncovered is due to the power of prejudice which seldom permits the victim to see clearly or reason correctly: 'the Money power prolongs its reign by working on the prejudices' (Lincoln). Every means has been employed to deceive the masses. Ridicule and derision have been applied to all opposition, while flattery and appreciation were showered upon the officials," (Mary E. Hobart, p. 49).

Mrs. Hobart's book "The Secret of the Rothschilds" would be excellent, had she not departed from the title and mistakenly accused England and "foreign Dukes and Lords." The European aristocracy was ruined and could not buy the American bonds.

"The money making is the world's curse" (Universal Christ. Conference).

Why not reveal that Rothschild made $4 billion out of this war?

ANGRY ROTHCHILDS PLUNDER THE U. S. (1864-1866)

All those "European capitalists" are the same Rothschilds and the 300 men, composing the "Hidden Hand,"

"During the Civil War the Jews were everywhere" (J. Burton Hendrick).

"Since 1865 everything is invaded by the German Jew; he became the absolute master in every place." (Ed. Drumont in "La France Juive.")

GOD made the rattlesnake noisy and the Jews boastful to warn us. Because of the boasting of some Jew, the London "Times" in 1865 published this Editorial:

"If this mischievous financial policy which had its origin in the North American Republic during the war (1861-1865) should become indurated down to a fixture, then that Government will furnish its money without cost. It will pay off its debts and be without a debt. It will have all the money necessary to carry on its commerce. It will become prosperous beyond precedent in history of civilized governments of the World. The brains and the wealth of all countries will go to North America. That government must be destroyed or it will destroy every Monarchy on the globe!"

...And they (the Rothschilds) began to "destroy" the American Government by killing Lincoln and soon after, in 1867 attempting to kill Alexander II. for having saved the U. S.

Of course, the author of the above appeal "to destroy the U. S." mentioned the Monarchies only to hide the real author. A Monarchy such as Russia, where the railroads were "nationalized," and the Czar was preparing to "nationalize" the credit could better resist the money power than could corrupt Republics, as is proved by Mrs. Hobart, Sen. R. F. Pettigrew and Ph. Francis.

This editorial confirms that the Rothschilds played a predominant role in the financial enslavement of the United States, which enables them today to practically rule this country and lead it to disaster at any moment.

The $450 million of "greenbacks" then being exhausted, Wall Street (Rothschild) demanded bonds with interest.

"The hour to stab the Republic had arrived. London sent gold by the million to buy up the 'Exception clause' greenbacks for 35 cents on the dollar and to redeem it in U. S. bonds at face value, or 100 cents on the dollar. The money mongers of Europe could buy up our money at 35c. a dollar and convert it into a bonded debt against us of 100 cents. Lincoln was opposed to this conversion!.. The assassin's bullet was in harmony with such diabolical plots. But under U. S. Grant, he being either willingly or ignorantly their (bankers') tool, the work of despoiling the American people began in earnest. The $450 million 'Exception clause' greenbacks were converted into $1,640 million of bonded indebtedness" (Mrs. Hobart, p. 58).

"What secret cabals may have been held, what diabolical plottings entered into, what sums of money have been expended?" (Mrs. Hobart).

"Immediately on receipt by Emperor Maximilian of the news of the death of Lincoln, he dispatched to Europe his adviser, Ellon, to confer with Napoleon (III), King Leopold of Belgium and the Emperor of Austria as to what should be done under the changed condition of affairs, the Empire in Mexico having been undertaken under the conviction that the United States were permanently disrupted" (New York Herald of July 29, 1865).

"The Judeo-Masonry means constant wars" (The Universal Anti-Jewish Alliance, the Aryan Committee, 33, rue Gioffredo, Nice, France).

179

THE "MYSTERY" OF THE CIVIL WAR

Bismarck knew the truth and revealed it in 1876 to a German, Conrad Siem, who published it ("La Vieille France," N-216, March, 1921). Bismarck said:

"The division of the United States into two federations of equal force was decided long before the Civil War by the High Financial Power of Europe. These bankers were afraid that the United States, if they remained in one block and as one nation, would attain economical and financial independence, which would upset their financial domination over the World. The voice of the Rothschilds predominated. They foresaw tremendous booty if they could substitute two feeble democracies, indebted to the Jewish financiers, to the vigorous Republic, confident and self-providing. Therefore, they started their emissaries in order to exploit the question of slavery and thus to dig an abyss between the two parts of the Republic. Lincoln never suspected these underground machinations. He was anti-Slaverist, and he was elected as such, But his character prevented him from being the man of one party. When he had affairs in his hands, he perceived that these sinister financiers of Europe, the Rothschilds, wished to make him the executor of their designs. They made the rupture between the North and the South imminent! The masters of Finance in Europe made this rupture definitive in order to exploit it to the utmost. Lincoln's personality surprised them. His candidature did not trouble them: they thought to easily dupe the candidate woodcutter. But Lincoln read their plots and soon understood, that the South was not the worst foe, but the Jew financiers. He did not confide his apprehensions; he watched the gestures of the Hidden Hand; he did not wish to expose publicly the questions which would disconcert the ignorant masses. He decided to eliminate the International bankers, by establishing a system of Loans, allowing the States to borrow directly from the people without intermediary. He did not study financial questions, but his robust good sense revealed to him, that the source of any wealth resides in the work and economy of the nation. He opposed emissions through the International financiers. He obtained from Congress the right to borrow from the people by selling to it the 'bonds' of States. The local banks were only too glad to help such a system. And the Government and the nation escaped the plots of the foreign financiers. They understood at once, that the United States would escape their grip. The death of Lincoln was resolved upon. Nothing is easier than to find a fanatic to strike."

"The death of Lincoln, was a disaster for Christendom. There was no man in the United States great enough to wear his boots. And Israel went anew to grab the riches of the World. I fear that Jewish Banks with their craftiness and tortuous tricks will entirely control the exuberant riches of America, and use it to systematically corrupt modern civilization. The Jews will not hesitate to plunge the whole of Christendom into wars and chaos, in order that 'the earth should become the inheritance of Israel.'"

Thus Bismarck, who knew the game of the Jews, spoke in 1876, just as did rabbi Reichhorn in 1869, and as is now verified.[*]

[*] "The Protocols of the Learned Elders of Zion," at "The Britons," 50c.

"If the key opens the door it is the right key" (Lord Acton).

The "Protocols" open all the doors and explain all the mysteries and the plan of our deadly foes. Ignoring them one cannot become a Statesman.

"I like CHRIST, because HE held the Jewish religion in contempt" (Robert G. Ingersoll, The Chicago Tribune, May 5, 1881).

"The bolsheviks are a lot of murderers and thieves" (Repr. F. A. Britten).

THE "MYSTERY" OF LINCOLN'S DEATH

The above two Bismarck's declarations were received by me long after I had already written the precedent pages on the Civil War and its real causes. The facts always confirm my deductions.

According to Bismarck the awful Civil War in America was fomented by a Jewish Conspiracy, and Abraham Lincoln, the hero, and national Saint of the United States, was killed by the same Hidden Hand, which killed six Romanov Czars, ten Kings and scores of Ministers only to easier bleed their nations.

The Great American Nation should not forget this, if it desires to earnestly prevent a new and much more disastrous Civil War and a Second World War, both staged by the Hidden Hand.

"It was both silly and dangerous for the Americans to insult so pointedly a highly sensitive people like Japan" ("Montreal D. Star", Sept. 30, 1924).

R. W. Page ("Dramatic Moments in Amer. Diplomacy") wrote:
"In their dire extremity, the Confederates promised Mexico to Napoleon" (p. 139). "Gladstone's and the PrimeMinister's (of England) natural sympathies were with the Southern half of the Country"... "Napoleon was himself a party to the construction of these 4 leviathans (ironclads of tremendous power) destined to destroy a friendly country..." (p. 142). "The Emperor made haste tŏ stop the sailing of the Confederate ships and to assure Bigelow of his friendship for the U. S." (p. 149).*

What happened that Napoleon abruptly abandoned his plan to annex Texas and Louisiana offered him by the Confederates themselves? R. W. Page childishly assures us that it was a letter written by my old late friend Mr. John Bigelow to the American Consul in Marseilles, in which he introduced a spurious story; that this letter was intercepted; and that Napoleon was frightened by this hoax... No! When the change occurred, French troops were already in Mexico and no fable about pirates could have frightened him. What made Napoleon alter his plans was the warning of the Czar, that an attack upon the United States would mean war with Russia and possibly with Prussia.

"Animosity toward the United States was plainly displayed in England. Napoleon was ready to recognize the independence of the Confederate Government. The Russian Government, however, refused to accede to the French desire for joint action among the powers" ("American History" by J. Alton James and A. Hart Sanford, p. 40.)

"England and America were brought to the verge of war by the affair of 'Trent' and later by the building of Confederate vessels in English shipyards" ("American Political History" by Miss Viola A. Conklin, p. 402).

"England recognized the Confederate States as a belligerent power. France and the other powers of Europe followed this example. Russia remained friendly to the Union cause, and in 1863, when the success of the cause looked doubtful, a fleet of Russian war ships came into the harbor of New York." ("The Student's American History" by Montgomery, p. 453.·)

* J. Bigelow learned about the 4 leviathans on Sept. 10, 1863 and at first disbelieved it. But already on Sept. 8, 1863, the Russian squadron of Admiral S. Lesowsky came to San Francisco and on Sept. 11, the first battleship of the Russian Atlantic squadron of Admiral A. A. Popoff was in New York. Both Admirals had orders from the Czar to "be ready to fight any power and to take their orders from Lincoln!"

ATTEMPT TO KILL ALEXANDER II IN PARIS (1867).

The salvation of the U. S. by Alexander II. made the Rothschilds furious. James was left without Mexico and the Southern States, and Lionel could not capture the North, as was planned in 1857. The days of the Czar were counted... Lincoln was murdered in 1865 and an attempt to kill Mr. Seward the Secretary of State was made the same night. Next came the turn of the Czar. On June 6 the Czar was driving with Napoleon in Bois de Boulogne, when young Berezowsky fired two pistol shots at him. But a chamberlain, Rambaud, seing the pistol, dashed ahead and covered the Czar with his horse. Alexander II. obtained from Napoleon the promise that Berezowsky would not be executed. M. Paul Lanoir in his "Espionnage Allemand" was inclined to accuse Bismarck of this plot, but it is absolutely improbable. Bismarck's policy was to keep Russia in the most friendly spirit, because it was at the culminating moment of the Russo-Prussian entente, and a new Czar might be less Germanophile. Berezowsky alone, without the aid of the Hidden Hand, could not have succeeded, nor could the last attempt to kill the Czar.

The Rothschilds were very anxious not to permit the wise motto of King George III "Anglo-Russian Alliance" to prevail. It was easy to fabricate a legend about Peter the Great's testament to his successors to invade India. If India had been mentioned by Peter the Great, he meant the South Caucasus and Asia Minor.

"The gulf that severed Western Europe from Russia during the latter half of the nineteenth century was dug and kept open by Jewish resentment. The power of International Jewry was the strongest of the influences which misled the world" (Wickham Steed, ex-Ed. of The Times,"Through 30 Years")

Yes. It was the revenge of the Hidden Hand for the Czar having checked its plan to disrupt the U. S.

If the Jews had been so badly treated in Russia as they complain of, why were they so anxious to re-enter that country, as proved the American-Russian "war" of 1911, which they imposed upon Pres. Taft, when the Commercial Treaty was dropped?

The threat of Alexander II· to declare war on France and associated powers. should their troops, which were in Mexico. be employed to aid the Southern States, frightened Napoleon III. and he sought a way to withdraw from Mexico "with honor."

Thus the plot of James and Lionel Rothschilds — to divide the United States — fell flat.

They ordered the murder of Lincoln and Alexander II. After several Jewish attempts the Czar was killed in 1881.

The Rothschilds decided to quit Napoleon and to start the "mass murder" through Bismarck. Napoleon became too good.

"In point of fact the Kaiser was no more a free agent than Lloyd George with his entourage of Sassoons, Monds, and Isaacs (Lord Reading), or Pres. Wilson with his Brandeises, Schiffs, and Warburgs" (Dr. J. H. Clarke).

EUROPEAN (ROTHSCHILDIAN) CONSPIRACY OF 1857-65.

American children are being taught that the Civil War occured, because the South did not wish to free the Negro-slaves. That is not exactly true: the South itself was ready to free them. Lincoln was re-inaugurated on March 4, 1865 and was shot on April 4-th, 1865 by an actor Wilkes Booth, who cried: "The South is revenged." **He was a Jew, but this has never been mentioned!***
Thus "History without Conscience" describes events!
"Most history professors are asses." (G. D. Eaton, Nov. 13, 1922).
Since 1864 the Hidden Hand has renewed orders to its press and valets to calumniate, blacken and even murder the Romanovs. Their every act, step or word was disfigured, misrepresented.
This satanic work was especially successful in America.
Authors and politicians found it profitable to lie about the Czars; to be silent about their many virtues and enormous services rendered to Civilization, and conceal the fact that the **U. S. would possibly have ceased to exist, were it not for the courage of Alexander II, who risked war with 5 European powers and the anger of the Rothschilds—to preserve the Union.**
Thus the Jewish N. Y. Times deliberately lied on Aug. 2 1925:
"The **myth of a Russian fleet**, cruising ostentatiously in American waters as a quiet hint of the Czar's friendliness, has often been cited as proof positive of the allegation that, but for Russian opposition, Great Britain and France would have perfected some plan of joint intervention."
This "plan" was known to John Bigelow, as R. W. Page stated.
All becomes clear from a few issues of the N. Y. Herald (1863):
"**Perils from England, Perils from France**" (headlines on Sept 11, 1863).
"Rebel ironclads were ready in the Clyde and in the Mersey to be sent out on their mission of destruction of American commerce" (Sept. 14, 1863).
Are ironclads needed to "destroy only the merchant ships"!?!
"Napoleon (III) wished to write a message to the French Legislative body of a most menacing character towards the U. S." (Sept. 14, 1863).
It meant a declaration of war upon the U.S. Why did he drop it?
Why did not the French and English ironclads attack the U. S.?
"**The Russian frigate 'Oslabia' arrived at New York**"** (Sept. 12).
"That a rupture (of Russia) with France is sooner or later inevitable continues to be the general impression" (Sept. 16, 1863).
* That the Civil War was not caused in order to free the Negroes is proved by the words of Lincoln in his inaugural adress: "I declare that I have no purpose, directly or indirectly to interfere with slavery where it exists"
** The frigate "Oslabia" ran at full speed across the Atlantic in order to take part in any battle at Lincoln's orders, thus making war between Russia and France and England inevitable, if they should assault the U. S. The Atlantic and Pacific Russian squadrons had the same Czar's orders. The assault upon the U. S. by France or England would mean a new Crimean War (from which they went out nearly bankrupt) and the eventual occupation of Paris by Russian and Prussian troops, as in 1815!!!
The American Envoys at St. Petersburg during the Civil War: Clay, Cameron and Taylor were repeatedly told by the Czar's officials, that any European assault upon America would be fought by Russia to the finish.
The American Ambassadors: A. D. Curtin and G. W. Lothrop (of Detroit) and Justice Field have seen the original orders to the Admirals to be "at Lincoln's disposal." Lincoln said to his friend B. K. Cook that he knew about these documents, as did also W. H. Seward, Secretary of State.

WHEN WILL AMERICA PAY HER DEBT TO RUSSIA?

"The change in the attitude of England,* who has suddenly beat a retreat, was attributed to her fears of an alliance between Russia and the U.S. Such a combination is by no means remote. Prince Gorchakoff (Russia's Vice-Chancellor) and General Clay have frequent interviews. The two diplomats are on the best terms" (New York Herald, Sept. 17, 1863).

Page describes the reception of the ex-Envoy A. Burlingame: "The Czar (Alexander II) was as polite as a bridegroom" (p. 195).

Burlingame was so pleased that he never left St. Petersburg.

"Two powerful steel-plated rams were ready for sea at Liverpool. France has opened the port of Brest to the privateer 'Atlanta' to repair damages, and a number of vessels modelled after 'Alabama,' are on stocks at Havre and Bordeaux, supposed to be intended for the rebel (Confederates) service. France and England are still agitated on the subject of the conclusion of a Russo-American alliance. The 'Invalide Russe,' the organ of the Czar, has threatened both countries with such result"... "War with England and France (headline). Better war a thousand times with the governments which are guilty of these mean and treacherous acts than to allow them to continue to furnish our enemies with the means of destroying us" (Sept. 17, 1863).

It is clear that Czar Romanov saved the United States. Who are the Romanovs? They are of the very best Nordic stock. The best Anglo-Saxon women were their wives and mothers.

Their education was of the highest order; their training most careful. They personified all that was good in the Aryan race. All Europe called Czar Nicholas I a "Demi-God" and a genius!

Even their name Roma-Nova (new Rome) was ancient Roman.

My advice to the late Czar (in his own newspaper "Zemschina" on Aug. 11/24, 1916) to reconcile the Greek and Roman Churches was checked by the Hidden Hand and, as I predicted then, the catastrophe occured 6 months later....

As America is collecting the war debts from Europe, it is time to pay her ancient debt to the Romanovs, who risked and lost so much to prevent the assault of 5 powers upon the United States.

The sons of the Russians, who saved it, are now here, as refugees. Why are they treated with hostility?

Because such is the will of the Hidden Hand!

The same Jewish N. Y. Times is joyously boasting:

"With Russian Generals working as porters in New York restaurants and enlisted as privates in the American Army," etc. (Aug. 21, 1925).

"Bad liquor creates a wave of insanity in America" (Dr. Kraepelin).

"What is wrong with America? Murder, crime wave, ignorance"(M.Macy).

The answer is: "Too many Jews." CHRIST foretold the above

THE END OF THE FIRST PERIOD.

The failure to disrupt the United States and to murder Alexander II, was disappointing to James Rothschild III, and he died in 1868. Thus finishes the first period (1770-1868) of Rothschilds misgoverning the World.

As soon as this book is spread, the next book will be printed. It is ready and exposes: the reigns of Alphonse Rothschild IV. and Edouard Rothschild V., the actual World Autocrat and World Assassin; their wars, revolts and murders (of Alexander II., Alexander III., Nicholas II., and many others) all staged by the Secret World Government—the Hidden Hand.

*"Punch's" cartoon of Lincoln holding a candle for the Russian Bear.

CONCLUSION

I have but few pages to add. To know the truth and save Civilization this book must be spread and supporters found to publish its continuation: the period 1866-1926, which is ready.

This first book, condensed to the limit, will briefly expose the dangers and point out the "remedies" in answer to the question: "Will Civilization Survive?," made by Mr. John D. Rockefeller, Jr.

Called "prophet" by the best Editors, I may assert that it will survive, if my very simple "remedies" are applied.

To save it, must be saved Great Britain and the United States, now the strongest powers and the chief targets of the Hidden Hand, i. e. of the Judeo-Mongol World Government, which is inciting against them the 1,200 million Colored. **We must daily combat it!**

"The World Government will not permit peace" (Hon. T. R. Marshall).

"There is no connection between peace and advertising" (Sir W. Veno).

No! Advertising is in the hands of the Jews, "the sons of the devil—the murderer and father of lies." **They hate peace and truth!** The press, controlled by them, **must always lie**, or "regularly fool us," as W. J. Bryan stated.*

"Newspapers can't print anything, but babytalk. Press flatters Americans. They believe it all" (H. H. Baker, Ed. of "Amer. Tribunal", Chicago).

"The worst agents of this International Bankers' Plunberbund here are the newspapers and magazines they control." (Philip Francis, ex-editor of the Hearst's papers, "The Poison in America's Cup," p. 59).

"In international relations England remembers nothing; Ireland forgets nothing; **America knows nothing**" (an American. The National Review).

"We can lessen our ignorance by earnest search of truth" (Pres. Lowell).

Yes! But you cannot find it in the Jew controlled press.

I am the Columbus of the "Science of Political Foresight" and of truthful History, both **indispensable to Americans.** Why?

"Britain possesses real statesmen that we lack" (Brisbane, N. Y. Amer.)

* The New York Times (April 2, 1925) lied, that P. R. Malone, member of the British Parliament, is a Conservative. He is a near-bolshevik, and married to a Jewess, i. e. a bolshevik. His blame of the Bulgarian Czar Boris, a noble and brilliant Nordic, is a calumny.

The New York World (May 15) assures, that it was Mr. Owen D. Young's "financial genius," which was responsible for the formulation of the Dawes' plan." Mr. Lloyd George stated that the Hidden Hand dictated it (see p. 38).

Hamilton York confirms it in "The Dawes Report and Control of World Gold." ("Beckwith Documents", Beckwith Press, 299 Madison Ave., N. Y. C.)

"The Dawes plan was made and inspired by Jews" (Gen. Ludendorff).

In the N. Y. Evening Post, June 16, one S. B. Conger deceives us by saying that Bethmann-Hollweg-Rothschild was "an unfortunate, but well meaning blunderer." No, he started this war as one of the "300". He read in his Talmud the "Kol Nidre" teaching that vows and oaths are not binding on a Jew, and said it. This raised the "scrap of paper" scandal.

Norman Hapgood finds a "mystery" (N. Y. American, Aug. 8, 1925) in the French mind. He says England "fears a brainstorm, which might send the French prancing around Germany, looting and seeking safety in the madness of destruction." It is because in Paris is seated the Supreme Council of the "300," headed by Ed. Rothschild V. The other "300" arrive daily for orders. It is an endless plot of wars and revolts. Though cautious and cowardly the "300" are boastful. One word here, one there. Paris is poisoned by this satanic work. The French feel it and the hidden danger, preferring an open war. The trial of the "300" would cure all this. What good could France expect being ruled by the Jews: Painleve, Caillaux, Schrameck, ets. and above all Rothschild!!! Hapgood is "fooling the public."

"Every school (Russia) is a nest of atheism" (Marcosson, Sat. Eve.Post).

185

THE SATANIC WORK OF JEWS EVERYWHERE.

"Ye (Jews) will do the devil's lust of murder" (CHRIST).

"The Jews supply 50% of the criminals" (Chief Police, Gen Bingham.)*

The Jews J. Schiff and Co. compelled Roosevelt to save Japan.

"Roosevelt will do exactly what I tell him" (Loeb, his Jew sec'y).

The same Jews compelled America to start the First World War by declaring war on Russia in 1911, because after the war and revolt of 1905 (both staged by the Jews), Russia did not want more of the "Trotzkies."** If Russia had no right to stop the invasion of **Judeo-Mongols,** what right has America to stop the coming of 10 times better Japano-Mongols?

Seeing the **"American-Russian War,"** the Kaiser also was persuaded by his Jews to fight Russia! This War, staged by them, caused 40,000,000 casualties, and 30,000,000 Russians died "thanks" to the Jewish revolution.***

This seems to enthuse Sen. W. Borah, who to please his Judeo-Mongol Secretary Miss Rubin Corah, demands to "recognize" the Judeo-Mongol Soviets (i.e. to help them to "bolshevize" America).

"Nothing would constitute a more needless and base betrayal of civilization than the recognition of the bolshevik tyranny" (Gompers, May 1, 1922).

America went to war in 1917 ONLY because the Jews wished to create the "Kosher" League of Nations and to obtain Palestine (as Lord R. Cecil implied here and as confirmed by the British Guardian of April, 1925). This was done **against the will of CHRIST** Who warned, that: **"your (Jewish) house is left unto you desolate,"** until the Jews would recognize HIM as GOD (St. Luke XIII, 35). When England was losing the war (Haig's "back to the wall"), the Jews offered her the help of America, if Palestine were granted to them. England was forced to consent. Then Brandeis**** **("who ruled the White House by secret telephone,"** as the Chicago Tribune mentioned); Baruch (who told the Senators that he, and not the President **was the most powerful man);** the Schiffs, etc. ordered their press and valets to shout against Germany.

"Thanks" to the Jews America challenged CHRIST'S order...

"Towards the end of 1916 the Zionists began to identify themselves with the Allied cause" (Wickham Steed in his "Through Thirty Years").

"America dishonored herself by entering the World War" (C. D. Eaton).

* Add to this figure many criminal Jews, camouflaged as "Russians," "Poles," etc. Thus, the N. Y. World (Aug. 1) called a Jew, "Norman Klein," "Russian." He threatened the excellent President Coolidge!

** I mention it in my book "Towards Disaster; Dangers and Remedies" (October 1913) as a symptom that the World War began in 1911. On Feb. 15, 1911 Schiff and Co. urged Pres. Taft not to renew the Commercial Treaty of 1832 with Russia. When he declined, Schiff refused to shake the President's hand, saying: **"This means war!"** The murders of Iuschinsky and of the Russian Prime Minister Stolypin and the World War followed.

*** H. Bernstein (of The Jewish Tribune, New York) by saying (1925) this revolution was "bloodless" for the Jews, confirmed that they staged it.

**** In "Democracy or Shylocracy," by Capt. H. S. Spencer (at The Britons) a telegram is quoted, in which the Jewish leader Wiseman says: "Brandeis cabled Rothschild" etc. As a sequel came the bloody events in Russia... (See The Gentiles' Review, No. 7). Thus the "liaison" of Justice L. Dembitz Brandeis, a Jew, with the Hidden Hand is proved. The N. Y. World (1925) exposed the devilish work of a Jew Trebitz Lincoln in China which eventuated in today's murders. Aaron Saenz (Zaienz?), Foreign Minister of Mexico must also be a Jew! America beware!

FOREIGN ASSAULT UPON AMERICA.

"Thanks" to the Schiffs, Otto Kahns, Kara Kahns, Loeb Kuhns and Bela Kuhns, Japan is arming herself to the teeth (an expert, R. R. Magill, N. Y. American, June 21, 1925). The same Jews are (as Gompers said) financing "the blowing up of America from within." The Hidden Hand controls $300 billions and is ready to spend it in "doing the lust of murder."*

"Thanks" to them Japan is a deadly menace to America.

Every expert knows that an assault by Japan is imminent!

"Japan is building twice as many ships, as America" (Sir H. Russell).

A naval expert Hector A. Bywater forecasts in his new book:

"Just before war is declared** a Japanese freighter is blown up in the Panama Canal and blockades it. Then follows the swift loss of the Philippines," etc. (N. Y. Evening Post, July 16, 1925).

Can America expect a revolt in Japan?

"The Monarchistic idea is too deeply ingrained in the Japanese. To be a Japanese means to believe in the godly mission of the Mikadô. The colonization of California by us is a life and death question for Japan" (Goto, ex-Home Secretary of Japan, N. Y. Times, May 26, 1925).

The Hidden Hand invaded Japan: a) by Mohammedanism (N. Y. World, May 1, 1921) which is led by Judaism (see "The Science of Political Foresight"); and b) by Satanism, viz., "worshipping Satan" (The Morning Post, Aug. 28, 1920). Sassoon Rothschild has his agents in every Asiatic town. His Bolshevism is growing in Japan and will compel her to go to war to avert a revolt.

Bolshevism is Satanism under various masks. In Russia it pretended to be a "patriotic" movement 'to obtain land, peace and bread. To Japan it is more attractive, its leaders being Mongols, who have adopted Talmud, a kind of by-laws of a gang of World gunmen, led by the World Assassin and Autocrat—E.Rothschild V.

* I proved (The Gentiles' Review, No. 8) the imminent bankruptcy of the Aryans; the Hidden Hand controls $300 billion and earns at least $20 billion per year. In 1935 it will control $500 billion and will earn at least $30 billion per year; in 1946 it will control nearly $1,000 billion. The Jews avidity and the "lust of murder" (moral, mental and physical) grow daily.

Thus the "Bible Students," led by a Jew, Rutherford, assert that CHRIST would come soon. Did HE not say: "ye shall not see me, until the time come, when ye (Jews) shall say, 'Blessed is HE that cometh in the name of the LORD' " (St. Luke XIII, 35). The Jews delay the coming of the Millennium.

Many assert that CHRIST meant only scribes, not all the Jews. CHRIST was angry not because they were writers, but because they wrote the satanic Talmud. And 95% of the Jews adhere to it and ignore the Mosaic creed.

"The Jews in Crimea were specially favored by the Russian Government. Why? Because they are non-Talmud Jews" (N. Y. American, Aug. 23, 1925).

"Domination by the Jews created pauperism" (Proudon).

** The Japanese will suddenly attack the American ships at night without declaring war. An airplane will blow up the gates of the water-reservoirs and for months the Canal will be "dead." Many experts have said that the islands could be taken any day, which "would compel America to make war" (see p. 16).

Bywater, a patriot, knows that the Hidden Hand will compel England to fight America. So he is lulling America, assuring us that "every country would be pro-American and anti-Japan." He sees a revolt in Japan, but "overlooks" 8,000,000 Judeo-Mongols, 12,000,000 Africans and 5,000,000 "discontented", utopians, "reds," etc., within America, all incited by the Hidden Hand, which is financing also the provocation of daily insulting the 25,000,000 Catholics (Roman, Uniat and Orthodox).

"Europe will make every effort to get her gold back" (I. Marcosson).

187

DOMESTIC ASSAULT UPON AMERICA.

"The promoters of the Russian revolution had in view the complete destruction of Christianity and its moral code. Nobody was admitted to the Communist party, unless he denied GOD. It is a foreign domination from without which Russia is suffering. Evil is enthroned in Moscow. The promoters are not Russian. They are Jews" (the famous Stephan Graham).

In every mass murder Jews are the instigators. By imitating the "ostrich, hiding its head in the sand," the Gentiles are betraying their own children, who must pay for their base cowardice. The Judeo-Mongols are "the twofold more children of hell" (St. Matthew, XXIII, 15). Concealing this we commit a crime!*

The Jews are fomenting here a Civil war by inciting Labor vs Capital; Protestants vs. Catholics**; Negroes vs. Whites; staging a clash between the Fundamentalists and the "Evolutionists"***; and imposing a "bolshevization."

"Baruch has definitely planned the communistic state which will come into being immediately upon proclamation of the next war"... "It will not be necessary for communists to stage a revolt, it will only be necessary to force patriots into a war, when the U. S. goes under communism in one day! Baruch said that his power exceeded that of any other man. But his power was puny compared with that proposed for the next war. Instead of one thing menacing us in war, now three things menace: war itself; the attempt at establishing communism as a war measure; the possible resistance" (The Dearborn Independent, July 25, 1925).

"The fate of the country in which the Jew is dwelling is of no interest to him" (the famous Ernest Renan).

"The Jews detest the spirit of nations in the midst of which they live" (A Jew, Bernard Lazare in his "L'Antisemitisme").

"The radical movement is spreading like smallpox, and the menace of radicalism has become very grave" (Senator George Moses).

In case of a revolt the Fords, Rockefellers, Mellons and other rich Christians shall be killed and plundered, while the Kuhns, Warburgs, etc. will quintuple their wealth! Churches shall be turned into Jewish movies and clubs. A Trotzky would be in the White House.

The great leaders of Labor: Gompers and W. S. Stone are dead.**** The new leaders are more radical and aggressive.

* Many Societies are "aiming to fight Bolshevism." But in each a Jew pays a fee and prevents revealing the truth, that Bolshevism is Judaism. Out of 100 bolshevist leaders in America 90 are Jews.

** Special reviews are paid by the Jews to vilify Rome. They have but two "proofs" of its "guilt": the lies of a renegade priest Chiniquy and words attributed to Lincoln, that "he foresees a cloud, coming from Rome," denied by his son. The Roman Catholics are attacked for their political allegiance to the President and their religious to the Vicar of CHRIST. Such "dual allegiance" was sanctioned by CHRIST:

"Render unto Caesar the things which are Caesar's; and unto GOD the things that are GOD'S" (St. Matthew, XXII, 21).

The foes of Rome are inciting the 25,000,000 Catholics (Roman, Eastern and Uniat), mostly hard workers and patriots, forgetting that each clash would be exploited by Japan & Co. for an attack.

*** Miss Helen Phelps Stokes financed the J. T. Scopes case (The National Bulletin, June 1925, of the Military Order of the World War, N. Y.) As W. J. Bryan declared that he will fight to the end this masked assault upon CHRIST, he "suddenly" died. The Americans find it "normal."

****When a general strike was decided in October 1922, I warned Warren Stone, Plumb and other leaders of Labor in Chicago that it might be exploited by the Hidden Hand for a circular assault. Amazed, they abandoned the strike. Labor is patriotic, but nobody tells them the truth.

THE WORLD CHRISTIAN CHURCH.

"Bishop Manning predicts World Union of Churches" (N.Y.Herald, July 28).

Behind the 1,200 millions Colored people (including Judeo-Mongols) is Satan's Hidden Hand. Scorning CHRIST'S warning we shall perish, unless we believe in HIM. What is to be done? "Do the reverse of what your foe wishes" (Napoleon I, a genius). The Jews are destroying the Christian Churches and rulers and enthroning the Judeo-butchers. Ibanez, a Jew, tried to upset the excellent King of Spain. In Bulgaria Friedman, a Jew, with the money of Joffe, a Jew, envoy of the Moscow Jews, blew up the Sofia Cathedral and sought to kill the good Czar. Their "Plan of Hell" (see p. 35) is exposed in the "Protocols."

To check them we must do the reverse: stop attacking the Churches and "merge" them; and support all good Monarchs.*

"The Roman Catholic Church was praised for its custom of advertising the spiritual, rather than the material side of life, by Rev. Dr. S. Trexler, Pres. of the Lutheran Synod of New York" (N. Y. Times, July 20, 1925).

Yes! It is the best organized Church. There are, of course, among its million clergymen, some Jews (the Pope Borgia and all the Great Inquisitors were Jews, according to a Jew, Ibanez, see the "Patriot," July 2, 1925), and a few rascals. But the Church stands high and its downfall would spell disaster for all Aryans.

"Never go fishing without taking CHRIST along" (Rev. Dr.F.B.Meyers).

We must daily remember CHRIST'S words and fight HIS foes. Let us listen not to the "300" or their valets (whom I have made known), but to one, who dares openly accuse Satanism—Bolshevism and whom 300,000,000 Catholics regard as the Vicar of CHRIST.

Pius XI appealed to "all right thinking men to combine in fighting Bolshevism" (N. Y. Times, Dec. 19, 1924.) This alone justifies His title of "Holy Father," and crushes the lies of the Jewish International Bible Students**, who, basing them upon the apocryphal addendum to the book of Daniel, falsely tried to connect Rome with Satan. Did not the Jews assert, that CHRIST co-operated with Satan? (St. Luke, XI, 15).

"Should Bolshevism really threaten world stability, Catholicism would become the rallying point of all the forces that oppose Bolshevism" (Dr. Inge, Dean of St. Paul Cathedral, Atlantic Monthly, February, 1925).

Bolshevism is more than really threatening World's stability.*** If the World would accept the Pope, as the Vicar of CHRIST, Christian Civilization could yet be saved.

*In nearly all the European countries an enormous majority of the decent people are for a Monarchy. But the Hidden Hand with its billions and press is against Christian rulers and wishes to have Jews or their valets in power. Even in Poland there is a group aiming to have a King of the old dynasty of Piast now represented by Prince Paul Salvator, known as Prince Riedelski.

** The Montreal La Croix (the Cross) on Jan 31, 1925 stated that the leader of the "International" Bible Students is a Jew, Rutherford.

"The Reformation was the period, when Christianity dipped itself into Judaism" (Bernard Lazare, a Jew, "The Gentiles' Tribune," April 20, 1922).

*** R. W. Chambers describes in "The Slayer of Souls" the old sect of Assassins or Yezidees, the Satan worshippers. His regent on earth is "Sanang." These Sorcerers control Bolshevism. They united all the secret Moslem, Hindu, etc, societies. "This Oriental League is of Mongolian origin" (N. Y. Times, July 1, 1919). Its aim is a joint revolution in America, etc. Cautious Chambers says about Sanang: "I thought he was a Jew" (p. 145).

THE WORLD COMMONWEALTH ON THE AMERICAN PLAN.

Every expert foresees a war within 1-10 years. **Let us avert it.**
As the Hidden Hand **"will not permit peace"** (Hon. T. R. Marshall),
we must choose "to have war" or **"not to have the Hidden Hand!"**
"Another war would be the cemetery of civilization" (Hon. H. Hoover).
"Dr. H.E. Fosdick asserts: 'the next war will be the suicide of Civilization.'"
"War will break out once more, if the U. S. and England do not take
definite action" (I. McBride, ex-Secr. to the late Sen. H. Lane).
"Britain and the U. S. are the Chosen people" (Col. W. G. MacKendrick).

The wars could yet be averted, if the world would be reorganized on an "American Plan." The Americans are a people of gigantic "mergers," and should organize the "World Christian Church" and "The World Commonwealth."*

The British Commonwealth and other nations could then join it on an equal basis, as the "United States of the World" and no power could compel America to fight.

Having dethroned the Emperors of Russia, Germany, Austria and Turkey, the Hidden Hand is proceeding to "blow up" through Bolshevism—Great Britain, the strongest bulwark of Civilization.**

If we would join the Vatican in its war on Bolshevism, our Civilization could yet be saved.***"**The best defense is an attack.**"

England represents the Aryan World Police. Every Aryan profits by British culture. England's foes should consider the consequences to the Aryans if she were destroyed or even weakened. Britain's Dynasty is ideal and is, next to the Vatican, the second greatest asset of the White Race. The Prince of Wales merits to be considered by the whole Aryan Race, as its **"Dux Supremus."**

The "American Plan" would unite the World Christian Church and the World Commonwealth, which would have far reaching consequences: no wars and millions of Englishmen, Irishmen, Germans, Russians, etc, would starve no more.

What advantage would America derive from this plan? **An assault upon her would become impossible!** Taxes would be cut down by one half. The 135,000 murderers, who according to Supreme Justice M. Cavanaugh of Chicago, are at large, would be hanged. Murders in New York would fall from 335 per year to 33. The Americans (U. S.-ans or Usans) would become "World Citizens" with full privileges everywhere, etc., etc., etc.

But this would be too good for the Aryans, and the Hidden Hand through its press and its valet-statesmen will not permit it. Thus, in order to abolish war, **we must abolish the Hidden Hand!**

* This does not prevent England, Germany, Russia, etc., having Emperors, Kings, or Presidents, as Germany had many Kings, and a Super-Monarch.
** The press asserted that the distress of Ireland was attributable to the British misrule. But E. O'Reilly, Pres. of the Celtic Fellowship reveals that it is the rain falls during harvest time the consequences of which could be prevented by drying machines. (N. Y. Times, July 25.)
*** In my 4th letter "How to Save England" (The Financial News, Feb. 17, 1920), I advised Mr. Lloyd George not to rush weekly to Paris to see Clemenceau (a valet of Mandel Rothschild ,as Mr. Wilson was a friend of E. Mandel House), but to go to a great Britisher, Cardinal Bourne... Soon after Clemenceau "went to the dogs," but the excellent Cardinal remained. Now Lord Halifax, Pres. of the Anglo-Catholic party wisely pleaded:
"**Let the Roman and Anglican Catholic Churches be united.**"

INDISPENSABLE TRIAL OF ROTHSCHILD AND THE "300"

The Chicago Tribune of April 8-9, 1924, reported that a Jew, Zaharov, (of the "300") opened immense credits to buy war material for Russia! Thus were staged the subsequent murders in Sofia, Cairo, Morocco, Mexico, China, Syria, etc.*

"The Jews are the cause of nearly all the World's ills" (the Kaiser).

"We, Jews, have made the World War. We are the World's seducers, incendiaries, executioners. Our last revolution is not yet made" (Dr. O. Levy).

"Japan and the U. S. are engaged in a struggle for China. Russia will be ready to stand with Japan" (Radek, a Jew Soviet Commissar).

"All signs point to further war" (N. Y. Times, May 24, 1925).

"A new war is coming! If we wish to stop it, we must do so now" (O. Garrison Villard, Editor of The Nation, on March 6, 1924).

Mr. Lloyd George and Prof. G. Ferrero wrote that "bolshevist Russia is fomenting rebellions; a colored cyclone is coming; an inevitable war is brewing" (N. Y. American, July 26, 1925). "Bolshevist" means "Judeo-Mongol."

"Paul Hymans, ex-Minister of Belgium's Foreign Affairs said in its Chamber: 'America refused to ratify the treaty and considered void the signature of the man, who went to Europe to act in her name.' Hymans was followed by Foreign Minister Vandervelde, who declared this account was strictly accurate" (N. Y. Evening Post, July 16, 1925).

Whence this "anti-Americanism?" Because both are Jews (the latter is married to Speyer, a rich Jewess, as was Sembat, the French socialist leader), as are: Painleve**, Caillaux*** and the French "Dictator"—Abraham Schrameck, the Home-Secretary.

All this talk about "peace" and the Jewish League of Nations World Courts, "Outlawing Wars," "War to End War," etc., are Jewish tricks to "fool us regularly" (as W. J. Bryan said) and "to keep us busy." The only way of salvation is the trial of the Hidden Hand. How to start it:

Summon to Court any one of the "300". Seize a pretext:

"Repres. Hamilton Fish, Jr. of New York, proposed that the criminal code be applied to Americans who misrepresent the attitude of the U. S. in its negotiations with foreign nations. Fish suggested that a trial be made of Otto Kahn, for what he was reported to have said about the debt note in the presence of Premier Painleve," etc. (N. Y. Eve. Post, May 27, '25).

As Kahn is immensely rich, Fish became silent as his namesake, though Kahn is guilty as the following cable proves:

"Stockholm. Propaganda by certain 'American' bankers in Europe has convinced the public that America is responsible for Europe's ills! The 'Village,' a leading paper, quotes Warburg and Otto Kahn of Kuhn, Loeb & Co. to prove, that America contributed to bring about the European chaos. They have been repeatedly pointing it out. Kuhn, Loeb & Co. have since the war acquired considerable interests abroad, the value of which would be immensely increased, if the war debts were cancelled" (Chic. Tribune, Aug. 25, 1922).

* As Gompers stated (Chicago Tribune, May 1, 1922) the "Germano-Anglo-American" bankers are financing the "blowing up of America." Always the same Warburgs, Otto Kahns, Kara Kahns, Loeb Kuhns, Bela Kuhns, etc. Kahn is a "Germano-Anglo-American" Judeo-Mongol. His trial is a duty. Instead of trying these men, the Aryans wished to try the Kaiser. Now that he knows how basely they betrayed and fooled him, the Kaiser would be an ideal ruler for Germany, whose Dictator has been a Jewess Rosa Luxemburg (as I foretold in my "Alliance Franco-Allemande" in June 1914), and now the "Dictator" is G. Streseman, married to a Jewess Kleefeldt, and is himself a Jew (see Hvem er Hvem by M. Sylten).

** According to a Jew, Salzberger, Pres. of the Hebrew United Charities.

*** According to "Hvem er Hvem i Joedeverden" by M. Sylten, Editor.

191

"SAVE ARYAN RACE COMMITTEE" (SARC)

Sen. Robert Owen, Feb. 1924, proposed a Committee of Inquiry as to "Who Started the World War." Let us beg every Congressman to speed the work. It must not be composed of persons trembling for their jobs or votes.* It should be presided over by H. Ford, a genius, one of the greatest Americans that ever existed. He has revealed the deadly danger of the Jews. His weekly, "Dearborn Independent," is the only paper in America which tells the truth.

Ford knows that the Hidden Hand is urging Japan to attack, and he wishes to check it by creating a huge Air defense. But it is too late... Japan knows it and also that an eventual return of a Czar Romanov to Moscow would mean no assault upon America.

Ford's work alone might save America. He has boldly stated that "History" is 'bunk." I have proved it.

"We, Jews, have invented the 'Chosen people' myth" (Dr. O. Levy)

A few honest, clever, bold and patriotic Aryans could yet be found to compose the "Save Aryan Race Committee" (Sarc).** Their one meeting would be more effective than 20 Peace Conferences, composed of the "Jewish boot lickers." The score of Editors who stated that the Rothschilds can break Empires, start wars and revolts or suppress them, must help us. Any honest inquiry would prove the guilt of the "300". Then the Committee will request the powers to compel the "300" to repay $100 billion grabbed by them.

"Make Rothschild pay" (Senator Gaudin de Villaine).

* To obtain control of the Committee of Inquiry, Baruch offered $250,000 to "find the profiteers." All "inquisitors" would be his clerks.

Since Mr. B. Baruch is suspected of being one of the greatest profiteers owing to his dominant position during the war and his intimate contact with those accused of gross profiteering, he should have no difficulty in putting his finger on the key note of all political profiteering; thereby saving his $250,000, which might be more profitably employed in some real patriotic endeavor, to be controlled by Americans whose integrity cannot be challenged.

"The Jews have millions of Christians to fleece" (Rev. Dr. Dean Inge)

** Henry Ford—in America. Mrs. Nesta Webster; the Duke of Northumberland; Lord Sydenham of Combe; Hillaire Bellock; G. K. Chesterton; Dr. John H. Clarke; H. H. Beamish; Prof. Charles Sarolea; — in England. Mgr. Jouin (Editor of "La Revue des Societes Secretes," Paris); Sen. Gaudin de Villaine; Urbain Gohier, Editor; Felix Siry, Nice; Leon Daudet (Editor); Georges Batault, author; Roger Lambelin; Andre Cheradame — in France. Roberto Farinacci (Secr. General of Fascisti); Pietro Mataloni (Ed. of the "Agenzia Urbs," Rome), the Editor of "La Vita Italiana", Rome—in Italy. Dr. H. Kraeger (Ed. of the "Deutscher Folkswart"); Th. Fritsch (Ed. of the "Hammer," Leipzig); Dr. Kurt Kerlen—in Germany. A. E. Graefe; Prof. G. V. Below; Prof, L, Kahrenkrok; H, Kipper (Ed, of the "Michel," Graz)—in Austria. Gen. Nechvolodov and the Editor of the "Gentiles' Review"—in Russia. M. Sylten (Ed. of "Nationalt Tidsskrift," Oslo)—in Norway. Prof. W. Lutoslawski*** (Kowno); Pres. of "Rozwoy"; the Editor of the "Dwa Grosze"; H. Olszewski (Ed. of "Pro Patria"); the famous author N. Breshko-Breshkowski—in Poland. Prof. A. C, Couza and Z. C. Codreanu—in Roumania. Hon. Tiburce v. Eckhardt, Pres. of the "Awakening Hungarians"" and Editor of the "Courrier Danubien" (Budapest); Editor of "Nep" (Budapest)—in Hungary. Theo. N. Van Der Lyn (of the Pan Aryan League, Amsterdam)—in Holland. Joseph Begin (Ed. of "La Croix"—The Cross)—in Montreal, Canada. Grigory Bostunich, famous author —in Yugo-Slavia, and a few others, who know and tell the TRUTH.

All those ought to be named the "World's Citizens of Honor."

***Author of "The World of Souls" (Allen & Unwin, London).

$100 BILLION TO RESTORE THE ARYANS

"It is certain that if there be another such war, civilization will never recover from it" (Viscount Grey, the British ex-Foreign Minister).

Yes! We will go down in a Second World War and lose $400 billion more or we must try the Hidden Hand and recover $100 billion, which it grabbed in 1914-18. To disarm America the Hidden Hand is "chloroforming" her defenses.

Another reason for trying the "300"—is the loss of $32 billion by the farmers "thanks" to the "help" of the Jews: B. Baruch, Eug. Meyer, A. Shapiro and of Warburg's Federal Reserve Banks.

The "300" should be sent to some island for life. The $100 billion should be distributed to the nations which took part in the World War, according to the number of their populations. This would restore Europe. And the Hidden Hand, this "plant of wars" would be stopped. Europe would repay all her debts without ill-feeling and would again become the best customer of the U. S.

"Corral the 50 wealthiest Jews and there will be no wars" (Henry Ford).

"Wars are the Jews' harvest" (Prof. Werner Zombart, a Jew).

"To suppress the wars, suppress the Jews" (the Aryan Committee of the Universal Anti-Jewish League, 33 rue Gioffredo, Nice, France).

"It is the Jew, who lies when he swears allegiance to another faith who becomes a danger to the World. The (World) Conspiracy is among those Jews who are or seem ashamed of their origin. Among them will be those who may seize power for their own ends" (Rabbi S. Wise, N. Y. Tribune, March 2, 1920).

He confirms that Kahns, Baruchs&Co. "may seize the power."*

To encourage Japan to attack (1904) Schiff promised a revolt in Russia. Now Baruch has assured 'bolshevization" here, i. e. a Civil War! Are all the Gentiles cowards, vile, stupid and blind? Are there no Americans who would dare to prevent the disaster, staged by the Baruchs, Kahns, Kara Kahns, Warburgs (one of whom gave $10,000,000 to Trotzky to start tumult and murder), etc.

The Jews are being held responsible for the crimes of the "300" about whom most of them profess ignorance. Mass pogroms are imminent, unless the "300" are tried. Jews and friends of the Jews should urge their trial. When the Jews shall renounce their Talmud, which teaches: "Kill the best Gentiles"; when the daily "bleeding white" of the Aryans** by the Hidden Hand shall cease; then we can open our arms to the Jews.

Let us demand the appointment of a "Committee of Inquiry"; encourage the creation of the "Save Aryan Race Committee"; and insist that it be invited to participate in the work.

Only the restoration of a Romanov Czar, would make impossible a Japanese assault upon the U. S. and its "bolshevization" by the "300". All this could be attained, if a few millions were spent in spreading the truth and proving, how right is CHRIST.

* "Why would the rich Jews stage a revolt here, which may cost them money?" — The Jews will know exactly when to start it. And a little earlier they will sell or mortgage their estates and transfer the money abroad. Only Christians will lose all, even lives. When the rich Christians shall have been killed, the Jews will declare (as in Russia) that "war on Capitalism is a mistake," and rebuy all for one fifth. Always remember their lust of murder.

** The killing of 800 French in Syria, was (see The N. Y. Times of Aug. 9, 1925) also instigated by the agents of the Moscow Jews.

ADDENDUM № 1: THE JEWS REMAIN TRAITORS

In his "Rotten to the Core" Mr. Hugh Bauerlein, of Denver, has well pictured a story involving Mr. Lloyd George in the dirty "Marconi business" by the Jews Rufus and Godfrey Isaacs, who like Franks. were kept out of prison. Rufus was even made Lord Chief Justice, Vice-Roy of India, and Earl Reading.

The two greatest cases of treason in France were committed by Jews: Dreyfus in the Army and Ulmo in the Navy. The Jew Zangwill in his "The Problem of the Jewish Race," p. 10 wrote:

"If Germany had no Dreyfus case it is because no Jew is permitted to a military rank." Yes! Germany could endure a 4-year war without betrayal because, as Zangwill confirms, she avoided the race, which gave Dreyfus, Ulmo, Franks, etc. What was the role of the Franks in the war? They helped the British to kill as many Americans as possible and vice-versa, and plundered both nations. That is all. They have their own mission as satanists, i. e., as mankillers, according to CHRIST. This mission, they accomplished with the greatest ardor and joy.*

Rev. D. J. Brouse, Pastor of Grace Episcopal Church, stated:

"The Jew never was a real true American. In this war the Central Powers were financed by the Jews with money from America, and this money was used to fight against our own homeland" (Jewish World, July 13, 1921).

Rev. William S. Mitchell, D. D. (Philadelphia) rightly said:

"If there is an ingrate in history, it is the Jew. In this land which befriended him he has conspired, plotted, undermined, prostituted and corrupted, and (hiding to this hour behind the braver screen of other folks), dares to contrive and scheme the death of every Christian principle which has protected him."

"Assimilation of nations in America was condemned by Louis Marshall," a Jewish leader (New York Times, March 2, 1925).

"Religion for Pupils opposed by rabbi S. Schulman of New York" (New York Times, March 2, 1925).

"Rabbi N. Krath of New York denounced censorship of the theatre" (New York Times, March 2, 1925).

This means "white slavery" for the American girl.
"The part which Jews all over the world play in white slavery is one of the foulest blots on our people" (Jewish World, March 18, 1914).

Wherever the Jews are, there a revolt is being staged.
"They only simulated to separate from Judaism, just like fighters who adopt the armour and the flag of the enemy only to strike more surely and annihilate with more strength," ("History of the Jews," by a Jew, Graetz).

The well known Professors Ph. Marshall Brown, of Princeton and A. B. Hart, of Harvard, confirmed the words of E. Renan:
"The Jews do not give wholehearted allegiance to any one land!"

* General Percin revealed that the Jews, who served as artillery officers in the French army were purposely directing their guns in such a way that the shells killed an enormous number of French soldiers.

ADDENDUM № 2: THE BLUNDER OF TWO EDITORS

"What happened in Russia is briefly this: the few, educated in literature and in commerce, taking advantage of the mismanagement of the war, procured the abdication of the Czar. They were, however, utterly unable to establish a functioning government. They were soon forcibly dispossessed by the present gang of cut-throats, who adopted the methods of wholesale slaughter. Lenin and Trotsky are neither of them Russians, nor either of them Communists."

Such was the puerile statement given as an explanation of the revolution in Russia by Robert McCormick, the editor of The Chicago Tribune, in May, 1922.

Mr. McCormick completely ignores history. He believes that "few men educated in literature" could upset the Czar and dissolve into thin air his 17,000,000 soldiers. As his Chicago Tribune is read by millions of Americans, one can understand how fitting were the remarks of the eminent Ambassador of Great Britain, Sir Aukland Geddes, when he told the delegates to the Pan-American Conference of Women in Washington, that **"the trouble with you—women, is, you are too ignorant. Unless you get out of this ignorance you are a positive menace."** How much greater a menace is an editor who believes that a revolution in a country of 180 million souls could be brought about by a "few men educated in literature."

"A few years ago some very stupid men set the world on fire. The men, who ostensibly did this, were the Czar Nicholas, the Kaiser Franz Joseph, the Kaiser Wilhelm, the King of Great Britain, etc. These men were all tools in the hands of more cunning men"

declared Mr. Philip Francis, ex-Editor of The New York American, who, as he says, "was in a position to see behind the scenes and to watch the secret workings," in his otherwise clever booklet "The Poison in America's Cup."

When he states, that the King of Great Britain was a "tool" of "more cunning men," that means, that these could not be Britishers, as one would understand from his writing. Who were these "super-cunning men?" The same "300" of the Hidden Hand who are now staging the Second World War against the United States, perhaps in 1926, unless the Americans open their eyes by spreading the message of this book, which exposes this Hidden Hand.

There are numberless proofs, that the Jews never sought the improvement of any nation, but that their aims were to murder and de-Christianize. They are like worms in the finest apple.

"We Jews have spoiled the blood of all the races. We have tarnished and broken their power. We have made everything foul, rotten, decomposed, decayed" (Dr. Kurth Munzer, a Jew, in his "The Way to Zion.")

"Triumph of Jews is voiced by rabbi Israel Goldstein (New York). He referred to the great growth of Jewish influence" (N. Y. World, Sept. 21, 1925).

Alas! This influence means **demoralization and "satanization!"**

"AUTOCRAT OF THE WORLD" BY CHOICE OF SATAN
AND BECAUSE OF LAWLESSNESS

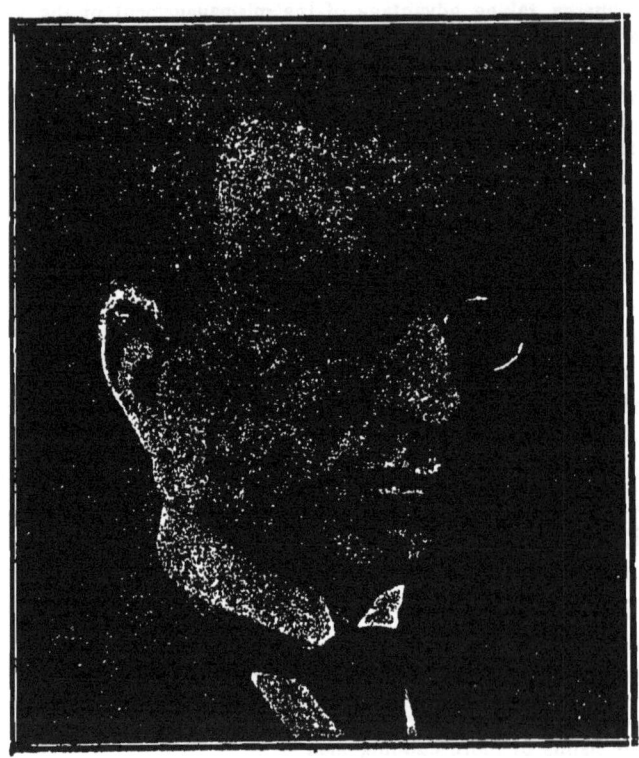

EDWARD ROTHSCHILD V.

The "World Autocrat and Assassin," the Vicar of Satan on earth, the grandson of James Rothschild III, who, through his agent, a Mongol- talmudist, Judah P. Benjamin (the Secretary of State of the South), started the Civil War in America in 1861. Through his Mongol-talmudist, Benjamin Disraeli, he also arranged the landing in 1863 at Mexico of the troops of five powers in the hope of smashing the Northerners and annexing the South to his "Mexican" Empire, with Emperor Maximilian as the Gentiles' front.

It was also Edward's great grandfather, Amschel Rothschild I, who equipped and sent here 16,800 Hessian soldiers to crush the American patriots who started the War of Independence.

The leaders of Bolshevism are Jews,—Edward's mere agents.

"The only real experiment in the setting up of Communism had resulted in a tyranny being replaced by a tyranny ten thousand times more hideous" (Rev.D.Kennedy-Bell, Vicar of St. John's, London, The Daily Mail, Aug. 1925).

THE ANTI-BOLSHEVIST PUBLISHING ASSOCIATION

15 East 128th Street, New York City